A SOCIAL HISTORY

OF

THE AMERICAN FAMILY

Vol. II: From Independence
through the Civil War

UNIVERSITY PAPERBACKS

A SOCIAL HISTORY
OF
THE AMERICAN FAMILY

Vol. II: From Independence
through the Civil War

by ARTHUR W. CALHOUN

BARNES & NOBLE, INC. • NEW YORK

PUBLISHERS • BOOKSELLERS • SINCE 1873

Printed in the United States of America

To
MY MOTHER

CONTENTS

CONTENTS

INTRODUCTION

The evolution of the American family during the period that accomplished the nationalization of the federal union manifests the operation of several large groups of formative factors that were present at least in rudimentary form in the colonial period. The chief of these was the influence of pioneering and the frontier, the development of urban industrialism, the rise of city luxury marked by conspicuous consumption, and the culmination of the chattel slave system. All of these agencies, it will be observed, are essentially economic and their outstanding importance supports the large lines of the economic interpretation. The first was a phenomenon of the westward-moving forefront of settlement—the most distinctively American factor in our history. The long persistence of a genuine frontier continually brought a considerable part of the population under the direct influence of pioneer life and has profoundly affected conditions even in the older sections of the country. Notions and usages brought from the various European backgrounds were inexorably modified by contact with the rough, large, free life of the New World. To a considerable degree the frontier acted equally on the North and South, but the fullness of its influence was reserved for the free section where there was no servile class to constitute a buffer to its hardships and to modify its liberalizing power. The rise of industrialism, urbanism, and high life were in the main peculiar to the North. The slave system, on the other hand, had by the end of colonial days surrendered its potency in northern life. In the period covered by this volume its direct influence is confined to the South, where its climax and decadence tinged with gruesome yet romantic color the family institutions of a nation within a nation.

It is to be remembered that in the epoch covered by this volume North and South were growing apart—losing the high degree of similarity that marked the two sections in the early days of colonization. It is possible, nevertheless, to generalize largely as to many elements in the family institution of the whole union—elements due to the fundamental sameness of origin and to the relative identity of many environmental influences peculiar to the New World. The South even had a touch of the Industrial Revolution that captured the North; and the North developed a new and more effective slavery of its own which manifested many of the degenerative influences that marred the social system of the South. It is continually apparent in the following pages what matter is relevant to the nation as a whole and what is peculiar to East or West, North or South.

I. MARRIAGE AND FECUNDITY IN THE NEW NATION

Conditions in the new American nation favored marriage, early marriage and high fecundity, and so long as pioneer conditions persisted mating and breeding went on apace. Independence signified no fundamental revolution in the currents of social life, and colonial traditions passed on unbroken into the folkways of the republic; for until the Civil War the population was distinctly rural, and urban sophistication had acquired no dominant influence over the thoughts, standards, and habits of the major part of the inhabitants of the United States. The pioneer environment and the pioneer spirit were still in their prime and tinged the whole people by reason of the currents of movement between East and West.

Inasmuch as the pioneer settler's time was divided mostly between home building and home protection, the psychology of domesticity was supreme; the family was the one substantial social institution in a nation that had discarded hierarchical religion and that had reduced government to the minimum, while business corporations had not yet attained notable development. On the frontier at least was the case thus. The field was rather bare for the unmarried man or woman; neither sex could get along comfortably, and woman could scarcely get along at all, without a partner. Wilderness rigors and lack of suitable employment in the settled regions impelled woman to marry, irrespective of love, as alternative to a rather impersonal and perhaps menial existence in the home of parent or other relative; while on the other hand, even in the cities, facilities for comfortable bachelorhood were not great in the early days, and in the wilderness a wife was valuable for her labor, her companionship, and as the presumptive mother of numerous sturdy workers.

Nor was there anything to discourage early marriage so long as the abundance and cheapness of land, together with the simplicity and easy procurability of equipment for farming or trade, offered an outlook and a leverage for labor and maintained thereby a reasonably high standard of well-being even in the older states. Simplicity of life, abundance of the prime necessities, certainty of subsistence, and the shortage of population and labor promoted marriage and procreation. Such facts appear in numerous writings of the colonial and nationalizing periods.

Benjamin Franklin before the Revolution drew an impressive contrast between the old settled countries where all berths were full and the new world where the abundance and cheapness of land and the relative ease of subsistence banished forebodings and led to readiness for early marriage; so that "marriages in America are more general, and more generally early than in Europe. And if it is reckoned there, that there is but one marriage per annum among one hundred persons, perhaps we may here reckon two." At the time of Independence marriage was the regular thing; sports and recreations turned largely on the mimic choice of a partner; the unmated player was the butt of ridicule. Thus did merrymaking reflect the status of "the mincing spinster or the crusty old bachelor."

As early as 1776 people were marrying in Kentucky.

The newcomers had to settle in forts and contact was sufficiently close for courtship. Many of the first Westerners married at fifteen or sixteen. In pioneer Kentucky, "a marriage that sometimes united a boy of sixteen to a girl of fourteen was an occasion of merriment and brought out the whole fort." Schoepf, who travelled in the Confederation, notes that people "generally marry with less forethought and earlier" than in more artificial civilizations. He was informed, for instance, by a gentleman of Petersburg "that he would be sending his son to Edinburgh to make a doctor of him, since he now doubted whether he would ever marry and take a plantation, his age being already twenty-one years."

Colonial conditions persisted far into the national period so that in writings of the early nineteenth century we find frequent reference to the facility and prevalence of marriage in the United States as compared with Europe. Instances are recorded of the marriage of boys of fifteen and of girls in the early teens or younger. Bernard, an English comedian who was in America at the beginning of the century, observed that Virginia ladies bloomed early. "A lady here was in the habit of marrying nearly ten years earlier than a European, so that at twenty, if she had proved a fruitful olive, her husband's table was surrounded with tall shoots sufficient to supply him with shade for the remainder of his days."

According to report, the girls of North Carolina married so early that grandmothers of twenty-seven years of age were frequently found.[1] Early marriages were usual in all the states. Even girls of the "higher" classes often married at thirteen. Men were in excess;

---

[1] Hunt. *Life in America one hundred Years ago*, 77.

so 'here were few spinsters; widows remarried if young; and widowers sought new mates anyway. Hodgson wrote from Charleston in 1820 that patrician damsels "are frequently married at sixteen or eighteen . . . and generally under twenty." In Kentucky early marriage was common; "men at eighteen or twenty; girls at fourteen or sixteen." One writer of about 1820 says: "The American youth of both sexes are, for the most part, married ere they are two and twenty; and indeed it is usual to see a girl of eighteen a wife and mother. . . No care is taken to prevent contracting early engagements." Another a little later writes: "Perhaps a great majority of the females marry before the age of twenty, and it is not an uncommon thing to see them mothers at sixteen, seventeen, or eighteen."

Nothing was more natural than such promptitude among pioneers where one needed merely to go to the other side of the spring, put up a cabin and start a clearing. A German-American writing in 1826 said that in the country as soon as a young fellow had gathered a few dollars, seldom over one hundred, he thought of marriage. The wedding gift to a son consisted of a horse, farm implements, and seed; a girl received a bed, a cow, kitchen utensils, and maybe a clothes chest, tables, and chairs. The young man procured a hundred acres of forest; relatives put up a house and stable; and in two or three years he was tolerably well-fixed, for the pair were used to work. A visitor of 1831 speaking of the vicinity of Springfield, Ohio, said:

> Any man who is able and willing to work for his livelihood, can always, in two or three years, make himself master of a farm, in this or any other part of the Union. The average value of uncleared land is a hundred dollars for eighty acres. A single man can everywhere earn at least twelve dollars a month. Provisions are exceedingly cheap: a sheep or a deer

can be purchased for a dollar, wheat may be about two shillings the bushel.

On toward the middle of the century the phenomenon of easy marriage continued to attract attention. There was still an abundance of unoccupied soil, ample elbow room for the energetic and efficient man, and fruitful opportunity for judicious investment. In spite of the clever devices of grasping exploitation it still remained true that for the average spirited and intelligent young man opportunities for maintaining a family in comfort were far more abundant than in older countries. A bachelor's life did not hold out the charms that it did in Europe; a wife was a light burden if not a source of income and a conserver of values. For some years following 1850 the federal land law for Oregon was a great attraction to immigrants, for it enabled a man and wife to obtain a section of land. A single man was entitled to but half a section. The situation encouraged early marriages. Girls were in great demand. It was not uncommon to see brides of fourteen. Some persons tell of having found married women in the woods of the Columbia playing with their dolls.[2] Additional citations corroborative of the tendency to early marriage and indicative of the social effects of the situation might be given.

Moreover pioneers found large families desirable: vast empty spaces kindled ambitions for dominion; the labor of growing children was valuable; and a sufficiency of stalwart sons increased security against the Indian. The value of children for defense and labor is mentioned by numerous writers. Amid the boisterous cheer of a frontier wedding one might hear the toast: "Health to the groom, and here's to the bride, thumping luck, and big children." Says Doddridge: "This

2 Lyman. *The Columbia River*, 177.

was considered as an expression of a very proper and friendly wish; for big children, especially sons, were of great importance as we were few in number and engaged in perpetual hostility with the Indians."

The birth-rate of pioneers far outstripped the high death-rate; natural selection drew fecund women from the East and weeded out weaklings. In 1751 Benjamin Franklin said that "if in Europe they have but four births to a marriage . . . we may here reckon eight." About 1760 it was estimated that the common rate of increase in America "when unmolested by enemies is: doubling the population every twenty-five years, by births, exclusive of immigration." The long-suffering pioneer mothers did not rebel against the tragedy of incessant child-bearing; the continent called urgently to them, it offered no sterile "careers;" no age of surplus had yet bred delicacy and worldly wisdom; maternity was their portion and they bravely played their part. Pioneer women were grandmothers at forty; mother and daughter often had infants at the same time. For the Scotch-Irish, as for the Puritan, the scripture conspired with environment; families of twelve or more are not infrequently encountered in the earlier records. Irving refers to the New England pioneer who buries himself in the wilderness and is soon surrounded by "some half a score of flaxen-haired urchins, who by their size seem to have sprung up all at once . . . like a crop of toadstools."

Adam Smith's reference to American fecundity is well-known.

Those who live to old age, it is said, frequently see there from fifty to a hundred, and sometimes many more descendants from their own body. Labor is there so well rewarded that a numerous family of children, instead of being a burden, is a source of opulence and prosperity to the parents. The labor of each child before it can leave their house, is computed to be worth a hundred pounds clear gain to them. A young widow with four or five young children, who, among the middling or inferior ranks of people in Europe would have so little chance for a second husband, is there frequently counted as a sort of fortune. The value of children is the greatest of all encouragement to marriage. We cannot, therefore, wonder that the people in North America should generally marry very young. Notwithstanding the great increase occasioned by such early marriages, there is a continual complaint of the scarcity of hands in North America.

In 1784 Franklin, writing advice as to migration from Europe, calls attention to the rapid increase of inhabitants "by natural generation," which multiplication he attributed to salubrity of climate, abundance of good provisions, and the facility of early marriage. He said that persons of moderate means

Who having a number of children to provide for, are desirous of bringing them up to industry, and to secure estates for their posterity, have opportunities of doing it in America, which Europe does not afford. Small capitals laid out in lands, which daily become more valuable by the increase of people, afford a solid prospect of ample fortunes thereafter for those children. . . It is easy for poor families to get their children instructed; for the artizans are so desirous of apprentices, that many of them will even give money to the parents, to have boys from ten to fifteen years of age bound apprentices to them, till the age of twenty-one; and many poor parents have, by that means, on their arrival in the country, raised money enough to buy land sufficient to establish themselves, and to subsist the rest of their families by agriculture.

Like considerations appealed of course to native Americans. Imlay writing from Kentucky spoke of "the extraordinary fecundity it is observed everywhere prevails. . . Plenty . . . is essential to occasion that fecundity which distinguishes the rapid population of most infant countries after they have overcome the first difficulties of establishing a settlement."

Michaux said of Kentucky at the beginning of the new century that few houses had less than four or five children. At that time "everything in the United States favors the progress of population . . . above all, the abundance of the means of subsistence."

In the *Literary Magazine and American Register* of 1803-1804, an article on the progress of population in the United States exhibited the following facts: 1. States and parts of states containing new land and now settling contain the greatest percentage of children; for migration to new lands is chiefly by young and middle-aged and such hardy people are prolific. 2. The excess of children in Kentucky and Tennessee shows mildness and salubrity of climate favorable to the rearing of children. 3. Massachusetts, Connecticut, and Rhode Island, owing to emigration, show the greatest percentage of people over forty-five, and the smallest percentage of children under ten. 4. More children under ten occur and fewer persons above forty-five as we go southward. The difference is chiefly in the flat country. [At this point one is moved to interrogate the mosquito.]

In Ramsay's *Sketch of South Carolina* there is the statement that

In many instances, from seven to ten, and in a few, from ten to fifteen children have been raised to maturity in South Carolina from a single pair. There are now eight families in Broad Street between the state-house and the western extremity of that street, in which sixty-nine children have been born and of these sixty-five are alive. In that part of Meeting Street . . . between Tradd . . . and Ashley River, from six marriages (which with the exception of one, have taken place since . . . 1782) forty-two children have been born, all of which, except three are now alive, and the eldest . . . is little more than fourteen. Within the same limits, seven other couples have fifty-two children living, the youngest of whom is twelve years old, and forty-seven are grown to maturity. Greater instances of fecundity frequently occur in our middle and upper country, chiefly among those who inhabit poor land, at a distance from the rivers. There is a couple in Orangeburgh district, near the road that leads to Columbia from Orangeburgh, who lately had fifteen children alive out of sixteen, and a fair prospect of more. Another couple live in Darlington county, fifteen miles from Lynch's creek, who lately had thirteen children and fifty-one grandchildren all alive; and of their thirteen children, twelve were married at the same time.

In the *History of South Carolina* Ramsay stated that one woman of Greenville district had had thirty-four children of whom but one pair was twins.

From sixteen to twenty-two have been brought alive into the world by individual mothers in the low country; but these instances are rare. . . From six to nine children are often raised in the western districts. Twelve is the largest number of children now living from one pair in Charleston, and only two such can be recollected; but there are several who have from eight to eleven alive; and many from four to seven. Some women have been mothers at fifteen, and a few grandmothers at thirty. The number of children born is great; but the deaths in infancy are also great, tho considerably less than was usual forty years ago.

Melish, who traveled in the United States between 1806 and 1811, wrote:

The Georgian ladies appear to be very fond of children, and, in the country at least, they seem to be sufficiently prolific; for we hardly ever passed a house without seeing a cluster of young ones; and often a child at the breast of a mother, whom, judging from external appearance, I would have reckoned past child-bearing.

Beaujour in a [French] *Sketch of the United States* in the first decade of the century noted that births were "more multiplied" than in Europe, and deaths relatively less frequent.

It is calculated that [the birth rate is one to every twenty of the population] and that the proportion of deaths is only one in forty. . . No human consideration . . . operates as a hindrance to reproduction, and the inhabitants swarm on the rich land in the same manner as do the insects.

Warden in 1819 gave the same birth-rate as Beaujour recorded, and set over against it an estimate for Europe of one birth to twenty-seven of the population.

Major Jonathan Hunter, writing on large families in a certain Virginia county, said:

In 1820 I passed by Mr. Watters and was shown five houses all in sight and farms adjoining with the old people living, and each with ten children making sixty persons in five families, and Major Morris' (living only two or three miles from Watters) wife died leaving nine children. Morris married a widow Harrison with nine children and they had a son Davidton . . . so there were twenty-one in the family. If you come across a farm as prolific in Cereals as that neighborhood was in children I would advise you to buy it.

Kingdom in 1820 advised mechanics, etc., with families or wishing families to come to America. In 1822 there was said to be "a greater proportion of children in the United States, under sixteen, to the general amount of the population than in any other country, on account of early marriages." Madison, writing after the census of 1820, stated:

It is worth remarking that New England, which has sent out such a continued swarm to other parts of the union for a number of years, has continued at the same time . . . to increase in population, altho it is well known that it has received but comparatively few emigrants from any quarter.

The fecundity of the Kentucky stock was subjected to a similar test. Singleton in his *Letters from the South and West* (published in 1824) remarked:

The Kentuckyans in general have numerous families, the fruitfulness of the climate extending even to the wives . . . brides who were as Rachels in the Atlantic states, having mi-

grated to the west, become as Leahs; and . . . they
esteem it no unusual compliment to receive even the double
blessing of Rebeccas.

It seems that for two or three generations the Kentucki-
ans scarcely intermarried with the people from other
states but into other families in the state, "perhaps even
of different nationality tho always Kentuckyans. The
result was that these happy, brave, strong, healthy people founded large families of children." In old Kentucky most families were large. It was not unusual to
have twelve to sixteen children. From 1820 or thereabouts to 1860 and later there was great emigration
from Kentucky to other Mississippi Valley states. It
has been estimated that Kentucky's contribution to the
white population of the other states amounted in 1860
to at least one million. If the figure is correct, the
fecundity of the Kentucky population in its first eighty
years must have been unsurpassed. Shaler suggests
several reasons: the original settlers were vigorous;
they came of their own initiative unforced by need of
subsistence; difficulty and danger deterred the weak.
The soil was rich; there was plenty of unoccupied land
for the rising generation; for a long time, children
were profitable to the agriculturist, and there was patriarchal pride in an abundant progeny. "The syphilitic
poison does not seem to have been common."

Tennessee enacted a law in 1829 authorizing any
man whose wife had three or more children at one birth
to take up two hundred acres of state lands for each of
the children. Buckingham noted in 1842 that in the
log huts of the Georgia mountains "the number of their
children appeared to be excessive, ten or twelve in each
hut at least." One woman not over thirty-five had
thirteen children. In 1839 Stephen Thomas, aged

eighty-eight, "the last of the Huguenots," died in South Carolina. His descendants consisted of between sixty and seventy persons, of whom three were his children and four his great-grandchildren. A North Carolina man born during the period under study in this volume had twenty-seven brothers and sisters. Numbers of South Carolinians had families of from nine to seventeen children. John R. Commons says, "From earliest colonial times until the census of 1840 the people of the United States multiplied more rapidly than the people of any other modern nation, not excepting the prolific French-Canadians."

A writer in the *Democratic Review* of 1844 said:

> The poor man in the new country has one aid not dreamed of in the older settlements – his children. These are elsewhere a subject of dread to those who depend on the day's labor for the day's food, and not always as welcome as they should be to some people who have plenty to eat. Here "the more the merrier" and the better off, too. For six months of the year hats and shoes are out of fashion, and drapery of an almost classical simplicity is quite sufficient for the younger children. [At seven or eight they begin to be useful. They become more and more useful until they reach their teens], when he must be a poor block indeed who does not pay back into the common treasury more than he takes from it. . . Our poor man counts each one of his half-dozen or half score a blessing . . . stout hands and active heads are the very things we need.

A family was an encumbrance to an immigrant in that it delayed his getting settled. But, said a traveller of 1849, "to the emigrant of small means and a large family, I would say let him not be discouraged. If his family are healthy, sober, thrifty, and industrious, they will be a fortune to him, and they make him independent, being a little, well-ordered community within themselves." Naumann in his *Nordamerika* noted: "The American regards a numerous family as a treasure, but often only for the reason that his children by their work until their majority are useful to him." A writer in 1852 tells us that

Each new babe is a new source of delight; and should the number surpass that of a common family, you cannot but smile in pleasant emotion with the father, who will tell you that he has the round dozen, or he can produce you "any quantity" of little ones.

Burn in his *Three years among the Working-classes in the United States during the [Civil] War* said: "Settlers with families of children able to work, as a general thing, will find no trouble in obtaining employment for them."

Conditions facilitated adoption. "One blessed custom they have in America," wrote an English visitor in 1848, "resulting from the abundance which they enjoy; a man dies, his widow and children are objects of peculiar care to the surviving branches of his family; the mother dies—her orphans find a home among her friends and relatives." Another visitor in a work published in 1852 said:

Observing how easily and frankly children are adopted in the United States, how pleasantly the scheme goes on, and how little of the wormwood of domestic jealousies, or the fretting prickle of neighbors' criticisms seem to interfere with it, one is led to enquire why the benevolent practice is so common there. . . The facility with which enough, and more than enough, is found to satisfy every hungry mouth on a farm, gives wonderful scope to the benevolent sentiment. [There is plenty of room in America. A fresh hand growing up is valuable to the sons of labor] who are quite as ready to adopt a child as the wealthy. [Absence of primogeniture favors adoption. The novelty of the plan of adoption] led me to enquire very carefully as to its results, and the statement was, that if one in a hundred tired or failed to do by the adopted as they would have done by their own, it was *but* one in the hundred.

Opinion as to the merits of early marriage varied.

An early writer remarked: "It is curious to see how soon these laughing maidens are metamorphosed into fond wives and attentive mothers; and these giddy youths into industrious citizens and thinking politicians." Another considered early marriage in some cases desirable as a spur to enterprise. Another said: "The facility of getting on in the world, and marrying young, is, upon the whole, most favorable to the morals of the community, altho it sometimes leads to uncongenial and unhappy unions." Another: "Early marriages offer to parents the great advantage of bringing up their children under the parental eye. . . There are certainly inconsiderate marriages, which ought to be disapproved, but still in this kind of lottery they cheat the less." These are the views of foreigners. A writer in the *Lady's Book* of 1836 expressed the opinion that as a rule early marriages are advisable.

Others noted ill effects. Mackenzie held that: "The youth of twenty, and the female of fourteen are ill-fitted for the cares, anxieties, and education of a family." Miss Martineau said that in the South and West, "owing to the disproportion of numbers, every woman is married before she well knows how serious a matter human life is." Cooper said: "It is far more common to find" American women "mothers of eight or of ten children, at fifty, than mothers of two or three. . . These early marriages . . . have an obvious tendency to impair the powers of the female and to produce a premature decay." A visitor noted that American womanhood decays early. By thirty "nothing remains but the traditions of former conquests, and anticipation of the period when her reign of triumph will be vicariously restored in the person of her daughter." Another considered the early fad-

ing of woman's beauty attributable "to the great assi-
duity with which American ladies discharge their duties as mothers. No sooner are they married than they
begin to lead a life of comparative seclusion, and once
mothers they are actually buried to the world." Bunn,
a mid-century author, thought women should "not marry at so tender an age, nor have half-a-dozen children
before they ought to have one." It is only fair to say
that part of the decay was doubtless due to the inactivity and indulgence of incipient luxury. But degeneracy could not have gone very far in the ante-bellum
period. F. A. Walker said: "There is not the shadow
of a statistical reason for attributing to the native
American population prior to the war of secession a
deficiency in reproductive vigor compared with any
people that ever lived."

II. THE UNSETTLING OF OLD FOUNDATIONS

The same economic basis as stimulated marriage and procreation in the new nation operated in the direction of general liberalization and even radicalism. The abundance of natural resources hampered the designs of such as aspired to establish the prerogatives of aristocracy by means of narrowed holdings of wealth; it reduced the importance of vested riches, and created a social optimism that measured men by their future possibilities rather than by the tokens of the past. Thus conditions eventuated in lessened regard to property considerations and social gradations in the making of matches and opened the field for unhampered crossing of strains, a tendency which was augmented by the free circulation of population untrammeled by the meager systems of exhausted countries. The frontier created also the economic basis for egalitarianism inasmuch as the axe and the rifle "made all men equally tall;" hence there arose an individualistic democracy akin to anarchy—a state of affairs quite in harmony, moreover, with the paucity of public enterprises in a region where the government even left the settlers largely to their own devices against the Indians. In so far as grasping Easterners retarded government paternalism in the West lest population should be drawn thither and wages raised in the old states, they were really furthering that fierce democracy that was to mean so much in the way of general insurgency and social transformation. The whole weight of frontier freedom conspired with the modernist individualism imported from Europe to work that family disintegration whose later phenomena are so conspicuous today.

The relative absence of mercenary marriage in America was noted by various authors.   In St. John's *American Letters* it is reported of Nantucket:

> Every man takes a wife as soon as he chuses . . . no portion is required; none is expected; no marriage articles are drawn up among us, by skillful lawyers, to puzzle and lead posterity to the bar, or to satisfy the pride of the parties . . . as the wife's fortune consists principally in her future economy, modesty, and skillful management; so the husband's is founded on his abilities to labor, on his health, and the knowledge of some trade and business.

Mazzei reported in 1788 that it is not "rare for a girl to refuse a man whose face and fortune are his only recommendations." The utter absence of the European custom of parents' providing their daughters with marriage portions excited many comments among our French guests.

Lambert in his *Travels* of 1806-1808 tells that:

> Several young ladies in New York have fortunes of a hundred or a hundred and fifty thousand dollars, and often bestow their hand upon a favorite youth who has everything to recommend him but money. . . I understand that unhappy marriages are by no means frequent; and that parents are not apt to force the inclinations of their children from avaricious motives.

Several writers of the next decade referred to the absence of monetary considerations in the typical American marriage.   One remarked on the non-existence of family wealth, another on the rarity of dowries. A German traveller noted: "It is generally hard here for widows to get another husband, and likewise for girls of advanced years, for . . . Americans marry more from natural inclination than do Europeans."

For the period between 1825 and 1860 numerous writers might be cited in evidence of the non-commercial character of American marriage. Sidons says that "parents seek less to secure a rich match than a steady man for their child." Cooper in 1828 remarked:

> A young woman of the middling classes . . . seldom gives much of her thoughts towards the accumulation of a little dowry; for the question of what a wife will bring to the common stock is agitated much less frequently here than in countries more sophisticated. My companion assures me it is almost unprecedented for a lover to venture on any inquiries concerning the fortune of his fair one, even in any class. . . From all that I can learn, nothing is more common, however, than for young men of great expectations to connect themselves with females, commonly of their own condition in life, who are penniless; or, on the other hand, for ladies to give their persons with one or two hundred thousand dollars, to men who have nothing better to recommend them than education and morals.

Golovin in *Stars and Stripes* wrote:

> It is quite common among parents to give their daughters only their parental blessing for dowry, and to make them wait till after death for the inheritance. . . Fortune-hunters are despised here, and men take a wife with the same carelessness as they would take a glass of brandy, especially when "bound westwards."

Of course indifference to economic attractions in matrimony was more common in rural and especially in pioneer regions than among "the richer portion of the inhabitants of cities." There was certainly a tendency in the direction of sordid unions among the class that rose with commercialization and the waning of wilderness influences as well as among the beneficiaries of the slave system. These phenomena will receive treatment in a later chapter.

With neglect of pecuniary considerations went carelessness as to social rank. De Tocqueville commented

on the fact that democratic equality by obliterating social barriers opened the way to marriage between almost any man and almost any woman and thereby tended to lessen irregular sex relations such as occurred in
aristocratic countries where passion drew together men
and women whose permanent union would have been
unthinkable. To the pioneer, health and courage were
sufficient commendations of a prospective son-in-law
and standards scarcely less simple were of wide prevalence. There were certain limits, however, to easy tolerance, as for instance a case reported by an English
traveller who found at Buffalo a woman of English
birth, well-informed, good-looking, married to a negro,
seemingly owing to his fortune. Tho the man was not
an undesirable citizen, the wife was despised by the
wives of white citizens and both were shunned. White
etiquette would not let him attend her at their theater
box; they never ventured out together. If one did go
out, it was usually after dark. On one occasion the
man was mobbed and nearly lost his life.[3] Carlier,
whose work on *Marriage in the United States* appeared
on the eve of the Civil War, was struck by the elope-
ment of girls of good family with men of low station;
such unions were stigmatized by public opinion.

In so far as indifference to economic and social rank
prevailed, marriage and the preliminaries to it were
naturally simplified. Some of the French visitors of
the end of the eighteenth century were much impressed
with the American freedom of courtship. Mazzei
said: "The young girls and men see each other every
hour of the day, and that too without masks; they do
not marry unless both are pleased, and don't postpone
until too late the discovery that they have been de-

---

[3] Benwell. *Englishman's Travels in America*, 56-58.

ceived. The object of both sexes is to learn each other's character." Bayard reported:

> The time which passes between the proposal and the marriage
> is given over to mutual observation. The girls insist upon an
> absolute independence which they devote to testing the char-
> acter of their future husband. . . They yield to every
> fancy . . . and do everything they can to escape the re-
> proach later on of having concealed their imperfections. It is
> a contest of frankness, inspired by the desire for common hap-
> piness.

Especially numerous were the remarks made on the
fact that young women did not allow themselves to be
hampered before marriage by the jealousy of their
men. Additional light will be thrown in a subsequent
chapter on the sovereignty assumed by woman.

James Franklin in his *Philosophical and Political
History of the Thirteen United States of America*, said
of Pennsylvania and Delaware:

> The matrimonial state is so much the more happy, and con-
> sequently the more reverenced, as the freedom and sanctity of
> marriage depends entirely on the will of the parties. They
> choose the lawyer and the priest, rather as witnesses than as
> means of cementing their engagements. When they meet with
> opposition from their relations, the two lovers go off on horse-
> back together. The man rides behind his mistress, and in this
> situation present themselves before the magistrate, where the
> girl declares she has run away with her sweetheart, and that
> they are come to be married. Such a solemn avowal cannot be
> rejected, nor has any person a right to give them any molesta-
> tion. In all other cases the parental authority is very exten-
> sive.

Sidons in *Die Vereinigten Staaten von Nordamerika*
(1826) related that even before a girl's majority the
parents "seldom make objections . . . to her
choice, provided the suitor has the means to support
their child; and even about that the children usually are
more careful than the parents. If the lover is an en-

tire stranger, investigation is more exact." Another
writer of the same period says: "Taste and inclination,
rather guided than controlled by the prudence of older
heads form most of our matches." Given such freedom
of choice, couples had only themselves to blame for a
mismating and small excuse to justify infidelity; besides, it tended to enhance the chances of congenial
mating. The wider connections of the reign of freedom will appear in subsequent chapters.

New world life tended not only to make marriage
independent of economic considerations, social gradations, and parental constraint but also to loosen social
control. Even at the dawn of Independence, while
each community firmly upheld matrimony, the Protestant repudiation of Catholic doctrine was already por-
tending freedom in marriage and divorce that threatened to produce further laxity. The ceremony was in
general simple and complaint was made that the pair
were kept too long in the company, exposed to banter.
The doctrine of free love was bound to develop as an
ethical counterpart of laissez-faire economics; both are
anarchism; both were stimulated by the spacious freedom of the new world. An article in the *Literary
Magazine* of 1805 may perhaps be taken as corroborative of this assertion of tendency. It said that probably
the mischief that some moralists attribute to novels is
due to their exaggeration of the omnipotence of love
(with the inference suppliable that licentiousness is
justified thereby). "Those people who are willing to
indulge irregular desires have created [the doctrine
of the omnipotence of love] and the force of love is now
a part of the creed of almost every master and miss in
the reading world." Such might naturally be the case
under the influence of such liberalizing factors as previously detailed. It would seem that what had always

been a practice (licentiousness) was now investing itself in a theory, and thereby assuming a more frightful
mien.

Pioneer marriage relations sometimes became involved in strange vicissitudes. Sometimes a man detained long from home through capture by Indians or
otherwise returned to find his wife remarried. If one
thought dead thus came back, the neighbors and interested parties seem frequently to have held a sort of
court and to have decreed that the woman should make
choice between the two men. The other was to leave
the settlement. No one seems to have been disturbed
at the thought of possible legal irregularity in such
proceedings. Incidents of the sort are often mentioned.
Usually the woman returned to her first husband.[4]

Some hazards of pioneer marriages appear in the
following incidents.[5] In the history of early Tennessee
is recorded the account of a wife's becoming tired of
her husband and taking up with another man. She
left her husband sick and induced the party with which
they were travelling to leave him, doubtless to his death.
In the same state in early days a man named Bean, a
noted character, went with a cargo to New Orleans and
remained two years. On his return he found his wife
nursing an infant, the reputed child of a merchant.
The outraged husband left the house without a word
but later returned intoxicated, took the baby from the
cradle, and cut off both ears, muttering that he had
marked it so that it would not get mixed up with his
children. He was arrested and sentenced in addition
to other punishment to be branded; while his wife was
granted a divorce and married again. After the death

[4] Roosevelt. *Winning of the West*, vol. i, 129.
[5] Hale and Merritt. *History of Tennessee and Tennesseeans*, vol. ii, 345,
365-367, 370.

of the child and of her second husband, Bean remarried her. Another frontiersman, on his way home to Ireland to bring his family to the home prepared, heard in Virginia that his wife, believing him dead, had married again. The report turned out to be false; so in 1796 he set out for Ireland after an absence of twenty years and returned with wife and son. In 1819 a traveller writing from Jeffersonville, Indiana, observed that "runaway wives are frequently advertised."

Unconventionality sometimes attended the celebration of the marriage ceremony. At the beginning of the nineteenth century, upon the Tombigbee and Lake Tensaw (Alabama) the people still lived without civil government and without the rite of matrimony. For years the sexes had been pairing off and cohabiting with the mutual promise of regular marriage when ministers or magistrates should appear. In one instance where the parents of a rich girl objected to a pairing, she and her poor lover paddled off with a crowd of young people and begged the commandant at Fort Stoddart to marry them. He said he had no authority of the sort. They told him that the government had put him there as general regulator of affairs. He presently acceded and said: "I Captain Shanneberg of second regiment, U.S.A. and commandant of Fort Stoddart, do hereby pronounce you man and wife. Go home! behave yourselves—multiply and replenish the Tensaw country." The settlement pronounced them the best-married people it had known in a long time.[6]

The early settler west of the mountains received only occasional visits from ministers. McConnell in his *Western Characters* said:

Protestant ministers . . . were few [and the words] were usually spoken by a Jesuit missionary . . . or by some

---

[6] Pickett. *History of Alabama*, 465.

justice of the peace of doubtful powers and mythical appointment.   If neither of these could be procured, the father of the
bride, himself, sometimes assumed the functions.   .   .   It was
always understood, however, that such left-handed marriages
were to be confirmed by the first minister who wandered to the
frontier; and, even when the opportunity did not offer for
many months, no scandal ever arose – the marriage vow was
never broken.

Such free and easy arrangements speak strongly of a
new world with a clean slate.

The development of marriage law in the United
States is completely summed up in Howard's *History
of Matrimonial Institutions* and need not be detailed
here.   Its evolution has been largely a history of adjustment to new conditions caused principally by pioneer life and industrial evolution.   Thus owing to
shortage of ministers legal arrangements had to be made
for civil marriage.   A civil marriage that occurred in
1805 among the Spanish colonists of the South was
later declared valid by the United States Supreme
Court, the Council of Trent notwithstanding.   It is of
interest to note, on the other hand, what was happening
in New England, that early stronghold of civil marriage.   Dwight said in 1822:

Justices of the peace are throughout New England authorized
to marry, but are rarely, if ever, employed to perform the service, when a clergyman can be obtained.   As it is everywhere
believed to be a Divine institution; it is considered involved, of
course, within the duties of the sacred office.   An absolute decency is observed during the celebration.

An illustration of the breezy freedom of the frontier
marriage is given by an early settler in Wisconsin
whose servant girl, taken along from the East, contemplated matrimony.   As justice of the peace he was
asked to perform the ceremony but at first flatly refused
owing to unwillingness to lose the domestic until her

year was out. The offer of five bushels of turnips as wedding-fee proved a sufficient inducement and the rites were performed.   But just as the guests were about to leave, one of the bride's rejected suitors inquired "whether the *Squire* had seen the *license* authorizing the parties to be joined in marriage."   This question produced tremendous consternation.   "Was it a fact that a license was necessary; and if such was the fact, why had not our friend made it known before the ceremony was performed?"   The scandalous wight replied that he "thought it would be greater fun to let the ceremony go on, and blow it up afterward.   Then, you know, we could have another wedding!"   Vainly did the new husband remonstrate.

> They threatened to tear the house down if their will was not obeyed, and D—— was forced to submit to their mandate – to be separated from his bride – which he did with a very bad grace.   The next morning he procured the important document from Milwaukee.   The ceremony was repeated.[7]

That the adjustment to changing economic conditions was destined to prove a more ticklish problem than adjustment to wilderness needs becomes apparent at the time when slavery was becoming extinct in the North. Judge Platt of New York in 1822 delivered an opinion that marriage was legal where one of the parties was a slave and that if the mother was free the children were also free.   "The husband is not emancipated, nor is the wife enslaved by such a marriage."   But in 1827 it was held that a slave could not marry under common law.   The children of a slave could not inherit at common law.   But by a special law a slave could take possession of land granted for military service in the Revolution; hence all marriages and births involved

---

[7] *Western frontier life*, 520-522.

were legitimate, and the children of such a slave could inherit.[8]

The advent of male political democracy consequent on the free life of the frontier went hand in hand with an intense individualism akin to anarchism. The dominant idea tended to be "that the individual is superior to the community and that the latter should not exercise any restraints except in rare cases and from reasons of most serious moment." A disposition to govern marriage by some such principle became manifest. The progress of individualistic democracy was quite consistent with the reduction of social control over marriage, as in the abolition of banns and the dropping of the requirement of publicity as if the union of the individuals were their own exclusive affairs concerning no one else. A writer in 1823 noted that

> Marriage . . . in the United States, is considered a civil contract, therefore a justice can marry equally as well as a clergyman. In general a clergyman is employed. . . I was one evening at the house of a Baptist clergyman: he was called out of the room, and was not absent more than three minutes, but in that time he had tied Hymen's indissoluble knot. This facility of marriage is frequently attended with very injurious effects. I have known perfect children married, often to the great grief of their friends. [The government will have to intervene and require license.] [9]

Another writer said:

> If the youth be of age and the girl likewise they marry without asking leave of any one, and if not, they frequently do the same.[10]

Le Comte de St. Victor, who visited the United States (and liked to make out a bad case against America),

[8] Adams. *Neglected Period of Anti-slavery in America*, 239.
[9] Holmes. *Account of the United States*, 399.
[10] Sealsfield. *The United States*, 133.

wrote in 1832 that the laws seemed to make sport of marriage, turning it over to the bizarre regulations of the sects. A justice could marry a couple without any ceremony by a mere acknowledgment. The consent of parents might be agreeable, but was not necessary. A parson frequently married a couple on the spot without knowing who they were. Then they stayed married till they felt like getting a divorce. Marryat reported:

> Bigamy is not uncommon in the United States from the women being in too great a hurry to marry, and not obtaining sufficient information, relative to their suitors. . . When a foreigner is the party, it is rather difficult to ascertain whether the gentleman has or has not left an old wife or two in the Old World.[11]

Wyse said in his *America*:

> Marriage is regarded throughout the union as a purely civil compact. There is no mystical rite, no set form of words, or stated observance necessary . . . no particular class of persons appointed to preside at its ordinance, and requires the assent merely of the contracting parties, who may have the ability to contract and nothing further. . . Marriages contracted in England . . . are sometimes made subject to inconvenience, if disavowed by either on their landing; the laws generally in force . . . requiring under such circumstances a legal attestation of such marriage, under the seal of the archdiocese of Canterbury before they will enforce its obligations. Of this, many heartless and unprincipled individuals take advantage, and who cannot, without such evidence, be charged with the crime of bigamy, in the event of fraudulently contracting any other, or second marriage.[12]

One source of inconsiderate marriage was the dearth of women in new settlements. The demand was advertized and attracted a supply of women ready to take the chances of haphazard mating. But Görling in *Die neue Welt* saw a bright side of American freedom: "Every

[11] Marryat. *Diary in America*, pt. 2, vol. ii, 6.

[12] Wyse. *America*, vol. i, 298, 309. This author should be read with caution; for he says that marriages are less frequent in proportion to population than in the old country.

one can marry unceremoniously if he takes the notion and this fact totally removes many of our European evils." Naumann said: "To be married by a minister is optional, but is the prevailing custom."

In 1849 Miss Bremer was impressed with the way in which the marriage ceremony was sometimes hurried, in travelling costume, after the manner of American haste.

Carlier, the French historian, in his work of 1860 dilates on American laxity as to marriage. The American girl, he says, enjoys great freedom and is unguided in the choice of a husband. She is disposed to receive with great reluctance any parental opposition, and the delicate deference of daughter to mother is too rarely seen. Under such conditions is marriage very often contracted. The law does not require parental consent, but parents usually consent, or acquiesce in their child's choice. The common law does not compel publication of banns or require witnesses to the act or even the signature of the parties themselves and the marriage may be performed by a justice of the peace or a minister—no matter where they may reside—at any hour and in any place. No more paternal authority; clandestinity is substituted; the salutary office of the minister, who might lend solemnity to the occasion, is replaced by some obscure justice of the peace. These customs are not yet very widely spread but the law is sadly deficient. There are, it seems, two states where publicity is required but without penal enforcement. The fact of cohabitation suffices to render the judges very lenient in validating an imperfect marriage.

Eccentric forms of marriage occur, as in the case of the Maine railroad conductor who was married while making his run, the minister being taken on the train;

or of the couple who, unable to cross a swollen stream, did not wait for it to subside but called to some one to summon the minister, who came to the opposite bank and from there performed the ceremony. Mock marriages also occur and sometimes one party to the sport found to his dismay that the joke formed a legal bond which could be sundered only by divorce. Carlier is led to remark: In view of the "excessive readiness of the law in the formation of marriage, should we not be authorized in saying that it aimed only at a promiscuous intercourse, designed to increase the population, without regard to moral considerations or the future of the family?"

Certain religious bodies found it necessary to impose restrictions of their own beyond the scope of civil law. Such an incident occurred in 1796 at the General Conference of the Methodist Episcopal church where an inquiry was answered thus:

> We do not prohibit our people from marrying persons who are not of our society, provided such persons have the form and are seeking the power of godliness; but if they marry persons who do not come up to this description, we shall be obliged to purge our society of them. And even in a doubtful case, the member of our society shall be put back upon trial. . . We are well assured that few things have been more pernicious to the work of God than the marriage of the children of God with the children of this world. We therefore think ourselves obliged to bear our testimony, both in doctrine and discipline, against so great an evil.

The matter was again up in 1804 and was similarly handled.

The question that seemed most recurrent in the early days of the Presbyterian church was that of forbidden degrees. The church was in general very cautious in the handling of this question. Thus in 1797 a case came up respecting a man who had married his former wife's half-brother's daughter. It was resolved, "That though the Assembly would wish to discountenance imprudent marriages, or such as tend in any way to give uneasiness to serious persons, yet it is their opinion, that the marriage referred to is not of such a nature as to render it necessary to exclude the parties from the privileges of the church." In 1802 in a similar case the decision reflects uniquely the state of mind of an assembly face-to-face with the problems of a new, unsettled society. It was resolved

That such marriages as that in question have been determined, both by the late Synod of New York and Philadelphia, and by the General Assembly, to be on the one hand not forbidden by the laws of God, and on the other hand to be contrary to the general practice of Protestant churches and the feelings and opinions of many serious Christians among ourselves, and on that account to be discountenanced; therefore, resolved, that when such marriages take place, the session of the church where they happen are carefully to consider the case, and if they think it expedient, to administer such discipline as they may judge to be deserved, for that want of Christian tenderness and forbearance that are incumbent on all the professors of our holy religion, or for violating any municipal law, if this has been done; and then to admit or restore them to good standing in the church. And if the session judge that the state of society is such, where these marriages take place, as that neither the duty of Christian tenderness and forbearance, nor the laws of the state have been violated, they may admit the persons concerned to Christian privileges without censure.

Later this action was reconsidered and it was resolved: "That the decision given by the General Assembly in the year 1797 . . . may be adopted on this occasion."

In 1804 such cases were left to the decision of lower courts of the church on account of apparent diversity of opinion in different parts of the country. Similar action was taken in 1810 touching marriage with a deceased wife's sister, and for the same reason. In 1811, "The committee appointed to draught a letter to the joint sessions of Bethel and Indian Town on the case of a person marrying the sister of a deceased wife, prayed to be dismissed from further attention to this duty, and their request was granted." On another occasion the Assembly showed itself reluctant to settle a case of marriage with a brother's widow. It returned the case to the session. "Difference of opinion" among the people was the ground of the difficulty. The Assembly seemed to act consciously on the principle that folkways can make a thing right or wrong, at least within bounds.

In 1821 it was decided that marriage to a deceased wife's sister was to be discouraged, but treatment was left to the session. In 1857 there was a proposition to refer to the presbyteries the question of erasing from the Confession "the last clause of the fourth section of the twenty-fourth chapter" on marriage within prohibited degrees. The motion was laid on the table. Similar action was taken in 1859, and again in 1860.

The Presbyterian church was confronted very early with the problem of sex-irregularity. The Assembly of 1790 gave a careful solution of a case such as was probably not uncommon in the new world. A man had come from Ireland some years before, leaving his family behind. Three times he went back for his family but his wife refused to come and finally refused further cohabitation. He returned to America and lived single for ten years. Then he married and had children. Should the man and his wife be admitted to communion? The case is of value as a further illustration of ecclesiastical circumspection. The Assembly thought such a man ought not to be admitted to privileges because it did not appear that he had procured a divorce and in the eye of the civil law was living in vice.

> It does not appear . . . that he has used the proper means to obtain a legal divorce, nor even to authenticate the facts. . . But . . . if it shall appear that this man has separated from his wife by her wilful and obstinate desertion, and that he has taken all just means to obtain a divorce to which he was lawfully entitled, but was prevented and oppressed by the power of antagonists or of unjust courts; and if he shall . . . produce such evidence . . . as would ntitle him to a divorce by the law of the land and of the church, then . . . it is the opinion of the General Assembly that such a man, behaving himself otherwise as a good Christian, may be admitted to church privileges. [But great caution must be used that the church] may not be inconsistent with the civil law, and that a door be not opened to laxness.

This incident throws interesting light on several points: (1) The church tacitly accepted the patriarchal theory of the family. Else why was not the man considered the deserter inasmuch as he had come away and left his family in Ireland? Evidently the assumption was that to the man belonged the right of determining the place of abode. (2) A disposition on the part of the church to review the acts of civil courts; yet not in conflict with civil law. (3) A spirit of reasonableness, yet of firmness in discouraging marital irregularity.

It will be observed, in fact, through its national history that the Presbyterian church has pursued by no means a fanatical course in the matter of marriage and divorce. It was a recurrent question. The church did, indeed, act ecclesiastically, yet not without regard to a wider social viewpoint. Matters were not settled offhand. Thus in the Assembly of 1808 arose a question:

> If a living child is born in five months and twenty days after

the marriage of its parents, shall the parents be dealt with as guilty of ante-nuptial fornication?

The answer was that as the question was in the abstract

And decisions on questions of this nature must, in most instances, depend on attendant circumstances . . . the Assembly do not judge it proper to decide on the abstract question.

Democratic independence in America tended to easy divorce. The precedents set by colonial New England were in that direction. At the beginning of Independence there was little show for divorce in America nor was legal separation frequent or easy.[13] For the evolution of divorce, Howard's *History of Matrimonial Institutions* should be consulted. It must suffice here to illustrate sparingly the trend.

After Independence, divorce by private statute continued for more than half a century in most states. Gradually, however, general statutes began to emerge and jurisdiction began to pass to the courts. Georgia, Mississippi, and Alabama were the first to abolish legislative divorces, tho the approval of a two-thirds majority was still required after the court had made its decree. In the other states, legislative divorces were used on occasion till about the middle of the century when in the majority of states the method was abolished.

In the early part of the nineteenth century divorce was not a momentous danger. Rhode Island had a singular law to the effect that if a married couple gave to a magistrate a mutual declaration of desire to separate by reason of incompatibility and then lived apart for two years conducting themselves with propriety they might obtain on application annulment of the marriage. A writer of 1818 told that few sought the benefit of this

<hr>

[13] On family troubles see chapter vi.

act and of those that did, some broke the stipulation in-
side of the two years.[14]

Miss Martineau about 1834 wrote:

> In Massachusetts divorces are obtainable with peculiar ease.
> The natural consequences follow: such a thing is never heard
> of . . . protection offered by law to the injured party
> causes marriage to be entered into with fewer risks and the
> conjugal relation carried on with more equality.

Marryat declared

> In the United States divorces are obtained without expense, and
> without it being necessary to commit crime as in England. The
> party pleads in forma pauperis, to the State Legislation, and a
> divorce is granted upon any grounds which may be considered
> as just and reasonable.

A few years later another observer remarked upon the
facilities afforded for persons to get rid of innocent
partners, who perhaps did not know of the application.[15]   Brown in 1849 asserted:

> There are more divorces in one year in the state of Ohio than
> there are in ten in the United Kingdom. In the year 1843
> there were 447 bills of divorcement sued out in that state, and
> they were principally at the suit of the women, whose husbands
> had behaved ill, neglected them or . . . run away.[16]

Two other mid-century writers remarked, however, on
the rarity of divorce in the Unitel States.

The laxity of individualistic laissez-faire democracy
borders on Owen's scheme according to which

> They unite and part as it pleases them, while the children are
> brought up at the general expense of all. It is true, that far
> from encouraging libertine life, he assumes that man, being a
> monogamous animal, may be permitted to choose a companion,
> to whom, after a slight previous intercourse he might be more
> attached, than if bound by lawful wedlock.[17]

[14] Wright. *View of Society and Manners in America*, 425.
[15] Wyse. *America*, vol. i, 300.
[16] Brown. *America*, 48.
[17] Murat. *America and the Americans*, 107.

A Southerner who had lived in the North wrote in 1860:

> The socialists and free lovers argue against the marriage rela-
> tion because married people are always quarrelling and running
> off to Indiana to be divorced.[18]

In 1858 the Presbyterian General Assembly sustained the deposition and excommunication of a minister who had married a woman divorced on an unpermitted ground, and in so doing took "occasion to call the attention of the churches . . . to a tendency, manifest in some portions of our country, to relax the sacredness of the marriage tie;" and to express abhorrence of "any attempt to diminish its sanctity or to extend beyond the warrant of the Holy Scriptures the grounds of divorce."

Carlier observed that each state had its own divorce law, though there was a tendency to adopt uniform reasons for deciding divorce. Besides absolute divorce there was divorce *a mensa et toro*. The latter was allowed in very few states and met with no favor. It was considered immoral, was conducive to adultery, and punished the innocent more than the guilty. He gave the following variety of causes for divorce sanctioned in different sections: bigamy; adultery; voluntary desertion for one, two, three, or five years; absence continued for five years; imbecility or mental alienation; union with a negro, mulatto, or an Indian; vagrancy; cruelty or abuse; slighting conjugal duties; habitual drunkenness during a certain time; the excessive use of opium; imprisonment for certain crimes; impotence; non-support; immorality; membership in the Shaker sect. Kentucky had made a law that when a husband announced in the papers his intention of not paying the debts of his wife, she had sufficient cause for a divorce.

---

[18] Hundley. *Social Relations in our Southern States*, 148.

Carlier said that much depended on the judge. In some states the Legislature decided cases in concurrence with the courts. This participation of the Legislature was a source of abuse. The almost indefinite power granted to the caprices of married couples in America tended to nothing less than indirectly producing polygamy. In Ohio a judge remarked

> That there was no law more abused in that state than that of divorce; and that a majority of the inhabitants thought, of all contracts, marriage was the least obligatory, and nothing further was necessary to dissolve it than to make an appeal to the competent tribunals.

The courts of Indiana were crowded with cases, whose movers were very often citizens of other states, an evidence of the superior facilities there afforded. Simple affirmation proved residence and no one hesitated to lie in so trivial a matter. An Indiana judge was reported to have said

> That the advocates of "free love" . . . could not ask a statute more favorable to their views than the law of divorce in Indiana, and that the polygamy of the Mormons was preferable; for it at least obliged husbands to provide for the subsistence and protection of their wives.

Carlier added

> Throughout the States, it is thought that all which tends to separate the married contributes to the increase of population, and that facilitating the dissolution of the tie is of social utility; because it allows the parties to seek another union, better assorted, destined to fulfil the ends of marriage.

The majority of the divorces were granted at the request of the wife. The step was often in consequence of the husband's abandoning her to seek his fortune in the West, especially in California where the thirst for gold lured. The one that gained the case had a right to remarry. The lot of the defendant varied. Some states allowed an immediate second marriage; others withheld this privilege during the life of the other partner. The law could be evaded, however, by moving to another state.

Horace Greeley, who was so radical on fundamental social questions, was ultra-cautious in this matter. A *Tribune* editorial of March 1, 1860, opposed the loosening of New York divorce law and referred to Indiana as the paradise of free lovers

> Where the lax principles of Robert Dale Owen, and the utter want of principle of John Pettit (leading revisers of the laws) combined to establish, some years since, a state of law which enables men or women to get unmarried nearly at pleasure. A legal friend in that state recently remarked to us, that, at one county court, he obtained eleven divorces one day before dinner; "and it wasn't a good morning for divorces either." In one case within his knowledge, a prominent citizen of an eastern manufacturing city came to Indiana, went through the usual routine, obtained his divorce about dinner-time, and, in the course of the evening was married to his new inamorata, who had come on for the purpose and was staying at the same hotel. [They vent back and ejected his astonished ci-devant spouse.]

Owen replied correcting misstatement and upholding the morals of Indianans. He asserted that they then required one year's residence and timely notice to the absent partner.

> It is in New York and New England, refusing reasonable divorce, that free-love prevails; not in Indiana. I never even heard the name there. [Indiana law allows the court to grant a divorce for any cause it sees fit.] You have elopements, adultery, which your law, by rendering it indispensable to release, virtually encourages; you have free love, and that most terrible of all social evils, prostitution. We . . . have regulated, legal separations. [You believe a poor woman should be kept bound to a brute, subject to his rape.] In no country have I seen marriage and its vows more strictly respected than in my adopted state, where the relation, when it engenders immorality, may be terminated by law. For the rest,

divorces in Indiana are far less frequent than strangers, reading our divorce law, might be led to imagine. [People are more disposed to suffer what is sufferable than to break bonds.]

Greeley was able to reply that New York granted *separation* to Owen's supposititious poor woman. But what of South Carolina, one of whose judges said that in that state "to her unfading honor, a divorce has not been granted since the Revolution"? Bishop cites a case in which "a man took his negro slave-woman to his bed and table and compelled the unoffending wife to receive the crumbs after her" and the state refused any remedy to the wife! The legislators of this state thought "necessary to determine by a special statute what portion of his property a married man may give to his concubine, even under pretext of a compact previous to adultery."[19] In the South, general conservatism retarded the introduction of divorce. In the southern rural community there was small facility for separation, even, in case of estrangement. In the old South a person divorced save for adultery was tabooed. Separation meant ostracism. Yet "it is precisely in the South," says Howard, "that legislative divorce was tried on the widest scale and bore its most evil fruit." On one occasion the Louisiana legislature divorced seven couples in two days.

The South of course had no tolerance for loose views as to the family! Radical opinions developed in the North might echo toward the Gulf but were certain to meet with professed abhorrence. The family pride of the slave power could not contemplate with equanimity community care of children or the abolition of inheritance. A British visitor who was in the United States

[19] Kitchin. *History of Divorce*, 222; Carlier. *Marriage in the United States*, 109-110.

during the War records the following utterance from
the Richmond *Sentinel*:

> Rationalism, introduced by the Puritans, is gradually under-
> mining all religious and political faith and all conservative
> opinions at the North. The marrage institution, reduced by
> them to a mere civil contract, begat frequency and facility of
> divorce, led next to Mormonism, and we suppose has cul-
> minated in free love. But pure Yankee reason is about to
> achieve a still higher triumph . . . miscegenation. . .
> Beginning with liberalism and free inquiry, the North seems
> about to wind up with free love, amalgamation, infidelity,
> agrarianism, and anarchy, while the South becomes daily more
> conservative.

The full force of this contrast will be made apparent
later in a chapter on the family of the South.

It is evident from the foregoing considerations that
the stability of marriage institutions in the past has
been a function of economic pressure. Decrease the
importance of family wealth by throwing open a virgin
continent; and a crude anarchistic individualism throws
off traditional checks and puts personal fancy on top.
We might ask whether marriage has since developed
spiritual sanctions that will guarantee stable monogamy
in the absence of economic necessity for permanent
wedlock.

III. THE EMANCIPATION OF CHILDHOOD

The nineteenth century witnessed a very remarkable revolution in the status of the child in America. As the vastness of the unfolding continent and its needs impressed themselves more and more on the minds of men, the valuation placed on childhood rose. In a society whose population is small as compared with available resources, children always occupy an important position. Moreover, as in colonial days, child-rearing seemed to present special difficulties in the New World. The climate was different from that of the historic habitat of the race. As late as 1848 an Englishwoman remarked that "the difficulty of rearing children until they have passed the second summer and gone through the troubles of teething, makes the American mothers more solicitous than we are in English nurseries." Another writer said: "Children's diseases are hasty and come with a fell swoop, desolating cities and hearts."

The utter dependence of the frontier children on the parents' care in absence of physician's aid increased the parents' burden of responsibility. Pioneer women suckled their own children and cared for them themselves. Until schools and churches came, child-training was of necessity exclusively a family affair; consequently of the simplest character. The pioneer was not sentimental.

His children were never "little cherubs," "angels sent from heaven," but generally "tow-headed" and very earthly responsibilities. . . . He looked forward anxiously to the day when the boys should be able to assist him in the field or fight the Indians, and the girls to help their mother make and mend.

In a new world men face the future and worship, not ancestors, but posterity. "For the children" was the motto of many a pioneer, who endured the wilderness hardships that the next generation might have a better chance, might grow up with the country and enter into their inheritance. The struggle for existence had not yet closed the door of hope.

In addition to its direct stimulus, the pioneer environment created a specific economic situation that tended to emancipate childhood and youth. Family wealth or even surplus was small among settlers, but facilities for making one's way by labor were abundant and thus children began early to produce for themselves. This economic self-sufficiency, uninvaded by any lure of artificial pastimes, matured and emancipated children from undue prolongment of parental control. Where parents stretched their prerogatives or tried to retain jurisdiction past the majority of the boy, estrangement was likely to ensue.

The general preoccupation of the ordinary American husband and wife with the urgent economic problems of life contributed to throw youth upon its own resources and to raise it to sovereignty. This was true even in the cities, or perhaps one should say, particularly in the cities. The rush of the new country left the men no time to be fathers; they were away all day and children came to be left entirely to the care of their mothers. The wives of the laboring class, doing all their own work, seldom looked after their children with due care. They sent the little ones to school to be rid of them or let them run with chance associates, exposed to dangers that they were not fitted to meet.

"Baby citizens are allowed to run as wild as the Snake Indians," said Oldmixon in 1855, "and do whatever they please."

The well known effect of pioneer environment and the economic processes engendered by it is to produce an extremely libertarian democracy bordering on anarchy. The most familiar instances of this operation are in the realm of politics but it goes on in every other phase of life, partly through direct influence and partly through reflection from democratized politics and other agencies of social control. Such lines of causation can be traced in the liberalization of the American family.

Many observers, commenting on the freedom allowed to children in the new nation, attributed it to the spirit of republicanism. The decay of patriarchism is a natural corollary of political democracy; for the government recognizes, not families, but individuals. The father counts no more as a citizen than does his grown son and the lingering of paternal authority beyond the majority of the son would be incongruous. The premonition of the youth's coming citizenship casts its shadow before and anticipates the day of his majority. At the ends of the first quarter of the nineteenth century a visitor to the United States wrote: "The American woman sees in her son the future citizen, and therefore she has a certain feeling of respect even for her child." Moreover in a democracy the idea of "superior" fades before the idea of equal sovereignty. All men are sovereigns. Personality is exalted; and the political status overflows and democratizes family institutions.

De Tocqueville asserted that "in America, the family, in the Roman and aristocratic significance of the word, does not exist." During the infancy of children, the father did, indeed, exercise unopposed the necessary domestic authority. But as young America approached manhood the ties of filial obedience were relaxed and the youth became master of his own thought and conduct. This result was not the outcome of a struggle between parent and child. The parent did not care for the possession of authority. The father yielded as a matter of course and the son entered naturally on the enjoyment of his freedom.

American conditions encouraged practical utilitarianism. In a new country, reliance is less on tradition and more on a study of existing fact. The son's opinion seems likely to be as valid as the father's (at least that is the assumption underlying manhood suffrage) and the hold of ancestral and paternal prestige diminishes. Thus the austere, the conventional, and the legal elements in parental authority go with the passing of the aristocracy and a species of equality grows around the domestic hearth. Rules and authority recede before tenderness and confidence, and spiritual values in kinship are free to assert themselves.

Mrs. John Adams related that her little grandson every day after dinner set "his grandpa to draw him about in a chair, which is generally done for half an hour to the derangement of my carpet and the amusement of his grandpa." If such was the amusement of the distinguished vice-president, and a New Englander at that, we can guess what the later trend must have been. An educational journal of 1833 contains an interesting description of the new cult of childhood. "The attention now bestowed on children forms an interesting feature of the day. An interest seems to be rekindling, analogous to that which animated the ancient philosophers."

There was something spontaneous and charming about the new unfolding of juvenile life. The little ones went and came unquestioned and unconstrained, unceremonious and frank. Beaujour remarks quaintly on the children that "sparkle in the streets of American towns like field flowers in the springtime." To Miss Martineau "the independence and fearlessness of children were a perpetual charm." Duncan found in

> The little citizen . . . a companion who will do you a service, get you information, or ask it from you as the case may be. . . The first impression produced by their manner is, that they are brave, bright, pleasant, little "impudent things." But . . . the "impudent thing" is gradually dropt, and . . . you adopt "intelligent" or "independent."

The new freedom evoked an astonishing competence on the part of childhood. Whether it was the nine-year-old girl doing the honors at table in the absence of her mother; or the barefoot Irish newsboy on the streets of New York rushing to sell you a paper with the remark, "Fait', it's little mudder or daddy cares what I does, it's not the like of them as will mind me"—in any case, the blessed years had come into their own, for good or for ill. Duncan was moved to record that

> Little creatures feed themselves very neatly, and are trusted with cups of glass and china, which they grasp firmly, carry about the room carefully, and deposit unbroken, at an age when, in our country mamma or nurse would be rushing after them to save the vessels from destruction.

Precocity was a natural correlate of the emancipation. The child was willing enough to play his rôle. Children came quickly to maturity. The new country was not ready for the "prolonged infancy" that marks advanced civilization. "[American children]," said Duncan in 1852, "receive education with facility and smartness, but those who are destined for commerce are so generally mounted on a tall desk-seat in their four-

teenth or fifteenth year, that they much require exact
and strict moral discipline before that . . . period." In 1859 Grattan said: "A 'Boston boy' is a
melancholy picture of prematurity. It might be almost said that every man is born middle-aged in that
and every other great city of the union. The principal
business of life seems to be to grow old as fast as possible."

Owing to the preëminence of the young, American
"Society" came to be marked by a gaiety that some
would call frivolity. "Pert young misses of sixteen"
took things into their hands. The mother, eclipsed by
her daughters or oppressed by household cares, sometimes did not even appear at parties. This reign of
youth was in part attributable to the fact that children
were enabled to enjoy opportunities that their parents
had lacked and were thus able to act as authorities on
social matters. It is evident, therefore, that the sway
of the young in social affairs corresponded to that bourgeois construction of society which offered room to the
man that was "on the make" and enabled his children
to qualify for acceptance in approved circles. No
doubt one underlying characteristic of the play life has
always been a function of sex, and social amusement
has been primarily in the interests of mating. But in
a static society such functions are presided over by
tradition, conventionality, and maturity; whereas in
America they followed the normal trend of a dynamic
civilization which transfers power to the young.

One form taken by the new freedom was correlate
with the overcoming of the age of deficit. "The simplicity, the frugality of the parents, contrasts often dis-
agreeably with the prodigality, the assumption, self-
assertion, and conceit of the children," says Gurowski

in 1857. "In European domestic life the children even of the highest aristocracy, are educated with more comparative simplicity than is the case in America."

The wave of youthful freedom colored theology. Lyman Beecher felt called upon to deny that Calvinists teach infant damnation.[20] A Baptist convention at Savannah in 1802 "agreed that in the tenth chapter of our excellent confession of faith, the elect infants, mentioned as dying in infancy, are not opposed to non-elect infants, who, we are humbly of opinion, never die in infancy—but to those elect infants who, in possession of rational powers, arrive at maturity."[21] Doctor Humphrey, president of Amherst, indicated the trend in 1840. He said: "There is a great deal of fine, hot press poetry to be found 'now a-days,' in booksellers' windows and ladies' parlors, about the angelic sweetness of infancy. . ."

Beaujour said, at the beginning of the nineteenth century, that some fathers "gave no religion" to their children in order that these might pick one for themselves when they reached the age of reason. Harriet Robinson, one of the early mill girls of Lowell, went to the Congregational church and Sabbath School.

> We were well taught in the belief of a literal devil, in a lake of brimstone and fire, and in the "wrath of a just God." The terrors of an imaginative child's mind, into which these monstrous doctrines were poured, can hardly be described, and their lasting effect need not be dwelt upon.

No wonder that the mill girls and boys were to a large degree drawn away to the liberals.

A liberal revolution in the field of law and penology was well under way in the ante-bellum period. According to the Northwest Territory code of 1788, chil-

---

[20] *Autobiography*, etc., vol. ii, chapter xvi.
[21] *Georgia Analytical Repository*, vol. i, 77.

dren that disobeyed their parents might, on approval of
a justice of the peace, be sent to jail till, as the law put
it, they were humbled.   For a child that struck a parent
the law prescribed ten stripes.[22]   In antithesis to this
lingering Puritanism observe what Naumann says of
the United States in his *Nordamerika* (1848) :

> The law has seen fit to take children into its special oversight
> even at an age when with us they are still under the exclusive
> supervision and direction of parents and teachers.   If a father
> has chastised his boy somewhat severely, and it occurs to the
> lad, or he is put up to it by some foolish person, to complain to
> the justice of the peace, the father is punished by fine or im-
> prisonment.

In one most important particular, enfranchisement
of childhood came but slowly : education was primitive
and at first juvenile literature was lacking.   At the
close of the Revolution, says McMaster,

> Rude as was the school system of New England, it was incom-
> parably better than could be found in any other section of the
> country.   In New York and Pennsylvania a schoolhouse was
> never seen outside of a village or a town.   In other places chil-
> dren attending school walked for miles through regions infested
> with wolves and bears.

A French visitor of the latter part of the eighteenth
century observed that though children are happy while
in the bosom of the family, "the age of iron succeeds
rapidly to that of gold."   Bayard said that the American school-teacher was dreary and pedantic, better suited for training slaves than citizens.

> Dr. Benjamin Rush has in vain recommended the humane
> methods of J. J. Rousseau.   [Better whip scholars than let
> them go, and lose your fee!]   The unfortunates who toil
> under the direction of these pedants soon lose that sweetness of
> character which they took to school, and you see them emerging
> from their torture-chamber tormenting and beating each other.

---

[22] McMaster. *History of the People of the United States*, vol. iii (1902),
114.

It is relief to find Bayard speaking of one school-master who "had neither the air of a pedant nor of a missionary, but of a father of a family."

At the end of the eighteenth century there was no real juvenile literature and in many places schools could be maintained only with difficulty if at all. Michaux in his *Travels* told that

> Throughout the western country the children are kept punctually at school . . . supported at the expense of the inhabitants. . . Upon the Ohio, and in the Barrens, where the settlements are farther apart, the inhabitants have not yet been able to procure this advantage, which is the object of solicitude in every family.

In Kentucky and Tennessee in early days the gentry made every effort to bring about the erection of academies where their boys and girls could be well taught. But in the highlands many that bore the names of distinguished Virginia families raised children that could scarcely read or write. Even in the venerable East the masses were long devoid of adequate educational facilities. Education remained a special privilege. Willard Hall wrote that when he settled at Dover, Delaware in 1803,

> There was then no provision by law in the state for schools. Neighbors or small circles united and hired a teacher for their children. . . The teachers frequently were intemperate, whose qualification seemed to be inability to earn anything in any other way. . . Even in the best neighborhoods teachers of the young frequently were immoral and incapable.[23]

From 1809 to 1835 the laws of Pennsylvania provided education for the children of those that were willing to take a pauper's oath. This condition put a stigma on the public schools. In Delaware and Maryland the schools were little better and were frequently taught by redemptioners and indentured servants. A

[23] Powell. *History of Education in Delaware*, 142.

Delaware act of 1817 appropriated one thousand dollars to each county for the education of the poor. The measure was never popular because it drew a hard and fast line between poor and rich. Governor Cochrane said: "It is not surprising that a provision which invited an independent people to have their children schooled as paupers proved a failure."[24] In Connecticut, about 1830-1840, women teachers of district schools received four to six dollars a month and board. Parents were indifferent.

By 1830 there were in Boston two infant schools supported by charity for the poor. The first infant school in New England seems to have been established about 1828. Neilson wrote (in his *Recollections of a six Years' Residence in the United States of America*):

> Education for children may he had on various terms; but even poor people are at no loss in regard to this, for at least the most useful branches. There are several free schools in New York, supported chiefly by the state, where people may have their children educated on very low terms; or if they cannot at all afford it, they are taught gratis.

The *Man* of March 17, 1834 cited the Brooklyn *Star* as noting "several flourishing infant schools" there, that were supported, or should be supported, by charity. From the point of view of labor this was wrong. "Education is the right of every child, and it is the interest of the community that the right should be possessed and exercised by all."[25] About this time a committee of Philadelphia workingmen outlined a scheme of education, including kindergartens.[26] The *Man* of February 18, 1834 contained an extract from the Philadelphia "Operative" recommending the abolition of West

[24] Oneal. *Workers in American History*, 207; Powell. *History of Education in Delaware*, 140.

[25] *Man*, March 17, 1834, p. 86.

[26] Simons. *Social Forces in American History*, 183.

Point, an aristocratic institution good only to enable a few privileged persons to have their sons educated at public expense. The issue of May 14 contained the information that a professor had been appointed to teach the young Tories at West Point "to draw at the expense of the people, many of whom are not enabled to teach their own children how to read!"

In September, 1834, Pennsylvania provided for tax supported schools. Three months later petitions for repeal of the act were received from thirty-eight counties out of fifty-one and only a hard struggle saved the law.[27]

The *National Gazette* of Philadelphia in editorials in 1830 ridiculed the public school as an impractical dream and as class legislation. The public school would place a premium on idleness.

> A scheme of universal equal education . . . could not be used with any degree of equality of profit, unless the dispositions and circumstances of parents and children were nearly the same; to accomplish which phenomenon, in a nation of many millions, engaged in a great variety of pursuits, would be beyond human power.

The first state education convention of Delaware, at Dover, 1843, said:

> The report of the Massachusetts Board of Education declares that the cardinal principle . . . at the foundation of their education system is that all the children of the state shall be educated by the state. . . This is not the principle of our school system . . . our school system is founded upon the position that the people must educate their own children. [All the state can do is to help and encourage.] [28]

Margaret Fuller cited a circular which estimated that the country needed sixty thousand additional teachers.

Progress in an appreciation of child nature and needs

[27] Oneal. *Workers in American History*, 207.

[28] Oneal. *Workers in American History*, 207-208; Powell. *History of Education in Delaware*, 146-147.

gradually accrued. An educational journal in 1833 recorded the impression that

> Mothers have derived new ideas on education, and entered with increased intelligence and zeal into the discharge of their duties. . . The infant school has become an assistant, an observatory to the mother; and the season of infancy and childhood a period of progress and enjoyment. [Children have not hitherto been properly trained. The dominion of passion and appetite is too obvious. Little has been done to help mothers in the training of the young. The books are inadequate. Mothers are deemed more as nurses of the child, than its mental and moral guide.] [29]

Certain magazines for women essayed to remedy the shortcomings of maternal care. They gave some wise hints as to the nature of children and the appropriate treatment. One contained an interesting article by T. S. Arthur relating an incident in the history of a friend written for the benefit of a mother. In this tale a woman guilty of passionate punishment of her unruly children was reproved by her bachelor brother who demonstrated that an explanation of reasons for prohibitions would accomplish more than violence. He maintained that "no child is ever improved by scolding; but always injured." Few children escaped this injury. "No cause is so active for evil among children as their mother's impatience." The old gentleman had found that the vandal children respected his property and that to forbid an offender to come into his room for a while was a cure. He said:

> We . . . expect children who do not reflect, to act with all the propriety of men and women. . . They must regard our times, seasons, and conveniences, and we will attend to their ever active wants, when our leisure will best permit us to do so. Is it any wonder . . . that children are troublesome? [30]

[29] *American Annals of Education and Instruction*, vol. iii, 16-19.
[30] *The Ladies' Wreath*, vol. iii, 113-124.

Doctor Humphrey had some interesting ideas on "Domestic Education." He thought that infants "are generally, except in very poor families, kept too much from the air, especially in fine weather." Mothers were inclined to keep the child from creeping: "till the poor child can walk like other folks, it must not move at all." Most American fathers had much leisure but many intelligent and excellent men "lose by spending so many of their evenings abroad."

Children of pious families have by far too many religious story books put into their hands, and are kept too long upon milk, essences and high-seasoned condiments. The same objection lies against almost all the family reading of the present day [though] . . . a certain amount of such easy and familiar reading, in childhood, is very useful. . . The Bible is not read half so much in religious families, as it was thirty years ago. . . Within the last thirty years, the [shorter] catechism has been gradually falling into neglect, and has been to a great extent displaced in pious families, by simpler, and in too many cases extremely superficial substitutes. The common objection is . . . that [the doctrines] are above the comprehension of children at the tender age, when it used to be committed and recited.

As to the doctrine of angelic infancy, "All this is . . . very well . . . if we understand it right." But the learned doctor urges that we always should

Carefully distinguish between the social affections, and the state of the heart in the sight of a holy God, so as not to leave the impression, that there is anything in all this infantile and juvenile loneliness, to set aside the teachings of Scripture in regard to native depravity. . . I conceive the great laxness of family government, which characterizes the present age, may be traced very often to erroneous views on this very point. . . The opinion seems to be gaining ground, in some respectable and influential quarters, that punishments are rarely if ever necessary in family government. It is said, that if parents would begin early, and cultivate the social affections of their children, and enlighten their understandings, and bring the

whole force of moral influence to bear . . . there would
be no need of resorting to punishments.

Most parents, he continued, were probably not so well
versed in these persuasive methods as they ought to be;
perhaps in some families punishment could be avoided
but as a rule it was necessary.

The reader needs only to be reminded of the alteration that had taken place since the days of regnant
Puritanism, and of the modern controversy on the same
question of child nature between opposing schools in
the field of religious education.

Naturally the transition to child-freedom was dis-
concerting to such as could not discriminate between
the soundness of the fundamental trend and the inci-
dental evils attendant on the relaxation of constraint.
A "Stranger in America" wrote as early as 1807 that

> One of the greatest evils of a Republican form of government
> is a loss of . . . subordination in society. . . Boys as-
> sume the airs of full grown coxcombs. This is not to be won-
> dered at, when most parents make it a principle never to check
> those ungovernable passions which are born with us, or to cor-
> rect the growing vices of their children. . . Often have I
> with horror, seen boys, whose dress indicated wealthy parents,
> intoxicated, shouting and swearing in the public streets.[31]

In 1818 profligacy had become so common in New
York that a respectable inhabitant said: "There is not
a father in this city but who is sorry that he has got a
son." [32]   A writer of that year said:

> Strictly speaking there is no such thing as social subordination
> in the United States. Parents have no command over their
> children. . . Owing perhaps to the very popular nature of
> our institutions, the American children are seldom taught that
> profound reverence for, and strict obedience to their parents,
> which are at once the basis of domestic comfort and of the wel-

[31] Janson. *Stranger in America*, 297.
[32] Fearon. *Sketches of America*, 172.

fare of the children themselves. . . Nay the independence
of children on their parents, is carried so far, as to raise doubts
if a father or mother has any right to interfere in the marriage
of a son or daughter. A few weeks since, this question was
publicly discussed at one of our New York Debating Clubs, for
the edification of a numerous audience both male and female;
and it was determined by a stout majority, that in a free and
enlightened republic, children are at liberty to marry whom
they please, without any interference on the part of the
parents . . . and for this most sagacious reason, that the
child, and not the parent, is about to commit matrimony; it being quite an exploded prejudice, that parents can have any possible concern in the welfare and happiness of their offspring.
The doctrine doubtless is palatable to every needy and unprin-
cipled adventurer, who wishes to persuade some silly daughter
of an opulent father, to accompany him to the next trading
justice, who, for a few shillings, will perform the marriage
ceremony, and consign her to a husband, and disgrace and misery, for life.[33]

A German visitor to America about the same time,
wrote of the "indulgence shown by parents toward the
excesses of children in earliest youth (often I saw children in quarrel with old people pick up stones, and
threaten to fling them at the head of the old man that
wanted to punish them)." He often saw young girls in
convulsive anger at their parents.[34] An Englishman
who took tea in a family remarked that

The children's faces were dirty, their hair uncombed, their disposition evidently untaught, and all the members of the family,
from the boy of six years of age up to the owner (I was going
to say master) of the house, appeared independent of each other.
I have seen the same characteristics in other families – in some
decidedly the contrary; but these latter would seem to be the
exceptions, and the former the general rule.[35]

[33] Bristed. *Resources of the United States*, 459-460.
[34] Hecke. *Reise durch die Vereinigten Staaten*, vol. i, 42, 63.
[35] Mackenzie. *Historical, topographical, and descriptive View of the United States*, 357.

Abdy, a visitor of the early thirties, thought that "the Americans are too anxious to make money and too apt to spoil their children. . . . The boys are much more spoiled than the girls." In the daily *Man* [labor newspaper] of March 21, 1834, occurred a "modern catechism adapted to the times." The following questions are suggestive:

Who is the oldest man? The lad of fourteen who struts and swaggers and smokes his cigar, and drinks rum; treads on the toes of his grandfather, swears at his mother and sister, and vows that he will run away and leave "the old man" if he will not let him have more cash. In what families is there the best government? Those in which the children govern the parents. . . Who brings up his children in the way they should go? He that teaches them to spend money without earning it; mixes sling whenever he thinks it will do him good, and always saves the bottom of the glass for little Frank.

The Ladies' Repository of Cincinnati from 1841 to 1849 contained numerous comments on the problem of child control. It is observed that the young lack respect for aged persons. "In travel, especially on steamboats," said one writer, "I have often remarked the selfishness of the young, monopolizing sofas, rocking chairs, etc., sometimes even to the disregard of the invalid." In another number, it was asserted that the good old breaking-in of children could not but have happy results. "We have fallen on evil times. There is a fearful decline of family religion. . . Earthly good . . . has filled the parental eye, and the heirs of the covenant are sacrificed to this Moloch." Parents waxed careless and tended "to relax their personal attentions to the great business of educating their offspring, and to surrender them up almost entirely to their academic and Sunday School instructors." "Broken-hearted mothers are often seen mourning over the waywardness of their children."

An English woman in 1848 wrote:

> The indulgence which parents in the United States permit to
> their children is not seen in England; the child is too early his
> own master; as soon as he can sit at table he chooses his own
> food, and as soon as he can speak argues with his parents on the
> propriety or impropriety of their directions.

In his *Old England and New England*, Bunn said:
"Young America calls his father 'the governor,' his
mother 'the old 'un,' his sisters 'our gals,' and his
brothers 'pals.'"

Emerson quoted a man who said that it was a misfortune to have been born in an age when children were
nothing and to have spent mature life in an age when
children were everything.   Such must have seemed to
many the effect of democracy on family relations.   Certainly children were coming to the fore.   People taught
their children to show off before guests.   Duncan in
America as I found it said:

> The parents, full of frank, simple emotion, bring their little
> treasures under notice and ask you with pride and joy, "Don't
> you think my Charley is a brave little fellow?" . . . If
> the children are not at home, you will be shown their pictures
> and told their histories. . . They come, not with a "make
> your bow," or "courtesy to the lady," — that is not republican
> fashion; but with a becoming courage, looking straight into
> your eyes, and extending the right hand for a cordial shake. . .
> My surprise has also been excited by the lengths they are per-
> mitted to go in mischief without punishment, or scarcely ad-
> monition. . . As each child obtains a seat at the family
> table at meals as early as they can be trusted in an elevated
> chair, they are used to ask for and to receive all manner of
> varieties of food. . . [They are commonly allowed to sit
> up] to see the guests at evening parties and share oysters, jellies,
> and ices, fruits, and preserves . . . with all the heartiness
> and excess of "frugivorous children" . . . to see sensible
> people smile with secret admiration of the "spirited" exhibition
> of rebellious will on the part of their offspring, excites in an

English mind, a sense of lurking danger – as also to hear pupils
asserting boldly what they "will never learn."

Oldmixon said that the child got everything on his
plate and left half of it.

The phenomena of child enfranchisement recall the
waywardness of negro children after emancipation and
of the children of immigrants cutting loose from parental archaism. Like these two latter types the children
of the new American family were children of migrants
to a new civilization. As in the case of immigrants of
our day not all parents were reconciled to letting go.
There was still a good deal of cruelty to children, and,
moreover, a sturdy defense of paternal supremacy.

Doctor Humphrey in his work of 1840 sponsored
patriarchism. He conceived of the domestic relations
as prior to all others in time and paramount in importance. "Families, are so many divinely instituted and
independent communities, upon the well ordering of
which, the most momentous interests of the church and
the state, of time and eternity are suspended." No
power on earth has a right to interfere with the patriarchal head. He is amenable to God only, save in
the most extreme cases of neglect or abuse. A neighbor
may lack every patriarchal qualification. Perhaps his
children would be better off in another's charge "but
you may not thus interfere with one of God's ordi-
nances." Nor can government assume parental duties.
He thought the country was menaced by growing laxity of family government. It was more difficult than
half, or even a quarter of, a century earlier for parents
to "command their household after them." The author
was of the opinion that considerable progress at establishing parental control could be made "under six
months, if not under four; and that parental authority
ought to be well established within the first year and

a quarter. . . The young man of twenty, in his father's house, has no more right to say that he will use his own discretion, in regard to observing the rules and regulations of the family, than a child of ten." Children must submit to parental authority even after their majority if they choose to remain at home.

Writers in the *Presbyterian Magazine* of the fifties represented similarly the conservative point of view. One thought

> That the deficiencies which disclose themselves in the marriage relation must be ascribed mainly to an inadequate and improper training. . . It can excite no wonder, that young persons who have grown up without restraint – allowed to treat their parents with disrespect – indulged in all their whims and caprices – accustomed only to flattery and adulation – should be found very troublesome inmates in another household.

Another article asserted the entire authority of parent over child, and denied any one's right to intervene against the parent's will.

> The signs of the want of family discipline appear in the waywardness of the children while yet they are young. Given up to idleness, knowing no restraint but such as they are wont to defy, having no domestic exercise for entertainment and profit, and nothing to keep them at home but their bed and board, and dreading their home for their leisure hours as a place of confinement; familiar with drunkenness, profaneness, and all the captivating forms of youthful dissipation; what have the parents or the community to hope from such children?

In another number it was affirmed that "The levelling system of the present age is nowhere more unfavorable than in the family. . . Tyranny is offensive to God. . . But the parent's authority ought to be early, absolute, and entire."

It must not be supposed that the abdication of sovereignty by parents in the period of this volume was universal or due to indifferentism. There are indications of serious parental concern for the welfare and training of children and of the persistence of the old religious zeal. Children may have seemed to foreigners spoiled and pert but there was not lacking a large element of genuine filial devotion. An Englishwoman writing in 1848 on the excessive indulgence shown to children in America conceded that "this early development of republicanism does not injure so much as might be expected the future man, does in no way lessen the domestic affections."

Gurowski's work of 1857 observed that

American parents, allowing an almost unlimited choice to their children, spare nevertheless no hardships and pains to bring them up, and to educate them according to their conception of what is the best and the most useful for the mature duties of life. Parents love their children as dearly and intensely here as in Europe, but exercise less control, less authority. . . American parents are far more forbearing, nay meeker with their children than are those in Europe. What here results from freedom or a yielding disposition, to the European comprehension appears as irreverence. A slight or no constraint is imposed upon children in America; and as childhood . . . is eminently imitative, their good breeding depends upon the bad or good examples which in various quarters are freely set before them. Children accustomed to the utmost familiarity and absence of constraint with their parents, behave in the same manner with other older persons. . . Even in the serious decisions of life, children in America enjoy a fulness of independence not customary in Europe. They make freely the choice of their intimacies, then of their church, of their politics, their husbands and wives.

Especially noteworthy was the emancipation of girls in the new world. This was correlated with "the political order of things in America." There is not much surface connection between the political democracy of the nineteenth century and the emancipation of girls from parental control; for political democracy was a male affair and could not logically serve as a premise for reasoning about the status of woman in the family. But when the spirit of democracy is in the air it does not wait altogether for logical rules of procedure. The emancipation of boys, consonant with the new egalitarianism, could not but have influenced the status of girls despite their exclusion from political activity. Moreover the conditions of the new world operated to raise the position of woman as will be seen later.

The French visitors of the end of the eighteenth century were almost shocked at the freedom enjoyed by girls yet they admit that no harm came of it. Perrin du Lac said that "because girls may go unattended to parties, married women seldom go." It was a surprise to the Frenchmen to find the delicate business of marriage confided to the young people. St. Méry reported: "The chosen sweetheart comes to the house whenever he pleases, he takes his beloved out walking when he likes. . . Young people sit up spooning after their elders go to bed." Brissot adds: "You will see a young girl drive off with her sweetheart in a light carriage, and injurious suspicion never interferes with the pure pleasures of this trip into the country." Rochambeau hinted that unmarried girls did not waste time on married men.

John Quincy Adams wrote in a student diary of 1787-1788 (Newburyport):

[On a terrace in High Street we] saw a number of young ladies who seemed to expect to be accosted; and some of them finally sat down on the grass, perhaps to see if that would not call our attention to them; but we were . . . inexorable. . . Some of these young ladies were so much piqued at our apparent neglect of them that they revenged themselves with proper spirit by laughing loud at us as we past by them;

and what punishment could possibly be more severe than the ridicule of a young lady?

An interesting instance showing the common sense of the new daughter of America coupled with the old subordination to parental will is found in the letters of Eliza Southgate Bowne. At the age of eighteen she wrote: "I despise the conduct of those girls who think that every man who pays them any attention is seriously in love with them." Later she writes very sweetly and beautifully to her mother regarding. Mr. Bowne's attentions to her. "He knew I was not at liberty to encourage his addresses without the approbation of my parents, and appeared as solicitous that I should act with strict propriety as one of my most disinterested friends." She sizes him up very sanely. "I wish my Father would write to Mr. Derby and know what he says of Mr. B's character." This careful maiden married Mr. Bowne.

From sundry references in the period between 1800 and the War, the inference is that the American maidens enjoyed great freedom, cherished their independence, and used it cleverly. Unhampered acquaintance with young men put them in a position to choose their mate, perhaps not always wisely yet doubtless with results happier on the whole than the fruits of marriage in more conventional periods. If some maidens kept a keen eye open for "desirable" husbands – even foreigners – their unwisdom was probably not so much a spontaneous product of their self-will as a result of the artificial culture that was beginning to engulf the women of the more prosperous classes.

Shortly before the war Grattan in *Civilized America* said:

Female children of the most respectable parentage live, even before they are said to have quitted the nursery, in public. . .

> At the age of twelve or thirteen, when female children rejoice
> in the appelation of "Misses," they begin to enjoy all the priv-
> ileges of self-management.

Not all girls were sweetly sane. Fondness for fiction came to be a common source of parental regret. John Quincy Adams, about 1787, records a social function at which he danced with a girl, of whom he wrote: "She . . . has read too many novels, which render her manners rather fantastical and affected." The New England *Quarterly Magazine* of 1802 reprinted an article from the *Monthly Mirror* of 1797 to the effect that novel reading led to female depravity. Some boy too young to marry commits fornication with the novel-fed girl. A girl lures her chum's husband. The writer was acquainted with three such instances in as many years. The peace of several families was destroyed. Novel reading was responsible. (Perhaps it was also to blame for the desire of girls to be ethereal and slender, delicate and shrinking, which climaxed in the early years of the nineteenth century.) A writer of 1842 lamented the defective education that makes women more sentimental. Many pore over sickly novels regardless of duty as wife and mother. "Is it not a melancholy prospect for the country, that mothers so full of sentiment and romance are to train the future generations of this republic?"

Martha H. Whitehouse, in the *Ladies' Repository* of 1852 said that one cause that might be assigned for woman's inferiority was her morbid taste for light reading. "Our country, at the present day, is flooded to an unparalleled degree with the vain imaginings of man, and presented to the public for a recompense so slight that 'he who runs may read'; and our young ladies devour with eagerness such books." This unreal world, she believed, unfitted for the real.

De Tocqueville described the emancipation of girls from maternal control. To offset the risk of unconventionality and freedom, he said, democratic education of girls developed. They were permitted to learn what was what and were not shielded in "innocence" according to the method of older societies. "If democratic nations leave a woman free to choose her husband, they take care to give her mind sufficient knowledge, and her will sufficient strength to make so important a choice." De Tocqueville probably exaggerated the emancipation of girls from traditional seclusion; the foregoing quotation is doubtless hyperbolic in its eulogy. Apart from any specific efforts to enlighten girls in the ways of life the usage of coeducation could not but accomplish large results. De Tocqueville thought that the matter-of-fact treatment accorded to girls

> Tends to invigorate the judgment at the expense of the imagination, and to make cold and virtuous women instead of affectionate wives and agreeable companions to man. Society may be more tranquil and better regulated, but domestic life has often fewer charms. These, however, are secondary evils, which may be braved for the sake of higher interests.

The *Man* of 1834 contained an article to the effect that at fifteen or sixteen the young girl began to think of the mysterious subject matrimony. Her youthful imagination was captivated with its delights. It was a subject of ever recurrent interest among her companions. A little later she thought more intently about it. She believed herself destined to happy wedlock. Eighteen to twenty was the "witching time," the time for marriage. Most women became more thoughtful after that and "look before they leap." In another number Mr. Cobbett was quoted thus:

> The girls in America are beautiful and unaffected; perfectly frank, and at the same time, perfectly modest; but, when you make them an offer of your hand, be prepared to give it, for

wait they will not. In England we frequently hear of courtships of a quarter of a century; in that anti-Malthusian country, a quarter of a year is deemed to be rather "lengthy."

Susan B. Anthony was an American girl of the coming type. Her father always encouraged the children
in their independent ideas. Once when a spooler was
sick in the mill Susan and Hannah clamored to take
her place. The mother objected but their father let
them draw straws for the chance. The winner was to
divide her wages with the loser. Susan was the fortunate one. She worked two weeks and received three
dollars. With her dollar and a half she bought half a
dozen pale blue cups and saucers that she had heard her
mother wish for. She later taught. She said there
were plenty of beaux, "but I never could bring myself
to put anything about them on paper." She often refers to their calling, escorting her to parties, etc., but
there is scarcely any expression of her sentiments
toward them. One, of whom she says: "He is a most
noble-hearted fellow; I have respected him highly
since our first acquaintance," went to see a rival, and
she wrote: "He is at ——'s this evening. O may he
know that in me he has found a spirit congenial with
his own, and not suffer the glare of beauty to attract
both eye and heart."

Goethe's *Correspondence with a Child* exercised a
strong fascination upon young minds. It led more
than one young girl to form an ideal attachment to a
man far her senior but full of nobility and intellectual
power. Theodore Parker said of letters to him from a
young New Hampshire girl: "They are as good as
Bettine's without the lies." It seems that "this ming-
ling of idealism and hero-worship was strongly characteristic of the transcendental period when women,

having little solid education and less industrial employment, were full of noble aspirations and longings for fuller and freer life, which must find expression in some way." Louisa Alcott (born 1832) wrote letters to Emerson pouring forth her girlish longings and raptures, but never sent them.[36]

On the whole the South was probably more conservative than the North in its treatment of the young, particularly of girls. The general emancipation of childhood prevailed, nevertheless, to a degree in the South. Ramsay wrote in 1809 of South Carolina revolutionary spirit that the sons

> Too little accustomed to the discipline of a strict education, seem equally zealous for the rights of boys, and urge their claims so practically that many of the merchants import from Europe clerks trained to habits of obedience, rather than make vain attempts to subjugate the high-minded youths of Carolina. Their repugnance to subjection [is often excessive]. . . The too early introduction of young lads into company has an unhappy effect on their habits. [They are led to drink.]

Letters from Virginia (1816) relate that "Virginia youths . . . are not naturally overpatient of restraint, or submissive to authority, even of the most parental kind."

Buckingham in *The Slave States of America* wrote of Savannah:

> The youths of both sexes appear to be brought up in less subjection to parental authority than in England. The boys are educated chiefly at day schools: between the hours of school attendance they are under very little restraint, and do pretty nearly what they like; many carry sticks or canes with them, and some even affect the bravo, by carrying bowie knives, but it is more for show than use. The young-ladies being also educated at day schools, or at home, have much greater liberty allowed them in the disposal of their time, and the arrangement

---
[36] Cheney. *Louisa May Alcott, her Life, Letters, and Journals,* 57-59.

and control of their visits, than girls of the same age in England. The consequence is, great precocity of manners in both sexes, and often very early marriages.

The actor Tasistro in *Random Shots and Southern Breezes* remarked:

Southern children do not come exactly up to my notion of what children should be. Educated almost generally under the French system, which converts children into ladies and gentlemen before they are ten . . . they exhibit none of that hearty and most unceremonious gayety and good-humor which prevail among the younger branches of families in the North, particularly at . . . holydays, when the inroads of these little Goths and Vandals is the signal for the overthrow of any remaining stiffness and formality, and for the commencement of all sorts of trifling games and sports.

The distinctive features of child-life in the South are treated in a later chapter.

From all the foregoing items it is evident that the century of the child was under way. To old-fashioned people it seemed that the foundations were being destroyed; but the emancipation was a forward move toward family reciprocity, democracy, and spontaneous, unforced loyalty.

IV. THE SOCIAL SUBORDINATION OF WOMAN

The line of liberalizing influences surveyed in the foregoing chapters had a positive effect on the status of woman that requires to be detailed; but first it is important to visualize the relics of medievalism lingering in woman's status throughout the period under consideration.   Such "equality" as was enjoyed by woman in the nineteenth century was a stingy concession even though it may have looked large to European visitors. The "fathers" did not plan a democratic America; hence it is not surprising that suffrage was limited and that woman suffrage was eliminated.

When English law crossed the ocean with the seventeenth century colonists, the women had the constitutional right to vote and in some cases made use of it. Not one of the constitutions of the thirteen states explicity restricted the suffrage to men.   New York was the first state to tamper with its charter by adding the qualification "male" in the year 1778; state after state fell in line, concluding with New Jersey in 1844.[37] The constitution of this state had been carelessly made; so that during thirty-one years women had the suffrage. That they used it is evident from the traditions in many families of a great-grandmother or great-grandaunt who voted year after year and also from the law of 1807 which limited the franchise to free white males and de-

---

[37] Münsterberg. *Americans*, 573.

clared as a reason that women, negroes, and aliens had been allowed to vote.[38]

American democracy is to be traced partly to old-world ideals and partly to the influence of pioneer life. But it will be observed in either case that conditions did not favor the inclusion of woman in the circle of privilege. Paul's interpretation of woman's sphere was vivid in the minds of those in whom Calvin had broken ground for democracy. And in the new world a woman without a man was so helpless, having no protection against frontier perils and small opportunity for procuring a satisfactory livelihood, and civic life was still so obviously a man's world with its crudeness and fighting, that woman still ranked as a dependent on man as in the old days of ordeal and could not logically claim equality.

In the Pennsylvania *Packet* of September 23, 1780, occurred the following advertisement:

> Wanted at a seat about half a day's journey from Philadelphia, a single woman of unsullied reputation, an affable, cheerful, active, and amiable disposition; cleanly, industrious, perfectly qualified to direct and manage the female concerns of country business, such as raising small stock, dairying, marketing, combing, carding, spinning, knitting, weaving, sewing, pickling, preserving, etc. Such a person will be treated with respect and esteem, and meet with every encouragement due to such a character.

Even if this advertisement did point to economic independence for some woman (the only sure basis of equality), opportunities of the sort must have been few. It is more likely, indeed, that the person in question was shrewdly advertising for a wife.

The attitude of the public toward women in business is suggested in the prospectus of a "Lady's Journal"

[38] McMaster. *History of the People of the United States* (1902), vol. iii, 147.

(issued by Mrs. Carr of Baltimore in the early part of the nineteenth century). This prospectus states that she knew the malignant part of mankind would scoff at a woman editor but a mother would brave death for the support of her children and she had five.

Daniel Anthony, father of Susan, at Battenville, New York, was much criticized for allowing his daughters to teach as in those days women did not work for wages save from urgent necessity; but he was far enough ahead of his time to believe that every girl should be trained to self-support. But even at the middle of the century woman had no recognized individuality in any sphere of life. She toiled in domestic obscurity to educate the boys. The girl was a chattel with no career in prospect. The boy past twenty-one was free but the girl continued to work without wages after twenty-one as before. Marriage transferred her services to the husband. Food, shelter, and clothing were considered adequate reward. Almost every woman had to marry whether or not or else become an utter dependent, living after her parents' death with some married relative as family drudge without wage and usually regarded with disrespect by the children. To step out as a wage-earner was to lose caste and be barred from the neighborhood functions. No man would be brave enough to marry a woman that had unsexed herself by becoming a literary woman. It was believed to a great extent that any woman that attempted a vocation outside of domestic service was henceforth unfitted to be a wife and a mother.

Catherine E. Beecher, who was by no means an iconoclast, in 1851 recognized the real crux of woman's depression, for she said:

The grand source of the heaviest wrong that oppresses our sex is found in the fact that they are so extensively cut off from

honorable and remunerative employ in their professional vocation. . . There are now more than two million children in
this country without any schools! There are probably as many
more in schools taught by men, who could be far more appro-
priately employed in shops or mills, or other masculine pursuits.

She quotes Doctor Coombs as referring to inactivity of
intellect and feeling as predisposing to nervous disease,
of which females of the middle and upper classes were
the most frequent victims, "especially those of a nervous
constitution and of good natural abilities." Miss
Beecher went on to say:

The results of high cultivation on the character and happiness
of young ladies of the higher classes [after quitting school is
painful to me]. That restless longing for excitement, that
craving for unattainable good, that morbid action of the imagination, that dissatisfaction with the world, that factitious interest in trifles, and those alternations of high excitement and
brooding apathy – these are the secret history of many a gifted
and highly-cultivated female mind. . . The ability to secure
an independent livelihood and honorable employ suited to her
education and capacities, are the only true foundation of the
social elevation of women, even in the very highest classes of
society. While she continues to be educated only to be some-
body's wife, and is left without any aim in life till that some-
body, either in love, or in pity, or in selfish regard, at last
grants her the opportunity, she can never be truly independent.
And true freedom and equality are the essential requisites of
genuine affection.

Mrs. Stanton also said that woman must be taught to
be economically independent.

The two-fold situation of transmitted bigotry and
economic subjection tended to a mischievous effect on
family relations: it left the way open to patriarchal despotism, and tended to make the boys overbearing, while
the girls and mother were likely to be subdued with a
sense of "woman's place" that prevented the full expansion of their personalities. Thus the seeds of equal-

ity were slow to reach their normal fruitage and the status quo was slow to dissolve even under the liberalizing influences already portrayed. In sharp contrast to those signs of promise appear many relics of medievalism that encumbered woman's status down at least to the Civil War. Marriage reduced her to a subordinate and cramped position. She was expected to embrace her husband's religion, to confine her activities to the home, and to make her husband's pleasure her guiding star. Ignorant of her husband's business, subordinate in the church, barred from politics, and possessing a scanty or a silly education, it is not strange that she scarcely aroused in her husband a sense of "consciousness of kind" or a real sympathy. She did not have to think; hence it was but natural that light reading or trifling gossip satisfied her, that she accepted indulgence instead of justice, or even gloried in her degradation.

A hundred years ago a woman of polite breeding would have been offended if told that she meddled in public affairs. Her attitude is illustrated by the remark of an unusually intelligent woman to a Federalist whom she met shortly after her flight from Washington on the occasion of the British invasion. He said that the disaster argued for a standing army and she replied that she had always associated a standing army with despotism, but added: "I am not competent to discuss such questions, sir." Mrs. Madison enjoyed the friendship of many public men but we have no record of her views on public questions or that she ever influenced the political views or acts of her devoted husband.

About 1840 Catherine E. Beecher voiced the dominant theory of the relation proper to the nature of the sexes. She said:

Heaven has appointed to one sex the superior, and to the other the subordinate station, and this without any reference to the

character or conduct of either. It is therefore as much for the
dignity as it is for the interest of females, in all respects to conform to the duties of this relation. And it is as much a duty
as it is for the child to fulfill similar relations to parents, or
subjects to rulers. But . . . it is not . . . designed
that her duties or her influence should be any the less important or all pervading. But it was designed that the mode of
gaining influence and of exercising power should be altogether
different and peculiar. Woman is to win everything by peace
and love; by making herself so much respected, esteemed and
loved, that to yield to her opinions and to gratify her wishes
will be the free-will offering of the heart. But this is all to
be accomplished in the domestic and social circle. All the
sacred protection of religion, all the generous promptings of
chivalry, all the poetry of romantic gallantry, depend upon
woman's retaining her place as dependent and defenceless and
making no claims, and maintaining no right but what are the
gifts of honor, rectitude, and love. [Better education will fit
women to be school-teachers.] But if females, as they approach the other sex in intellectual elevation, begin to claim, or
to exercise in any manner, the peculiar prerogatives of that sex,
education will prove a doubtful and dangerous blessing. But
this will never be the result. For the more intelligent a
woman becomes, the more she can appreciate the wisdom of that
ordinance that appointed her subordinate station, and the more
her taste will conform to the graceful and dignified retirement
and submission it involves.

A writer in the *Ladies' Repository* in 1842 reduced the
duties of a wife to three heads: affection, reverence,
faithfulness.

The *Public Ledger and Daily Transcript* of Philadelphia about the middle of the century had an article
on "The Women of Philadelphia," in which occurred
the following effusion:

Our ladies . . . soar to rule the hearts of their worship-
pers, and secure obedience by the scepter of affection. . . Is
not everything managed by female influence? . . . A
woman is nobody. A wife is everything. A pretty girl is
equal to ten thousand men, and a mother is, next to God, all

powerful. . . The ladies of Philadelphia, therefore, under the influence of the most serious "sober second thoughts," are resolved to maintain their rights as wives, belles, virgins, and mothers, and not as women.

Miss Barber of the Madison (Georgia) *Visitor* says,

It is written in the volume of inspiration . . . that man . . . is superior to woman. He has a more stately form, stronger nerves and muscles, and, in nine cases out of ten, a more vigorous intellect.

H. P. Grattan, editor of the New York *Sunday Age*, loved women, on the proper pedestal. "If they give evidence of a knowledge of puddings and pies, how much happier they might be."

Margaret Fuller, writing on the wrongs and duty of American women said:

It is not generally proposed that [woman] should be sufficiently instructed and developed to understand the pursuits or aims of her future husband; she is not to be a help-meet to him in the way of companionship and counsel, except in the care of his house and children. [But] a vast proportion of the sex, if not the better half, do not, cannot have this domestic sphere. Thousands and scores of thousands in this country, no less than in Europe, are obliged to maintain themselves alone. Far greater numbers divide with their husbands the care of earning a support for the family.

Woman's education before the Civil War was of a most inferior sort. Nearly all girls' schools before 1800 were limited to terms of a few months and confined themselves largely to needlework, music, dancing, and the cultivation of morals and manners. Referring to the literature of the end of the eighteenth century, McMaster has said:

For young women there was a class of books designed to inculcate a morality of the most unhealthy sort. . . They were popular and the list is long. . . There was a collection of dramatic pieces designed "to exemplify the mode of conduct

which will render young ladies both amiable and happy when
their school education is completed" and containing such de-
lightful reading as, "The Good Mother-in-Law," "The Good
Daughter-in-Law," "The Maternal Sister-in-Law."

In the first half of the nineteenth century there were
no adequate facilities for the education of women.
Some did indeed receive a good education, sufficient to
enable them to prepare their sons for college. But inasmuch as woman was excluded from the walks of life
in which a broad education seemed requisite, slight attention was given to her education and she was denied
the proper means of intellectual development. Some
did get a good domestic education; others were married "without knowing anything of life but its amusements."

The New England *Quarterly Magazine* for 1802
contained the opinion of Doctor Rush that several circumstances in America required a peculiar mode of female education: 1. Early marriage made contracted
education necessary. It should be confined chiefly to
the more useful branches of literature. 2. Most citizens had to work. Women should be trained to be
stewards and guardians of their husbands' property.
3. Professional life often took men away from their
families. Women should be prepared to train children.
They should know how to instruct their sons in the
principles of liberty and government. 4. Servants
needed looking after.

One hundred years ago the object of female education was to enable girls to attract men, gain husbands,
maintain homes, and manage families. It would have
seemed absurd to give a girl the same course as a boy
beyond the first reader. Hunt thinks that

Addison's description . . . of the accomplishments of an
Englishwoman of high breeding in 1712, would have answered

with some modifications for the daughter of a well-to-do family in America in 1815:

"She sings, dances, plays on the lute and harpsichord, paints prettily, is a perfect mistress of the French tongue, and has made a considerable progress in Italian. She is, besides, excellently skilled in all domestic sciences, as preserving, pickling, pastry, making wines of fruits of our own growth, embroidering, and needlework of every kind."

The domestic arts were taught to rich and poor. All women were expected to learn to nurse. But the book education of women was better and more diffused than in earlier days. Women whose grandmothers could not write were able to write well.

Americans generally were in accord, however, with Rousseau's view that

The education of women should be always relative to the men. To please, to be useful to us, to make us love and esteem them, to educate us when young and to take care of us when grown up, to advise, to console us, to render our lives easy and agreeable; these are the duties of women at all times.

Women accepted the gospel according to Paul. Books written for young women's guidance cited Milton:

To whom thus Eve with perfect beauty adorn'd:
"My Author and Disposer, what thou bidst
Unargued I obey; so God ordains;
God is thy law, thou mine; to know no more
Is woman's happiest knowledge and her praise."

Books for women indicate what was expected of them. They were advised to cultivate the power of pleasing conversation. Married women were to concentrate upon husband and home. One author bade woman understand "that there is an inequality in the sexes, and that for the economy of the world the men, who were to be the guardians and lawgivers, had not only the greater share of bodily strength bestowed on them, but those also of reason and resolution." She was reminded that chastity was less important in man than in woman; that she should not expostulate with an unfaithful husband lest she alienate him, but should feign ignorance of his behavior and charm him back; that she should not expect the public to sympathize with a blazoning of her wrongs; and that to separate from her husband made her responsible for his later vices.

For woman was prescribed strong doses of reading, mostly religious books; but she could read the *Rambler*, the *Idler*, and the *Spectator*. Shakespeare was too coarse but selections from him were admissible. Byron was taboo but Young, Thomson, Milton, Cowper, and Goldsmith afforded desirable reading. Moral essays were regarded as her best pabulum. She was encouraged to read American history but was warned against novels, though *The Vicar of Wakefield, Don Quixote*, and a few others escaped the ban. The young lady even put up with Swift's insults.[39]

For at least fifty years longer the education of women was in general of this degrading type. Too much time was given to frothy accomplishments, to dress, to romance and unreality, and too little to a substantial intellectual development that would have enabled her to interest and hold her husband and to escape from stagnation and inefficiency. The saner people of the period realized the defects of the system and urged amendment both in the interest of woman's function and of her own happiness. At school, however, none of the men teachers would teach Susan B. Anthony long division or understand why a girl should insist upon learning it.[40] It looked as if women were "to be mere kitchen maids, without a particle of information, ex-

---

[39] Hunt. *Life in America one hundred Years ago* (a valuable general reference on women's status), 74-84.

[40] Harper. *Life and Work of Susan B. Anthony*, vol. i, 22.

cept it belong to mere labor of body," or if taught more, naught but flashy accomplishments.

Many periodicals and papers for women (some of them by women) were in existence in the first half of the nineteenth century. At the middle of the century the leading magazine was Godey's *Lady's Book* – filled with fashion pictures "and stories supposed to be adapted by virtue of their domestic imbecility to the taste of the women of the period." The *Ladiès' National Magazine* was of like character. Women of the fifties took intense delight in novels of a "domestic, semi-pious character" – books that to men seemed trivial and empty. More substantial reading was afforded by some magazines, such as the *Ladies' Repository* of Cincinnati, in which in 1841 a writer advocated literature for women on account of their large influence on the race.

The arguments that so long deprived women of liberal culture rested almost entirely on the assumption that education would beget distaste for the pleasures of domestic life and would unfit women for family and social duties. When reading was first taught women in America, it is said that opposition arose on the ground that a woman would forge her father's or husband's name if she learned to read and write. Geography was likewise opposed on the score of its tendency to make her dissatisfied with home and desirous of travel. The first public examination of a girl in geometry, given in New York in 1829, raised a cry of disapproval all over the land – "the clergy, as usual, prophesying the dissolution of all family bonds."[41] In 1841 Mrs. Graves wrote:

It is their general anti-domestic tendency which is the greatest defect in our modern systems of female education; and to this

[41] These absurdities are recorded in Gage, *Woman, Church, and State*, 533, *footnote*, and Hecker, *Short History of Women's Rights*, 170.

we may trace the restless craving for the excitement of public duties and public pleasures, which so strikingly characterizes the aggregate of female society at the present day.

Mrs. Graves may have been justified in her criticism of what passed for higher education of girls, curricula of showy pretention, but it is strange that it did not occur to the thinkers of the day to trace more fundamental causation of woman's unrest. What could be accomplished by seclusion and prudishness? Sufficient commentary on the old system should have been found in such experiences as that of Paulina Wright who in 1844 gave public lectures on physiology. "When she uncovered her manikin, ladies would drop their veils or run from the room; sometimes they 'fainted.'" [42]

When about 1848 the first woman presented herself at the Harvard medical course she was ejected. When in 1855 the Regents of the State of New York gave to a woman's college the right to grant degrees and offer courses similar to those given to men the presidents of other institutions were horrified. One college president wrote: "A few dreamers I understand are trying to develop a college for women in the village of Elmira. The idea of giving woman a man's education is too ridiculous to appear credible." In a public address a professor in a well known eastern college said: "I am informed that a charter has just been issued in New York State for the forming of a woman's college and that a foolish effort is being made to place young women on the platform before an audience. To my mind this borders on the vulgar." Dr. Jewett, who in 1861 was organizing Vassar, met with similar criticisms. [43]

We must beware of taking the subject of female edu-

---

[42] Parsons. *Old Fashioned Woman*, 219.

[43] Dugard. *La Société Américaine*, 184-185; Reitzel. *Trend of Colleges for Women*, 310.

cation entirely out of its perspective. It must be remembered that the formal education of men was likewise very narrow and futile. Mackay, who travelled in the United States in 1846-1847, said: "As a general rule, the men in America fall far short of the women in intellectual culture and moral refinement. Most of them enter upon . . . business at an early age." Gurowski reported: "The intellectual education of an American woman, especially in the Free States, averages a higher degree than in Europe, even in countries considered as foremost in civilization. . . The culture of the mind is superior and more generally diffused among women than it is on the average among men. [Men are too busy.]" (In this fact may be an explanation in part of the strength of the woman movement.)

Woman's legal status during the first half of the nineteenth century was medieval and permeated with injustice. The reality of woman's bondage is made vivid by a case in New York City in which a husband recovered ten thousand dollars damages from persons that had received, harbored, and sheltered his wife after she left him.[44] Mrs. Robinson, a Lowell mill girl, saw

More than one poor woman skulk behind her loom or her frame when visitors were approaching. . . Some . . . were known under assumed names, to prevent their husbands from trusteeing their wages. It was a very common thing for a male person of a certain kind to do this, thus depriving his wife of all her wages, perhaps, month after month. . . A woman was not supposed to be capable of spending her own or of using other people's money. In Massachusetts, before 1840, a woman could not legally be treasurer of her own sewing-society, unless some man were responsible for her.[45]

[44] Gage. *Woman, Church, and State*, 141.
[45] Robinson. *Loom and Spindle*, 66-68.

Margaret Fuller recorded that

[In innumerable instances] profligate and idle men live upon the earnings of industrious wives; or if the wives leave them, and take with them the children, to perform the double duty of mother and father, follow from place to place, and threaten to rob them of the children, if deprived of the rights of a husband, as they call them, planting themselves in their poor lodgings, frightening them into paying tribute by taking from them the children, running into debt at the expense of these otherwise so overtasked helots. Such instances count up by scores within my own memory. I have seen the husband who had stained himself by a long course of low vice, till his wife was wearied from her heroic forgiveness, by finding that his treachery made it useless, and that if she would provide bread for herself and her children, she must separate from his ill fame — I have known this man come to install himself in the chamber of a woman who loathed him, and say she should never take food without his company. I have known these men steal their children, whom they knew they had no means to maintain, take them into dissolute company, expose them to bodily danger, to frighten the poor woman, to whom, it seems, the fact that she alone had borne the pangs of their birth, and nourished their infancy, does not give an equal right to them. . . This mode of kidnapping . . . is frequent enough in all classes of society.

I could give instances that would startle the most vulgar and callous; but I will not, for the public opinion of their own sex is already against such men, and where cases of extreme tyranny are made known, there is private action in the wife's favor. But she ought not to need this, nor, I think, can she long.[46]

Emily Collins, speaking of the period previous to 1848 and thereabouts, said:

In those early days a husband's supremacy was often enforced in rural districts by corporeal chastisement, and it was considered by most people as quite right and proper — as much so as the correction of refractory children in like manner. I remember in my own neighborhood a . . . Methodist class-

---

[46] Ossoli. *Woman in the Nineteenth Century*, 32-33.

leader and exhorter . . . esteemed a worthy citizen, who, every few weeks, gave his wife a beating with his horsewhip. He said it was necessary, in order to keep her in subjection, and because she scolded so much. Now this wife, surrounded by six or seven little children . . . was obliged to spin and weave cloth for all the garments of the family . . . to milk . . . to make butter and cheese, and do all the cooking, washing, making, and mending . . . and, with the pains of maternity forced upon her every eighteen months, was whipped by her pious husband, "because she scolded." [47]

In 1845 Edward D. Mansfield set forth the legal status of women. He exhibited the marriage relation as a legal unity the object of which arrangement was to secure unity of family support and government. Husband and wife could not make legal contracts with each other. It was only through trustees that an agreement between husband and wife could be enforced. If a husband, in order to stimulate his wife's industry, agreed to allow her a share of the proceeds, the court of chancery would enforce the agreement. Agreements to live separate and to allow the wife the use of her property could be enforced. In general they could not be witnesses for or against each other.

The husband was the legal head. He held the external powers of the family with reference to property. The wife's being was largely merged in his. The husband had a right to the person of his wife and hence the sole right to redress for legal wrongs against her person. She could not sue alone, nor execute a deed or other instrument to bind herself and property. (In some states a wife might make a will or devise of her property.) She forfeited all personal control over her property so long as the marriage lasted. Her personal property vested absolutely in the husband. The hus-

[47] Stanton *et al. History of Woman Suffrage*, vol. i, 88-89.

band was liable for wrongs and frauds of the wife committed during marriage and for debts contracted by her before marriage.

The husband had the right to claim his wife's society; to reclaim her if she went away or was detained; to use gentle constraint upon her liberty to prevent improper conduct. If preventive means, within limit, failed he must hand her over to the law or separate. He might sue for injury to her person. He might defend her with force. "In marriage the legal control of the wife passes to the husband, not that of the husband to the wife." The public opinion of men required of woman a stricter observance of certain morals than it demanded of men; but they had not ventured in that age to put the idea into the criminal code. "Probably the greatest amelioration of American jurisprudence is the relaxation of the old English rules in regard to the husband's control over the wife. . . The free spirit which pervades the whole legal and social structure of the United States, has entered this branch of jurisprudence also."

The wife might take some measures to restrain her husband from wrong but not to the same degree that he might in her case. She had redress at law against improper treatment. She was entitled to protection and maintenance. Legal title to property might be vested in trustees for the use of a wife. Any act of the mother over a child had the same validity as if it had been performed by the father. Under law of assault or seduction the father could claim damage on the ground that his daughter was his servant.

Even in mid-century if an employer paid to a necessitous wife her own earnings he could be prosecuted by a drunken and improvident husband and compelled to

make payment again to him.   The wife had no right to
custody of her person or of her children.   The husband could apprentice the children at an early age
against her will and at his death could dispose of the
children by will even though they were unborn.   The
formula constantly used in legal decisions was: "The
wife is dead in law," or "Husband and wife are one,
and that one the husband."   According to English common law, which then prevailed in every state save Louisiana, a man might beat his wife to the point of en-
dangering her life without being liable to prosecution.[48]
At a Woman's Rights Convention of 1852 Mrs. Nichols
said:

> If a wife is compelled to get a divorce on account of the in-
> fidelity of the husband, she forfeits all right to the property
> which they have earned together, while the husband, who is
> the offender, still retains the sole possession and control of the
> estate . . . he . . . retains the home and chil-
> dren. . . A drunkard takes his wife's clothing to pay his
> rum bills, and the court declares . . . the action . . .
> legal because the wife belongs to the husband.[49]

In 1860 a veiled lady told this story: She was sister
to a United States Senator and married to a distinguished member of the Massachusetts Senate.   They had
three children.   He proved unfaithful.   When she
confronted him with proof, he threw her down stairs.
Later he had her shut in an insane asylum (a very easy
thing for husbands in those days to do).   She got out
on habeas corpus.   The children were in the father's
custody.   Her brother said that if she made more
trouble they would return her to the asylum.   She fled
with one child.   Miss Anthony took her to New York.
They could not get shelter at night as hotels would not

[48] Anthony. *Status of Woman*, 901-902.
[49] Harper. *Life and Work of Susan B. Anthony*, vol. i, 74.

6 **The American Family**

take ladies alone. Even Garrison and Phillips urged
her to return the "abducted" child. Later the father
kidnapped the child. Nothing could be done.[50]

The subjection of woman was even used as an argument to bolster up slavery. The reverend F. A. Ross,
D.D., Presbyterian pastor at Huntsville, Alabama, in
an attempt in 1857 to prove *Slavery ordained of God*
said:

> Do you say, the slave is held to involuntary servitude? So
> is the wife. Her relation to her husband, in the immense ma-
> jority of cases, is made for her, and not by her. And when
> she makes it for herself, how often, and how soon, does it be-
> come involuntary! How often, and how soon, would she
> throw off the yoke if she could! O ye wives, I know how su-
> perior you are to your husbands in many respects – not only
> in personal attraction . . . in grace, in refined thought,
> in passive fortitude, in enduring love, and in a heart to be filled
> with the spirit of heaven. . . Nay, I know you may surpass
> him in his own sphere of boasted prudence and worldly wisdom
> about dollars and cents. Nevertheless he has authority from
> God to rule over you. . . You are bound to obey him in all
> things. Your service is very, very, very often involuntary from
> the first, and, if voluntary at first, becomes hopeless necessity
> afterwards. I know God has laid upon the husband to love
> you as Christ loved the church. . . But the husband may
> not so love you. He may rule you with the rod of iron.
> What can you do? Be divorced? God forbid it, save for
> crime. Will you say that you are free, that you will go where
> you please, do as you please? Why ye dear wives, your hus-
> bands may forbid. And listen, you cannot leave New York,
> nor your palaces, any more than your shanties. No; you can-
> not leave your parlor, nor your bedchamber, nor your couch, if
> your husband commands you to stay there. What can you do?
> Will you run away with your stick and your bundle? He can
> advertise you! What can you do? You can, and I fear some
> of you do, wish him, from the bottom of your hearts at the bot-
> tom of the Hudson.

0 Harper. *Life and Work of Susan B. Anthony*, vol. i, 201-205.

In the *Presbyterian Magazine* for 1852 the following keen comment on woman's status appeared:

> Our . . . position . . . is, that the Bible does not favor the manhood of woman — that it is opposed to the idea of a perfect equality of the sexes. . . Maternity, which we will here confine to the single idea of taking care of children, brings woman more within the precincts of the home. . . Authority must be vested somewhere. . . This authority in the human race is vested in man, as the divinely appointed head of creation. "Wives submit yourselves unto your husbands as unto the Lord." . . Woman has a mission to perform, which dignifies her even among angels. . . To light up the household with joy and love, to nourish and train the immortal children within its precincts, to minister to the good government of the little family kingdom, to cheer the husband who is the "head" amidst the sorrows and trials of life, to be an example of faith and righteousness.

A western legislator tells how he urged the passage of a bill giving to the widow of an intestate dying without children one-third of the husband's real estate in fee absolute and two-thirds of his personal property. He pled the wife's contribution to success in a new country. "The legislature, brought face to face with the notorious fact that, throughout the toilsome farming life, the wife bears her full share of the burden and heat of the day took a first step in righting the grievous wrong done to her." (The old law entitled her, in most cases, to but one-third of his personal property, and the use during her life of one-third of his real estate.) The legislature passed his bill; the people approved; but later a codification commission left it out.[51]

In this matter of the distribution of property, sex discrimination lingered long. Men of liberal views whose outlook transcended the system that denied females equal opportunity to earn a livelihood could, in-

---

[51] *Western People and Politicians*, 262.

deed, provide preferentially for their daughters. Some such logic may be reflected in the observations of a writer who said in 1828: "Rich men, here, often give more to their sons than to their daughters, tho it is very common for men of small fortunes to make the daughters independent at the expense of the sons." But Görling in 1840 wrote: "Seldom does the American provide his daughter in proportion to what the sons receive. She is a girl; girls are in great demand; well, let them go and marry." At this period a Massachusetts farmer would usually leave his daughter a home on the farm as long as she remained single. Fathers frequently willed all their property to their sons.[52]

Various stirrings of unrest among women were visited with indignant reprobation. With reference to knowledge of sex phenomena a body of New England churchmen wrote in 1837:

> We especially deplore the intimate acquaintance and promiscuous conversation of females with regard to things which ought not to be named; by which that modesty and delicacy which is the charm of domestic life, and which constitutes the true influence of woman in society, is consumed, and the way opened, as we comprehend, for degeneracy and ruin.

Women's activity in behalf of anti-slavery, circulating petitions, raising money, attending meetings, and forming societies, was an object of condemnation. After the attack on the Boston Female Anti-Slavery Society and the mobbing of Garrison in 1835 the editor of a religious journal declared that such as persisted in a course that led to such a riot were as much to blame as the rioters. Another remarked that when matters of grave political reform were up it might be wiser "for the gentler sex to seek information at home." When

---

[52] Cooper. *Notions of the Americans*, vol. ii, 254-255; Görling. *Die neue Welt*, 43; Robinson. *Loom and Spindle*, 68; Anthony. *Status of woman*, 901.

in 1837 the Grimké sisters championed on the platform immediate emancipation, the religious pro-slavery crowd cried out against the indelicacy of women's taking an active part in affairs of religious reform and assailed "Women's Rights." The General Association issued a pastoral letter urging that the churches should be closed to anti-slavery lecturers and that church members should not countenance women lecturers, saying that it was very wrong to encourage women to play an obtrusive and ostentatious part in matters of reform or countenance any "of that sex who so far forget themselves as to itinerate in the character of public lecturers and teachers." Thirty-nine students of Andover Seminary sent out an appeal to abolitionists. As abolitionists they condemned public lectures by women.

In 1841 Mrs. Graves wrote:

The great principles of liberty and equal rights, which are about to overthrow the long-existing institutions of despotism, and are stirring the hearts of men of every station, in every clime, have penetrated even into the quiet haven of domestic life. . . "The Rights of Women" are almost as warmly and wildly contested as the "Rights of Man;" and there is a revolution going on in the female mind at the present day, out of which glorious results may arise. [Woman] is yet too often found either the petted, capricious plaything, or the toiling careworn slave; and thus she lives and dies without knowing or fulfilling her responsibilities as the helpmate of her brother man — a being intended to be a coworker with him in promoting the spiritual and intellectual advance of the race. . .

We lament the erratic course of many of our female reformers, believing that they have inflicted deep injury where they intended good, by drawing woman away from her true and allotted sphere — domestic life. Nor are our female lecturers and female politicians alone at fault; for it is to be feared that even some Christian ministers, with greater zeal than knowledge, have, by their impassioned appeals, sent women abroad into the highways and byways of life, thereby deaden-

ing their sense of home responsibilities and social duties, and
teaching them to violate that gospel injunction which plainly declares that women should be "keepers at home." . . Not a
few of those who come forward to advocate the mental equality
of the sexes, do so in order to show that woman is entitled to
the same political rights and privileges as man; a doctrine
which, if brought into practical exercise, would tend to the
total disorganization of the family institution, and even more
effectually than the spirit of the age, dissolve the domestic ties,
and destroy all that makes woman efficient as a moral helpmate of man. . . The opponents of the claims set up in behalf of woman, instead of entering into a philosophical and
scientific examination of those claims, resort to jests and witti-
cisms, and unwarranted assumptions. They would seem to
shrink from examining the subject fairly lest they should be
drawn to concede more than they wish to do. . .

Many who are strenuous in denying to women all interference in the affairs of the State, are no less zealous in urging
her to engage in those of the church. . . Every argument is
brought forward to induce them to labor in adding to the funds
to be appropriated to the building of a church, to the education
of young ministers, etc., but when do we hear the sacred doctrine of home duties enforced? . . . [If such lessons] are
left almost wholly untaught, and in their place public services
are constantly pressed upon woman's attention, can we wonder
at the result? . . . It is, indeed, deeply to be regretted,
that among the many praiseworthy efforts of Christians at the
present day there should be so much in the spirit and character
of those efforts that is anti-domestic. . . Have not many of
our females, by assuming public responsibility but little in accord with their nature, and more properly belonging to the
other sex, neglected those congenial, paramount, and untrans-
ferable duties imposed on them by the God of nature and rev-
elation! . . .

The supremacy of the husband as the head of the family
institution is similar to the supremacy of the governing power
in the state, and there is like obligation to obedience in both.
But there is nothing servile or degrading in this . . .
"merely an official relation held for the mutual good of both
parties and of their children." . . She is required, therefore,

not only to submit to man as her head in the marriage relation but she must not assume to herself any right of participation with him in the management or control of civil or political affairs.

The intense animus against the woman's movement can not be fully understood or elaborated until the background and nature of that uprising have been studied, as is done in the next chapter.

V. THE EMERGENCE OF WOMAN

The economic forces back of modern progress and of the democratic enthusiasm involved in it could scarcely fail to unsettle the subordination of woman. The influences of the new world contributed to her elevation. This result was due in part to the operation of the law of supply and demand. In the pioneer regions women were usually scarce and hence were highly esteemed. There came to be almost a commerce in unmarried females between the old East and the new West. The deficit of women on the frontier accounts for their superior standing in some of the newest states.

In 1781 there was a large migration of young unmarried women into the country south of the Ohio, resulting in the establishment of many new families. Regarding early Memphis,

> I would like to give an account [said one writer] of the young ladies that flourished here at that time. It is due to them to say that they did not generally partake of the rude spirit of the men, though the few who did were not for that reason excluded from society. They could not be spared, as all of them made but a small-sized party.

In 1824 there was no Society worthy of the name. There were a few young men, unbridled adventurers. There was no preaching. There were no ladies to visit. Indian women and black girls were in abundance; but not a respectable white woman was to be seen once a month. Two or three respectable men married Indian women, with the excuse that there were no white women about. In the Chattanooga region some Scotch settlers courted and married Indian girls. In California in Spanish days the Franciscan fathers tried to keep white men and red women apart but failed. The practice of selling young Indian girls to white men became so common that in some regions a red man could not get a squaw. "By taking Indian mates and rearing offspring round the camps, these Spanish soldiers struck their roots into the soil" so that they could not be removed tho the Spanish policy had been to leave California as missionary territory free from whites. Thus California developed the Latin miscegenation with its usual illegitimacy.

In a newspaper of 1832 it was recorded that: "Some humane person, not long since, in reference to Mat Carey's benevolent exertions to raise the wages of females proposed a scheme for transporting the excess of spinsters in our large cities to the new settlements where there is a great scarcity of the female sex." An editorial of 1836 commenting on the excess of women in the older states recommended that they go West, where few would remain single for many months. A paper of the next year noted that "a wagon load of girls for the western market lately past through Northampton, Mass."

The value of women in the young settlements is well illustrated in the narrative of a pioneer who in 1836 made preparation to migrate to Wisconsin. His wife's health was not very good and they had two small children; so it was necessary to secure a hired girl. All that applied were too young and good-looking; his wife said they would marry within a month and leave the household without help and bereft of the passage money. Finally they attained their aim, as they supposed, by securing the services of a coarse and ugly spinster who surely could not attract a man to matrimony. In order to clinch the certainty, however, it was agreed that in case of marriage within a year she should forfeit her wages. But their arrival in the new home created notable excitement. Betsy was the first single woman. Various remarks were overheard, such as, "She is not handsome, certainly;" "Better than none, tho;" "Too old to add much to the future population," etc. In a few weeks it became apparent that her days of service were numbered. Betsy soon had an offer of marriage; indeed, she had several offers. Tho she probably had never before had a beau, she now had a dozen, could put on airs, could pick and choose. So the marriage came to pass as related in a previous chapter. Of like significance was the request sent back by an emigrant to Texas who among other things asked: "also one wife for me, handsome, etc. Mother knows what will suit me."

Another factor contributing to the standing of woman was pioneer isolation. As European life moved westward, first came the hunter's cabin.

> The next cabin [said a writer on the West] was more pretentious. It was large enough for two. The man who built it had induced a woman to share his lot. The woman who had courage to so adventure had also muscle enough to lift one end of a log sufficiently long to build a cabin for herself and her husband. . . This pair came to found a home, to rear a family, and ultimately to own broad acres to enrich their posterity. In one of these built by a man and a woman the writer hereof was born.

Such a pioneer family, living in isolation remote from civilized neighbors and far removed from the conventionalities of old society was apt to experience some relaxation of traditionally rigorous family relations. The feudal lord, living remote from kindred spirits, was led, we are told, to cultivate the society of his family, a condition favorable to gentler and more kindly family relations.   Similarly the frontier helped to liberalize the American family.   "What woman was in the days of chivalry," says one writer, ". . .   she was in pioneer days. . .   The pioneer wife . . . was the ideal of courage, industry, and virtue in the settler's home.   Here she reigns as mistress."

To isolation was added heroism and fortitude. Much depended, of course, on the character of the pioneer couple.   There would be men whom isolation would render morose and despotic and women whom loneliness would drive to insanity.   In the sparse West, insanity among farm women was not infrequent.

> The silence, the monotony, the absence of all society, the never-ending vista of the snow-covered plains, deathlike in their silence, with no moving creature or thing to afford even a momentary diversion, unbalanced these women, their physical vitality lowered by the enervating climate and unremitting toil.[53]

It has been noted that women, having fewer opportunities for contact with other people, were more susceptible to excitement at camp-meetings.

The selection exercised by the frontier was rigorous but it was on the whole salutary.   The outcome attested the sterling qualities of the men and women that opened the West.   The elevation that came in the status of woman was earned by devotion, labor, courage, self-control, heroism.   Never was the adaptility of female character more strikingly displayed than in the opening of the West.   Women stood by their husbands' side and fought for life and little ones against human and other foes.   Ladies whose husbands had lost everything

---

[53] This factor in the production of insanity has perhaps been over-emphasized, however. Compare Romanzo Adams's *Public Range Lands*, 338, *footnote.*

threw aside ease and luxury and fared boldly into the far West where they endured without complaint toils, danger, sickness, and loneliness. Reciprocity in the marriage relation was the logical consequence where woman bore a man's share in the struggle for existence.

Women's toils were great. It required not only heroism but muscle to make and maintain a cabin home. It required incessant labor to provide for the numerous household; for "she was lonesome until she had a half-dozen children about her. She did not begin to feel crowded in the single room until the second dozen began coming." She had to spin, and usually to weave all the cloth for her family, and it required all a woman's efforts to keep her brood comfortable. Privation and toil were her portion and upon her devolved the entire education of her children. In 1800, "the farmers' wives and daughters labored on the farm, in parts of New York, Pennsylvania, and in all the settlements where German or Irish people dwell in considerable numbers. The arrival of the New Englanders among them banished the females from the fields. . . ."

Even in the South, pioneer conditions bore heavily upon women and were efficiently borne. On occasion woman was capable of assuming headship of the family and discharging its duties with success. In early Tennessee "calico was very scarce, and [women vied] with each other in making the prettiest cotton frock, and eyed each other very closely at church to see who excelled." They "had no predilection for the cult of lilies and languors." The pioneer women, in daily peril and weighted with racking cares, resorted to tobacco, perhaps as a sedative. Mrs. Andrew Jackson was only one of thousands of women that smoked. The habit of chewing "obtained among numerous excellent women of the rural districts of middle Tennessee until long subsequent to the close of" the Civil War.[54]

Among the Scotch-Irish pioneers women held to the traditional sacrifice of self for the sake of the education of son or brother and his advancement into the sacred ministry. Some refused "the gift of loving companionship with strong and loyal spirits who wooed them to wifehood, and so lived and died voluntary celibates for the glory of God and the honor of their family."

Some conception of the toils of ante-bellum women even in the East may be gleaned from the case of Susan B. Anthony's mother, who married in 1817. Mr. Anthony was a generous man, loved his wife, and was well able to hire help; but such a thing was unthought of. A housewife would probably have been piqued by an offer of assistance. When Green Mountain girls came to work in Anthony's cotton-mill they boarded in the proprietor's family as custom was. Mrs. Anthony, the summer her third baby was born, boarded eleven factory hands who roomed in her house and she did all the cooking, washing, and ironing with no help save a thirteen-year-old girl who went to school and did chores night and morning. When brick was being burned for a new house, Mrs. Anthony boarded ten or twelve brick-makers and some of the factory hands with no help but that of her daughters Guelma, Susan, and Hannah, aged fourteen, twelve, and ten. When the new baby came these three little girls did all the work, cooking the food and carrying it to their mother's room to let her see whether it was nicely prepared and whether pails were properly packed.[55]

The American women [said Marryat in 1839], have a virtue which the men have not, which is moral courage, and one

---

[54] Hale and Merritt. *History of Tennessee and Tennesseeans*, vol. ii, 404.
[55] Harper. *Life and Work of Susan B. Anthony*, vol. i, 12, 19.

also which is not common with the sex, physical courage. The independence and spirit of an American woman, if left a widow without resources, is immediately shown; she does not sit and lament, but applies herself to some employment, so that she may maintain herself and her children, and seldom fails in so doing.

But not only on account of the scarcity of women in the newer regions, not only on account of the softening influence of pioneer isolation, nor of the devotion, heroism, and fortitude of pioneer women did woman's status begin to improve. All these influences had their effect on the frontier – an effect that reflected eastward. But indirectly, by the way of the democratic spirit which its economic conditions promoted, the new world furthered the equality of woman. The social changes that worked to the equalization of father and son, employer and employee and levelled class barriers generally could not but elevate woman and undermine arbitrary sex distinctions. Amid such conditions and influences sex barriers began to weaken; a belief in the equality of woman to man began to emerge; and the western habit of co-education came to register the new outlook. (The modern sweep of the suffrage movement toward the East is a correlate phenomenon.)

Quotations might be multiplied to show how observers were impressed with the regard shown to woman in the new nation. One remarked that woman's treatment was "too good" as man's was in England. We must allow for idealization. The reality was certainly not ideal any more than was the reality of chivalry with which comparison has been made. But neither was it a matter of mere sentimentality. A substantial opening was made for a better future.

A survey of the period covered by this volume shows

us that woman had already attained a status markedly
superior to the usage of Europe.   Not only was the
wife's managerial capacity recognized and rewarded
with full sway over the domestic hearth but woman
exerted an exceptional influence in the larger world as
the adviser of her husband and the arbiter of social
standards, of morals, of propriety.   Women were not
sheltered and futile as in some older civilizations but
were free to travel in safety and to know the world.
The relationship between husband and wife was freed
from sentimentality yet husbands treated their wives
with notable tenderness and the outraged woman could
ordinarily count on law and sentiment to protect her
against abuse.   Easy divorce offered a release for dis-
illusioned wives.   The extreme courtesy shown to
ladies was based on a genuine and growing respect and
deference which found its reflection in a remarkable
air of self-respect on the part of all women.   Woman
was largely freed from field work and other heavy labor; men even assumed responsibility for the marketing.   If woman still "kept her place," if she was still
hampered by a lack of business knowledge, if she still
used the sex appeal and played upon her weakness, if
she still sanctioned duels and other social atavisms – all
these shortcomings were of the past and could not hide
the better future.

De Tocqueville commented pointedly on the evolution of woman's status in America.   He said that her
prospective equality did not mean identity of function;
American women did not manage the outward concerns
of the family, or embark in business, or participate in
politics.   Tho often possessed of "a masculine strength
of understanding and a manly energy" the women of
America generally "preserve great delicacy of personal

appearance, and always retain the manners of women."
The Americans still hold "that the natural head of the
conjugal association is man . . . and . . .
that . . . the object of democracy is to regulate
and legalize the powers which are necessary, and not
to subvert all power." Women seem to be proud of
the yoke; "such at least is the feeling exprest by the
most virtuous of their sex; the others are silent; and
in the United States, it is not the practice for a guilty
wife to clamor for the rights of women, whilst she is
trampling on her own holiest duties." The Americans
believe in keeping the spheres of the sexes distinct but
consider them of equal value.

> If they hold that man and his partner ought not always to ex-
> ercise their intellect and understanding in the same manner,
> they at least believe the understanding of the one to be as sound
> as that of the other, and her intellect to be as clear. Thus,
> then, whilst they have allowed the social inferiority of woman
> to subsist, they have done all they could to raise her morally
> and intellectually to the level of man; and in this respect they
> appear to me to have excellently understood the true principle
> of democratic improvement. . . Altho the women of the
> United States are confined within the narrow circle of domestic
> life, and their situation is, in some respects, one of extreme de-
> pendence, I have nowhere seen women occupying a loftier posi-
> tion.

The distinguished Frenchman thought that Americans did not recognize the "double standard."
"Amongst them the seducer is as much dishonored as
his victim. . . A young unmarried woman may,
alone and without fear, undertake a long journey."
Rape is still a capital offence. "As the Americans can
conceive nothing more precious than a woman's honor,
and nothing which ought so much to be respected as her
independence, they hold that no punishment is too severe for the man who deprives her of them against her

will." Somehow, in spite of his unfriendliness to democracy, De Tocqueville tends to exaggerate the virtues of America.

Miss Martineau speaks of

The prevalent persuasion that there are virtues which are peculiarly masculine, and others which are peculiarly feminine. . .
[Marriage is safer than in England owing to] the greater freedom of divorce, and consequent discouragement of swindling and
other vicious marriages; it is more tranquil and fortunate from
the marriage vows being made absolutely reciprocal; from the
arrangements about property being generally far more favorable
to the wife than in England; and from her not being made, as
in England, to all intents and purposes the property of her
husband.

Mrs. Bodichon in 1857 expressed the belief that

America is full of hopeful signs for women; the men are not so
dead set against the rights of women as in the old country. . .
Men of position and reliable sources of information have assured me that when in any State in America a majority of
women shall claim the suffrage, it will be granted them. . .
There is always hope of change in America; evils do not go
on for ever dragging their slow length as in England. . . .
The ideas of human liberty and justice are too widely spread
in America for any state of things in direct opposition to these
principles, to endure forever.[56]

Burn, who spent three years among the working
classes in the United States during the war, said that
in America female notions of equality and personal independence had to a great degree reversed the old state
of affairs in the relations of the sexes to each other. It
was common for the husband "to do a considerable
part of the slip-slop work." In the morning he made
a fire in the stove, emptied the slops, got his breakfast,
and, if his work was at a distance, packed his lunch,
and departed for work while his wife was still abed.
"Even among the trading classes who have private

[56] Bodichon. *Women and Work*, 20.

dwellings, it is quite common to see the men bringing parcels from the market, the grocer's, fishmonger's, or butcher's, for the morning meal." It might be supposed from man's bending to "dishclout service," he went on to say, that the husbands were examples of kindness and affection and that the ladies "are so many connubial doves!" But the conclusion would be hasty. . . Wives would not black their husbands' shoes.

For some time a real interest in the education of women had been developing. Many seminaries had been established. As early as 1830 literary and scientific men were devoting attention to the preparation of lectures on science for female audiences.[57] Better education was broadening woman's opportunity for usefulness. In ladies' periodicals of the forties or thereabout appear many assertions of woman's intellectual equality and the champions are frequently men. This idea was coupled with a demand for ample education as an offset to woman's seclusion from the world or in order to enhance her personality. To such objections as that education made women pedantic, disagreeable, and undomestic one writer remarked:

> For the consolation . . . of men, who fear that our system of female education will soon become so perfect that they cannot find ignorant women enough for wives and companions for them, we can assure them that do all we can to educate them, yet there will always be ignorant women enough for all such men. [Men of liberal minds and true politeness enthusiastically prefer a learned woman as wife.]

Oberlin College opened in 1833 and was from the start co-educational tho disposed to frown upon graduates that agitated for "women's political rights." It was in 1841 that it granted the first three arts degrees ever received by women in the United States. For

[57] *Ladies' Magazine* (Boston), vol. iii, 41.

almost twenty years Oberlin was the only institution to receive women on substantially the same terms as men. Mt. Holyoke Seminary was incorporated in 1836. Antioch College (coeducational) opened in 1853.

The life of the women at Oberlin in its first generation was "plain, earnest, industrious, pervaded and guided by highest ideals." Lucy Stone said: "Nearly every one of us worked. We were poor. We earned our way. . . We did our own cooking (most of the time) and our washing and ironing all the time. Some of the girls paid their way by washing for the male students."

Elizabeth Cady Stanton wrote in 1851:

The girl must be allowed to romp and play, climb, skate, and swim; her clothing must be more like that of the boy . . . that she may be out at all times, and enter freely into all kinds of sport. Teach her to go alone, by night and day, if need be, on the lonely highway, or through the busy streets of the crowded metropolis. The manner in which all courage and self reliance is educated out of the girl, her path portrayed with dangers and difficulties that never exist, is melancholy indeed.

The fundamental life factors of the new world could not but result in new aspirations on woman's part for freedom, opportunity, enlightenment, and sovereignty, and lead to a pervasive insurgency. Away back in Revolutionary times (not to speak of the colonial days and Ann Hutchinson, with her demand "that the same rights of individual judgment upon religious questions should be accorded to woman which the Reformation had already secured to man"), the spirit of female revolt was awake. In the following humoro-serious letter to John Adams from his wife we see how closely it was correlated with the male revolutionary activity.

I long to hear you have declared an independency, and by the way, in the new code of laws, which I suppose it will be necessary for you to make, I desire you would remember the ladies and be more generous and favorable to them than your ancestors. Do not put such unlimited power into the hands of husbands. Remember, all men would be tyrants if they could. If particular care and attention are not paid to the ladies, we are determined to foment a rebellion, and will not hold ourselves bound to obey any laws in which we have no voice nor representation.

The "we" connoted Mercy Otis Warren, Hannah Lee Corbin, etc. Dame Adams is sternly logical in her deductions from revolutionary principles. Male "democracy" is pseudo-democracy. John replied on April 14, 1776, in substance as follows: Our authority is nominal; I hope all would fight rather than give up this shadow of power. But he wrote to Warren that wives must "teach their sons the divine science of politics!" In 1778 Mrs. Corbin, sister of Richard Henry Lee, presented a protest against taxation without suffrage. Her brother replied that women were entitled to vote.[58]

The Duc de La Rochefoucauld-Liancourt, who travelled in the United States in 1795-1797, noticed at the house of General Warren that

His wife, of the same age as he, is much more interesting in conversation. Contrary to the custom of American women, she has been busy all her life with all sorts of reading. She has even printed one or two successful volumes of poetry, and has written a history of the Revolution which she had the modesty and good taste not to wish published until after her death. . . They assured me that the literary occupations of this estimable dame have not diverted her attention from the duties of housekeeping.

The fact that as early as 1794, Mary Wollstonecraft's

[58] Squire. *Woman Movement in America*, 47; Adams. *Familiar letters of John Adams and his Wife*, 155; Björkman and Porritt. *Woman Suffrage*, 6; Stanton *et al. History of Woman Suffrage*, vol. i, 32-33; Barnes. *Woman in modern society*, 64.

Vindication of the Rights of Women was republished in Philadelphia shows that her ideas must have had some vogue in America. A few American writers of the early nineteenth century wrote on the rights and wrongs of women but they did not gain a great following. There was present nevertheless the nucleus of the modern point of view. Some people saw that a worse thing than spinsterhood might befall a woman. Eliza Southgate Bowne, who was born in 1783, wrote in her girlhood:

> The inequality of privilege between the sexes is very sensibly felt by us females, and in no instance is it greater than in the liberty of choosing a partner in marriage. . . After a long calculation, in which the heart never was consulted, we determine whether it is most prudent to love or not. . . I congratulate myself that I am at liberty to refuse those I don't like, and that I have firmness enough to brave the sirens of the world and live an old maid, if I never find one I can love.

At eighteen she professes admiration for many of Mary Wollstonecraft's sentiments on freedom of woman. A year later she wrote: "I thank heaven I was born a woman. . . As a woman I am equal to the generality of my sex, and I do not feel that great desire of fame I think I should if I was a man." The murmurs of female derelicts scarcely constituted as yet a momentous social force.

Robert Owen preached absolute equality of all men and women. A writer in the *Ladies' Magazine* (Boston) in 1830 says it is foolish to make marriage your one end. Sale of yourself is degrading. Let women learn housekeeping, keep up with their children, learn to think for themselves. In 1834 during a turbulent strike of female operatives at Lowell against a reduction of wages, one was said to have made a radical speech on the rights of women. Susan B. Anthony, at school at the age of eighteen, learning that a young friend had married a widower with six children, comments in her diary: "I should think any female would rather live and die an old maid." Her father believed in giving sons and daughters the same advantages. The daughters were taught business principles. He encouraged and backed her in her desire to go into reform work. Her mother also supported her, not wishing her to take any time from her public affairs for home work. Her father, years before his death, wrote her brother: "Take your family into your confidence and give your wife the purse."

In the *Ladies' Magazine* (Boston) in 1833 appeared "A New Method of Improving the Complexion of Ladies." Persian ladies were quoted to the effect that a husband should always be kind and give his wife limitless money. "If the man be but a day-laborer, and do not give his wages to his wife, she will claim them on the day of judgment." On this text was made the comment:

> The early decay of female beauty in our country, has been often remarked by Europeans. Now we leave it for gentlemen to decide, whether the effect arises from climate, and the delicate constitution of our women, or whether it is caused by their being allowed too little cash.

In 1835 Ernestine L. Rose and Pauline Wright Davis circulated the first petition for property rights for women. The woman question was becoming a large one. By 1840 it had split the American Anti-Slavery Society. A faction seceded because of the appointment of a woman on the business committee. The executive committee disclaimed disposition to take sides on the woman question.

The periodicals of the day give us some hint of lines on which thought was running. Thus *Graham's Mag-*

azine for 1842 contained a story (written by a woman) in which a girl was not spoiled for matrimony by her scentific studies. The volume for 1845 portrayed a woman that had had three husbands, a spendthrift, a philosopher, and a gourmand, urging her niece to marry a fool – "a man that would let his wife have her own way in everything." If this be fiction, it may nevertheless be significant. In the *Ladies' Wreath* (New York, 1848-1849), Mrs. S. T. Martyn discussed three ways of managing a wife. First came a picture of an outlandish husband, tyrannizing over wife and child. The wife became an adroit dissimulator; the child was spoiled. The second exhibit was a husband who "yielded to his wife's choice" but always managed to bring her to doing what he wanted. The third case was that of a young man that married a girl ignorant of housekeeping. "Servants often leave in our country." He encouraged her to learn and she took hold and came out beautifully.

Louisa M. Alcott had an offer of marriage, about which she consulted her mother, telling her that she did not very much care for the lover. Her mother wisely saved her from the impulse to self-sacrifice, which might have led her to accept a position that would have brought help to the family. This was not her only chance but Louisa had no inclination toward matrimony. She could hardly look upon her own interests as separate from those of the family. She loved activity, freedom, independence. She "could not cherish illusions tenderly," and she always said that she tired of everyone and felt sure she should of her husband if she married. She never wanted to make her heroines marry but she gave in to public taste. Doubtless many a wife in those days was of essentially the same temperament as Miss Alcott.

The first organized body to formulate a declaration of the rights of women was at Seneca Falls, New York, in 1848. This first Woman's Rights Convention prepared a Declaration of Sentiments following closely the Declaration of Independence. For the present study it will suffice to quote a few of the charges made against man:

He has made her, if married, in the eye of the law, civilly dead.

He has taken from her all right in property, even to the wages she earns.

He has made her, morally an irresponsible being, as she can commit many crimes with impunity, provided they be done in the presence of her husband. In the covenant of marriage, she is compelled to promise obedience to her husband, he becoming to all intents and purposes her master – the law giving him power to deprive her of her liberty and to administer chastisement.

He has so framed the laws of divorce, as to what shall be the proper causes, and, in case of separation, to whom the guardianship of the children shall be given, as to be wholly regardless of the happiness of woman – the law in all cases going upon a false supposition of the supremacy of man, and giving all power into his hands.

The declaration from which the above indictments are taken illustrates very clearly the then prevailing status of woman. The convention resolved that woman being man's equal ought to be enlightened as to the laws so that she would no longer be satisfied; "that woman had too long rested content in the narrow limits worked out for her by corrupt customs and a perverted application of the scriptures;" that women should now secure their rights. Two weeks later at Rochester the same convention resolved that women not being represented ought not to be taxed; that the assumption of the law to settle the estates of intestates that left widows was an insult to women; that the husband had no right to hire out the wife and appropriate her wages to his own use; that the promise of obedience in the marriage contract was a hideous barbarity that ought to be abolished.

The proceedings of the convention were ridiculed by the press and denounced by the pulpit from one end of the country to the other. (Since then most of the Seneca Falls demands have been granted.) The *Mechanic's Advocate* (Albany) seemed to see in the movement a mere bourgeois insurgency; for it said: "It would alter the relations of females without bettering their condition. . . It presents no remedy for the real evils that the millions of the industrious, hard-working, and much suffering women of our country groan under and seek to redress." The *Rochester Democrat* reported that "the only practical good proposed—the adoption of measures for the relief and amelioration of the condition of indigent, industrious, laboring females—was almost scouted by the leading ones composing the meeting." At Rochester Sarah Owen reported the complaint of seamstresses of the city "that they get but thirty cents for making a satin vest, and from twelve to thirty for making pants, and coats in the same proportion." She thought that husky men ought to quit selling ribbons. Mrs. Roberts

Made some appropriate remarks relative to the intolerable servitude and small remuneration paid to the working-class of women. She reported the average price of labor for seamstresses to be from thirty-one to thirty-eight cents a day, and board from one dollar twenty-five cents to one dollar fifty cents per week to be deducted therefrom, and they were generally obliged to take half or more in due bills, which were payable in goods at certain stores, thereby obliging them many times to pay extortionate prices. . . It did not require much argument, to reconcile all who took part in the debates, to woman's right to equal wages for equal work, but the gentlemen seemed more disturbed as to the effect of equality in the family. [Who was to be the head?]

Certainly Wendell Phillips was not guilty of overlooking the proletarian connections of great movements. At the Worcester convention in 1851 he referred to the pulpit's declaring

It "indecorous in woman to labor, except in certain occupations." . . The whole mass of women must find employment in two or three occupations. . . They kill each other by competition. . . From what sources are the ranks of female profligacy recruited? [In some cases the cause is giddy idleness.] But, undoubtedly, the great temptation to this vice is the love of dress, of wealth, and the luxuries it secures. . . There are many women, earning two or three dollars a week, who feel that they are as capable as their brothers of earning hundreds, if they could be permitted to exert themselves freely. Fretting to see the coveted rewards of life forever forbidden them, they are tempted to shut their eyes on the character of the means by which a taste, however short, may be gained of the wealth and luxury they sigh for.

In 1855 Lucy Stone called attention to the fact that society was keeping woman at home a dependent. Women working in tailor shops, moreover, were paid one-third as much as men.

Some one in Philadelphia has stated that women make fine shirts for twelve and a half cents apiece; that no woman can make more than nine a week, and the sum thus earned, after deducting rent, fuel, etc., leaves her just three and a half cents a day for bread. Is it a wonder that women are driven to prostitution? Female teachers in New York are paid fifty dollars a year, and for every such situation there are fifty applicants. . . The present condition of woman causes a horrible perversion of the marriage relation. It is asked of a lady, "Has she married well?" "Oh, yes, her husband is rich." Woman must marry for a home, and you men are the sufferers by this.

In the course of the mid-century movement, protest

was made against the legal nonage of the wife, against
the husband's control of property, against the wrongs
of slave women. Women were urged not to let a
drunkard beget children. It was recognized that the old
"dainty notions" had made women hot-house plants—
half of them invalids; that humanity was only just
emerging from the age when might made right; and
that superstitious fears and dread of losing man's regard smothered frank expression of woman's views;
women did not dare support their champions. It was
denied that any portion of the species had a right to
determine the sphere of the rest; and suffrage was demanded as a means of self-defense and education. It
was urged that rights and burdens, taxation and representation should be coextensive, that all civil and professional employments should be opened to women,
that there should be a single standard of propriety for
both sexes; that women should assume the right to woo;
that they should be given title to their own wages
and equal guardianship over children; that drunkards
should have no claim on wife or child; and that neither
law nor opinion should presume to hold together souls
not bound by love.

The bloomer costume and war against corsets sprang
up during the woman campaign. Amelia Bloomer's
followers thought that if woman was to take her place
as man's equal, competing with him in the professions,
in business, in the trades, she must adopt a rational
costume fitted to her new sphere. Jeering mobs followed the new-costumed women. In Easthampton,
Massachusetts, some young women that appeared in
bloomers were warned by their pastor that if they continued to wear such clothes they would be put out of
the church. Ridiculed by the press, hooted by the
crowd, discountenanced by other women, the mass of

devotees of short skirt and trousers speedily returned to the old garb.[59]

Fierce opposition developed against existing marriage laws. In 1832 Robert Dale Owen and Mary Robinson had married by signing a document written by the groom, with a justice of the peace and the immediate family as witnesses:

NEW YORK, TUESDAY, APRIL 12, 1832.

This afternoon I enter into a matrimonial engagement with Mary Jane Robinson, a young person, whose opinions on all important subjects, whose mode of thinking and feeling, coincide more intimately with my own than do those of any other individual with whom I am acquainted. . . We have selected the simplest ceremony which the laws of this state recognize. . . This ceremony involves not the necessity of making promises regarding that over which we have no control, the state of human affections in the distant future, nor of repeating forms which we deem offensive, insomuch as they outrage the principles of human liberty and equality. . . Of the unjust rights which in virtue of this ceremony an iniquitous law tacitly gives me over the person and property of another, I can not legally, but I can morally divest myself. . .

ROBERT DALE OWEN.

I concur in this sentiment, MARY JANE ROBINSON.[60]

Another couple protested similarly in 1855. They declared that they did not sanction or promise

Voluntary obedience to such of the present laws of marriage as refuse to recognize the wife as an independent rational being, while they confer on the husband an injurious and unnatural superiority, investing him with legal powers which no honorable man would exercise. . . We believe . . . that marriage should be an equal and permanent partnership, and so recognized by law. . . We believe, that, when domestic difficulties arise, no appeal should be made to existing tribunals; but all difficulties should be submitted to the equitable

[59] McMaster. *History of the People of the United States* (1913), vol. viii, 122.

[60] Stanton *et al. History of Woman Suffrage*, vol. i, 294-295.

adjustment of arbitrators, mutually chosen. Thus, reverencing law, we enter our earnest protest against rules and customs which are unworthy of the name, since they violate justice, — the essence of all law.

The officiating minister, the reverend T. W. Higginson, wrote a letter to a newspaper, as follows:

> I never perform the marriage ceremony, without a renewed sense of the iniquity of our present system of laws in respect to marriage, a system by which man and wife are one, and that one the husband. It was with my hearty concurrence, therefore, that the . . . protest was read and signed, as a part of the nuptial ceremony; and I send it to you that others may be induced to do likewise.[61]

It may be wondered what was the character of the women that espoused the cause of revolution. Catherine Beecher, who certainly was not an ultra-radical, passed the following verdict:

> In my long-protracted and extensive journeyings I have discovered, that the Woman's Rights party, in this country, embraces many women whom even the most conservative can not but concede to be persons of superior talent and acquisition, of great benevolence, of great purity of motive and elevation of aims, and whom, saving where conventional points are antagonistic to their *principles*, all would allow to be women of modesty, delicacy, and refinement.[62]

The unthinking conservatives of the day had distinctly uncomplimentary views of the whole movement. An 1853 convention was marred by the riotous proceedings of "antis." The women of the revolt were "Amazons," "unsexed," "disappointed of getting husbands or perhaps of ruling over them," "a hybrid species . . . belonging to neither sex;" or else, perhaps, "dull and uninteresting, and, aside from their novelty, hardly worth notice." It was supposed that separation of interests would cause domestic strife and that suffrage would engender endless household quarrels. The idea that married women should possess their own wages and have equal guardianship of the children was a start toward "a species of legalized adultery." Jests were made about the possibility of women (whose names were appended) giving birth to children in the law-court or in the pulpit, and these pleasantries were not directed solely at married ladies. The Utica *Evening Telegraph* said that Miss Anthony in a public address urged women not to allow intemperate husbands to add another child. Shocking! a maiden lady! The "Editor's Table" of *Harper's New Monthly Magazine* for November, 1853, contained an illuminating discussion of the subject:

> The most serious importance of this modern "woman's rights" doctrine is derived from its direct bearing upon the marriage institution. The blindest must see that such a change as is proposed in the relation and life of the sexes cannot leave either marriage or the family in their present state. It must vitally, and in time wholly sever that oneness which has ever been at the foundation of the marriage idea, from the primitive declaration of *Genesis* to the latest decision of the common law. This idea gone – and it is totally at war with the modern theory of "Woman's Rights" – marriage is reduced to the nature of a contract simply. . . That which has no higher sanction than the will of the contracting parties, must, of course, be at any time revocable by the same authority that first created it. That which makes no change in the personal relations, the personal rights, the personal duties, is not the holy marriage union, but the unholy alliance of concubinage.

As late as the Woman's Rights Convention in Philadelphia, in 1854, an objector in the audience called out: "Let women first prove that they have souls; both the Church and the State deny it." [63] In Massachusetts in 1857 an attempt was made to grant greater rights to a surviving wife. One of the opposing sena-

---

[63] Gage. *Woman, Church, and State*, 57.

tors maintained that wives were already too much disposed to rid themselves of their husbands. The senator
alluded to certain crimes of a short time before, which
were imputed to a desire for succession. The judiciary
committee of the New York Assembly to whom in 1856
women's rights petitions were referred reported that
when both husband and wife had signed the petitions
"they would recommend the parties to apply for a law
authorizing them to change dresses . . . and thus
indicate the true relation. . ."

The generation before the War witnessed positive
improvement in the legislation governing woman's
status and rights. By the early thirties nine states had
abolished imprisonment of women for debt, viz. Massachusetts, Connecticut, New York, New Jersey, Pennsylvania, Ohio, North Carolina, Alabama, and Mississippi. In some states a woman was allowed to retain
some or all of her property in her own hands after marriage. Miss Martineau heard decided criticism of
existing laws. "I heard a frequent expression of in-
dignation that the wife, the friend and helper of many
years, should be portioned off with a legacy like a sal-
aried domestic."

As early as 1809 Connecticut granted to married
women the right to will property. In Alabama, about
1830, the "Ladies' Bill" to give women the right to hold
after marriage property that belonged to them before
was warmly debated in the legislature. In 1839 Mississippi placed the control of her own property in a
married woman's hands. During the forties and fifties several states granted property rights to wives. The
California constitution of 1849 provided that the real
and personal property belonging to a woman before
marriage was to remain her separate property after

marriage.   In the new Texas instrument it was provided that all real and personal property owned by the wife before marriage or acquired by gift or device after marriage was to be her separate property.   The legislature was required to enact laws clearly defining the rights of the wife and providing for the registration of her property.

A spirited debate attended the progress of the radical innovation.   Use was made of the case of the Massachusetts heiress, worth fifty thousand dollars, who married and in a year was widowed and endowed by her generous husband with the fifty thousand dollars for so long as she should remain his widow.   When the Tennessee Senate passed a bill to secure to married women enjoyment of their own property, the Nashville *Union* said:

> Under the old law, which has been miscalled the "perfection of wisdom," how many worthy women have been reduced from competency to beggary? how many have been victims of worthless fortune hunters? how many have suffered cruel privations from miserly husbands? how many have been left penniless widows, their property being taken to pay their husbands' debts . . . The measure injures no one . . . and last, though not least important in its consequences, it will diminish the number of old maids, who now refuse to marry lest their effects should be squandered.

In the New York convention it was pointed out that law as it had been, protected wives from cruelty to about the same extent as animals.   Final passage of the New York law was due in large measure to two facts:

> Some aggravated cases of cruelty in families of wealth and position had just at that time aroused the attention of influential men to the whole question; [and, second], among the Dutch aristocracy of the state there was a vast amount of dissipation; and as married women could hold neither property nor children under the common law, solid, thrifty Dutch

fathers were daily confronted with the fact that the inheritance of their daughters, carefully accumulated, would at marriage pass into the hands of dissipated, impecunious husbands, reducing them and their children to poverty and dependence.

The bill was originated by a conservative member who had all his life tried to keep his wife's property distinct, so as not to risk its loss, but felt himself hampered by the old laws. Another member had been at great pains to draw up a trust in order to safeguard a bequest to his daughter but was not sure that it would hold. "When the law of 1848 was passed, all I had to do," he said, "was to burn this will." What the New York reformers intended was "to strike a hard blow, and if possible shake the old system of laws to their foundations, and leave it to other times and wiser councils to perfect a new system." [64]

The enemies of the reform pointed out that the question had often been before the New York legislature and asserted that the people had not demanded a change. They urged that such a separation of interests would cause domestic strife. The cry of injustice to women was represented as a figment of delusion, an attack on foreign adventurers in the interests of the daughters of millionaires, not for the benefit of the daughters of the plain people. Some conservatives alleged that if women were given the new right they would be brought into contact with the roughest scenes of life, their sensibilities destroyed, their dependence on man weakened and thereby one of their loveliest charms removed.

The New York law allowed the wife to engage in all civil contracts or business on her own responsibility, rendered her joint guardian of her children, and granted both husband and wife a one-third share of each other's property in case of the death of either. Step by

[64] Stanton *et al. History of Woman Suffrage*, vol. i, 63-65.

step the Middle and New England States modified their laws. In Massachusetts constitutional convention, however, a resolution to secure married women's rights was reported adversely. In 1857 the Ohio legislature passed a bill that no married man should dispose of any personal property without consent of wife. The wife was empowered in case of violation to commence civil suit in her own name for recovery. Any married woman whose husband deserted or neglected to provide for the family was to be entitled to his wages and those of her minor children. Not until 1860 did the New York legislature grant to married women possession of their own wages and equal guardianship of their children, and in the midst of the War, finding women off guard, the solons took away the right of equal guardianship and control by widows of property for minor children.[65]

In the background of this transition period men and women lived and worked in normal wise. Wives were reminded of their husbands' business stress and of the need of gentleness and love. Complaisance was suggested as the way to control the man. Very likely such advice was sound. We can not suppose that the typical American wife was as cramped and oppressed as the law would allow. Legal changes came more slowly than the modification of social ethics; legal advance was slow down to the Civil War. It remained for the more decided economic revolution of the post-bellum period to complete the emancipation set on foot by the push of new world liberty, equality, and mutuality.

[65] Harper. *Life and Work of Susan B. Anthony*, vol. i, 219.

VI. THE FAMILY AND THE HOME

American family life seemed to the observer from Europe to be strangely lacking in closeness and warmth. Count Carlo Vidua wrote in 1827 on American manners as follows:

Paternal and filial affection is not [very] lively among them. In a large family the sons gather together at meal time, each coming from his business; each enters the room, says not a word to father or brother; opens not his mouth, in fact, except to put something therein; devours in a few instants the few ill-cooked dishes, and whoever is first satisfied, without waiting till the others have finished, rises, takes his hat and is off. . . A son who goes off . . . to establish himself in Kentucky or Missouri has no more to say in the way of adieu than if he were going to see a festa in a neighboring village. The father on his side, welcoming some other son returning from China, will say to him, cool as a cucumber, "Good day, John" and at the very utmost do no more than throw in a shake of the hand.[66]

Another visitor wrote: "Domestic life in America has the appearance of being cold and formal. . . The American conducts himself towards his wife and children with very little more familiarity than towards his neighbors."[67] There is seeming want of feeling on parting from children. St. Victor in 1832 wrote that the child in the lower classes quit his parents readily, "almost like the animal does." Parents saw with indifference the departure of their children. There were numerous cases of children abandoned by parents on

---

[66] *Decay of the family affections*, 291.
[67] Sealsfield. *The United States*, 118-119, 125.

leaving for distant states.[68]   Naumann remarks in 1848 that the relation between parents and children often does not impress the observer as joyous.

> Generally they treat one another coldly and soberly; mutual love and cordiality often seems foreign to them. . . [At majority, children feel that they have discharged their duties to parents.   Usually the son leaves the father's house to establish his own hearth.]   Farmers, who generally can not well conduct their affairs without the aid of their children, often, in their later years arrive in a very unpleasant situation, owing to their children's leaving them.

The father of the frontier bride usually gave her "a bed, a lean horse, and some good advice: and having thus discharged his duty . . . returned to his work."   Letters of 1840, even to children, began thus: "Respected Daughter."   They were likely to be taken up mainly with the weather and sickness in the family, of which there was an appalling amount.

The seeming coolness in American family relations, which so impressed Europeans, may be attributed in part to native temperament, but was evidently due also to the economic largeness of the new world which made family wealth and backing less significant and to the exaggerated individualism and independence that came with the spread of anarchistic democracy.   The situation illustrates the general principle that the family is not an end in itself but varies in strength in proportion as it is needed for race conservation and proves capable of serving that end.   The abundant opportunities of the new country, the relative ease of getting along, the certainty that the children would be able to find good openings, tended to loosen family attachments; for children past their earliest years were not essentially dependent on the father and necessity did

---

[68] St. Victor. *Lettres sur des États Unis*, 222.

not enter so strongly as in old countries to bind the family closely together. The family ceased to be an economic unit: each member could follow a calling to taste. The ease with which the son could start for himself upon attainment of legal majority tended to make previous relations with the father a period of quasi-servitude which tended to beget estrangement and make separation easy for both.

Moreover a people alert to grasp fresh material opportunity crowding upon them in profusion will tend to be matter-of-fact and unsentimental. The strenuous life of a society whose prime business was production rather than consumption lessened family endearment. Paternal preoccupation left wife and children a larger scope. Men were too busy to know their little ones, to enjoy much of their wives' society, or to lavish affection. One writer accounted for the intensity of the maternal affection of New England women by the fact that it was almost their whole romance, inasmuch as the men were too busy to be very affectionate. "I have hardly ever seen that tender affection – that union of souls, in which two persons require nothing but each other's consent for the completion of their happiness." . . Suppose a man to marry a woman with tastes, disposition, and character essentially different from his. The points of contact are so few that he might become the father of a large family and die without discovering his mistake. He has no time to be unhappy. Women are left all day to themselves: the life is monotonous. Hence they love their offspring passionately, "while for their husbands they feel a sort of half distant respect."

A considerable factor in this attitude of women toward men, however, must have been the fact that woman was under necessity of marrying for the sake of a home even tho she had not experienced love. At the end of the eighteenth century, Eliza Southgate wrote to Moses Porter:

> I may be censured for declaring it as my opinion that not one woman in a hundred marries for love. [I mean] she would have preferred another if he had professed to love her as well as the one she married. . . Gratitude is undoubtedly the foundation of the esteem we commonly feel for a husband. . . [One is surprised] at the happiness which is so generally enjoyed in families, and that marriages which have not love for a foundation on more than one side at most, should produce so much apparent harmony.[69]

An article in the *Literary Magazine and American Register* of 1803-1804 stated that nothing was more common than marriages where the parties were unequal in capacity and dissimilar in feelings. Misery was a result.

Other factors in the obscuring of family sentiment were the binding out of the children of the poor, a usage that killed filial affection; the stress put by nascent capitalism on contract and free competition as opposed to status and fixed restraints; the fact that parents were under no legal obligation to adult children and could disinherit them freely; the cult of democracy which made the son a citizen in every respect independent and attached him positively to social responsibilities, so that a mother's apparent indifference at seeing her son go to the ends of the earth was not lack of love but a recognition of civic and social needs. Moreover respect for the independence and rights of women and children tended to replace sentimentality with a certain deference. Sometimes, of course, man's rut of business kept him so narrow that he was not much of a

---

[69] Bowne. *Girl's Life eighty Years ago*, 37-40.

companion for his more cultivated wife. Lack of
suitable reading and other home attractions must be
taken into account as a factor in the lessening of family
fondness; males sought recreation abroad. One writer,
attributing superior domesticity to the Bostonians, gave
their taste for reading as a contributory cause.

Woodruff (in his work of 1862 on *Legalized Prostitution*) saw a great lack of proper knowledge. He
pointed out that in marriage the question whether "nature has made them for each other" was "left for the af-
ter-clap." The form of law was followed with dignity,
but "the spirit of the act they commit they are ignorant
of." The majority of those whose connubial relations
were normal contracted them ignorantly. School education avoided the problems of life.

> Life in its reality constitutes no part of the modern scholar's
> study. . . Young ladies are falsely and artificially educated
> and grow up to know comparatively nothing of the relations of
> life or the duties they are to fulfill. . . They are taught to
> show the outside rather than the inside; to cultivate taste in
> dressing their bodies rather than their minds; while young
> men are but little better instructed save as they spend more time
> in the busy world. . . With so much of wrong educational
> bias given to the young, with so much falsity in society, we can-
> not have marriage as it should be.

Certain factors of American life worked against
familism. Political democracy is congenial with
equality among brothers. The superior position of the
eldest brother that prevailed in old societies does not
appear or yields to the general spirit of democracy.
The laissez-faire spirit of nascent capitalism could not
tolerate, in the new world, governmental interference
in the form of entail, which made competition unequal
among the members of the upper caste. Sentimental
democracy, also, entered the lists against the survivals

of feudalism. The abundance of land minimized the prestige of primogeniture. Jefferson attacked entail on the ground that it defrauded creditors; was unjust to unprivileged members of the family; and supported an aristocracy. It was argued that to permit land to remain in the same family prevented "that equal distribution of property which was the legitimate reward of industry," and discouraged the poor from the hope of "ever gaining any part of the property" guarded by entail. In Virginia entail was abolished in 1776. After 1800 the traditional influence of the old families had in large degree disappeared with their great landed possessions. Many early settlers, such as the Livingstons in New York and Calvert and Carroll in Maryland, attempted to introduce entail and to found manors as the basis of a titled aristocracy. But all these air castles mouldered with the bodies of their founders and primogeniture was not allowed permanently to obstruct the agricultural development and the industrial settlement of the country.

Thus in the nineteenth century, equality among children came to pass. Carlier found public opinion opposed to disproportionate bequest. Equal division of property among numerous children prevents the formation of family wealth. In the absence of the custom of primogeniture, said one writer in 1833 or earlier: "It will rarely happen that a father can bequeath to each of his children enough to render them independent." Property ties being thus weakened, family integration would be less distinct. Daughters and younger sons would not be dependent on their older brother and family cohesion would be less essential. Rapid movement and dispersion of population tended to obscure lineage, and to destroy the influence of the wider kinship group and the sentimental power of ancestral seats. The revolt of individualism against familism attacked the principle of inheritance. Even in 1829, Ebenezer Ford was elected to the New York legislature on a Labor Ticket, on a platform declaring hereditary transmission of wealth and poverty at the root "of all our calamities." [70]

During the first half of the nineteenth century the development of the public school and the spread of the Sunday school drew attention from the home as an agency of education. The great revival work and the tendency of the general work of the churches had a like effect. Moreover the spirit of democratic individualism was early manifest in religious differences, which often crossed family lines. The split-off of the Hicksite Quakers, for instance, divided many families. Sectarianism is a normal correlate of the capitalist régime of free competition and class rivalry. The alinement of the various sects runs back in part to fundamental economic cleavage (e.g. landlordism and the Episcopal church on the one hand, commercialism and the non-conformist churches on the other) but individual tastes might outweigh the economic undercurrent in determining the affiliations of individuals. There has all along been a tendency for wives to adopt the religion of their husbands and for children to grow into the church of their parents. It must have been hard for European visitors in the period of this volume to comprehend, however, the freedom and tranquility with which husbands and wives, parents and children, brothers and sisters exercised individual choice of church connection. Time and again this phenomenon is noted, sometimes in specific detail. Doubtless such facility for idiosyn-

[70] Simons. *Social Forces in American history*, 184.

cracy, together with the multiplication of religious
services furthered by sectarian competition, did much
to weaken the spiritual bond of family coherence and
to "draw attention away from the religious duties of the
family." In 1855 Schaff said that table prayer was almost universal; and daily family worship the rule—at
least in religious circles. But if so, not for long. The
forces of the new social order were turning the tide
away from the home center to which Puritanism had
originally directed it.

The family problems that beset the people of the
new nation were often the old-fashioned difficulties
such as inhere in the ordinary course of human relations and bear little formal relation to time or place.
In newspapers of the revolutionary period occurred
various instances of marital incompatibility, such as
advertisements for deserting wives: "She has left my
bed and board;" "She has been very unfriendly to me;"
"She has behaved badly with other men;" "Her impru-
dence has reduced me to great poverty and distress."
One man cited *I. Corinthians*, vii, 10-11. One offered
a reward for the arrest of the seducer. The wife sometimes responded in type. One said her husband had
become insolvent and used up the whole income of
her inheritance. Another said her husband's cruelty
drove her out. "I never ran him in debt one farthing,"
asserted a third, "neither has he ever purchased me or
his infant child one article of clothing, except two or
three pairs of shoes for almost two years." Another
said that her husband deprived her of the barest necessities and forced her to do servile work, such as caring
for cattle in winter and she exhibited an affidavit he
made shortly before, acknowledging her wifely good-
ness and obedience and his fault. Thus public opinion

was a favorite tribunal; but reconciliation, forbearance, or regard for appearances (a strong feminine trait) impeded many a breach.[71]

America had a due share of family troubles. In a magazine of 1821, for instance, was reviewed a *New England Tale* which the reviewer considered a perfect illustration of American society and manners. In the story Jane Elton was left an orphan, thrown on the bounty of a cruel relative. In the family that adopted her she was assailed by bad example and injustice; consolation came from her mother's domestic. Her foster mother had a son, whose moral cultivation was neglected and his nature spoiled by tiresome religious services and harsh doctrine. He drew on his mother, while at college, beyond her resources; and also seduced and deserted a girl. Jane found him robbing his mother's desk. The heroine finally married a Quaker.

Family troubles that in some countries would have been settled by main force or in family council, American democracy and independence took to court. St. Victor, the muck-raker, notes family quarrels – fathers accusing sons of insubordination; sons, their fathers of injustice; and he says that "among the persons tried [at one session of court] was a husband for assaulting his wife, an aunt for assaulting her nephew, a son for assaulting his father, a daughter for assaulting her mother."

A southern clergyman in defense of slavery declared in 1857:

I say deliberately, what one of your first men told me, that he who will make the horrid examination will discover in New York City, in any number of years past, more cruelty from

71 Schouler. *Americans of 1776*, 37-41.

husband to wife, parent to child, than in all the South from
master to slave in the same time.

There were doubtless too many cases of callousness and
heartlessness.   Thus Olmsted said in 1861:

> Every year some miserable wretch is found in our dark places
> to have a crazy father or brother whom he keeps in a cage in
> the garret, and whose estate he takes care of, and who is of the
> opinion that it will be of no use, but . . . a manifest de-
> fiance of . . . Providence, and most dangerous to life and
> property to let this unfortunate out of his cage, to surround
> him with comforts, and contrive for him cheerful occupation, as
> our State requires.

It has seemed best to marshal at the beginning of this
chapter such material as might be taken to indicate a
weakening of family bonds and then to array on the
other side the more vital facts of family integrity and
strength.   Certainly the Americans had not fallen into
indifference to fundamental values.   They were eminently a domestic people; home was still home – the
center of affection and the school of sociability.   Lack
of surface sentiment did not betoken absence of happiness.   Generalizing from the testimony of a host of
observers we may assert that in the United States before the War, marriage was on the whole a happy consummation marked by mutual esteem and respect.
Morality was high.   Though women received what
seemed to Europeans great adulation, they were not
spoiled.   Flirts settled down into staid and efficient
domesticity.   After marriage, if not before, women
became thoughtful, responsible, and painstaking.   Domestic order and comfort were marked.   Affection,
fidelity, and good management on the part of wives
conserved the best interests of husband, children, and
home.   The very reserve and mutual respect that ex-
isted tended to obviate collisions and to render Ameri-

can families largely free from "that brutality which too often disgraces the lower classes of other nations." Gurowski in his *America and Europe* stated:

Americans stand out best in the simple domesticity of family life. It is the only normal condition growing out of their earliest traditions and habits; it is their uninterrupted inheritance. The domestic hearth, the family joys and hardships must have formed almost the exclusive stimulus of existence for the first settlers; therein they concentrated all their affections and cares. . . Religious convictions, local impossibility, the limited means of the colonies, prevented them at the outset and for a long time afterwards from recurring to public joyful gatherings. . . The day spent in hard labor or in professional duties, was cheerfully ended in the family circle. Even now, notwithstanding the rapidly increasing wealth and expansion in large cities, out-door pleasures seem rather exotic to the American life. At any rate far more so in America than in Europe, the family hearth is about the only preventive against gross and often degrading recreations; it alone assuages the tediousness and burdensomeness of existence even for the rich.

American homes are warmed by parental love. The relations between parents and children, harmonizing in their outward manifestations with certain conditions and modes special to the development of Amercan society, being misunderstood or not thoroughly examined by several European writers and visitors, have created the erroneous opinion of the want of parental feeling. At the outside, however, the reverse is apparent; less filial affection, or at least a less demonstrative one from children towards parents, seems noticeable; less so than is customary in Europe. Family ties seem to be looser, because generally Americans bear small affection to the spot of their birth; young members leave it or change with indifference, and parents do not make undue sacrifices to keep their children around them. Events providentially enforced upon Americans this unconcern, otherwise the task of extending culture and civilization would not have been fulfilled.

The outbreeding promoted by American freedom from inertia and caste lines afforded that enjoyment of novelty which bulks so large in the quota of happiness. The crossing of strains was also favorable biologically—a fact that was not without recognition. A writer in the *Ladies' Magazine* (Boston) of 1833 spoke of several married couples that essentially resembled each other in looks and disposition and said that they had proved unhappy in their offspring. "Either they have no children, or their children die in infancy, or they are not such as their parents would desire." This writer thought that marriage of cousins should be prohibited.

Some specific illustrations may serve to make clear the spirit that prevailed in the better type of American families during the period we are covering.

Lyman Beecher said:

> I had sworn inwardly never to marry a weak woman. I had made up my mind that a woman, to be my wife, must have sense, must possess strength to lean upon. [When I became engaged,] we agreed, quite bravely, that if either of us repented we would let it be known.

In 1798 he wrote to the lady:

> You doubt the permanence of my attachment. Believe me, it is not the result of fancy or a sudden flush of passion. . . I discover in you those qualities which I esteemed indispensable to my happiness long before I knew you.

He worries for fear she is not converted in heart.

George Bancroft's mother, born in 1765, was "almost a child of nature." She cared nothing for solid education; read novels and blank "verse." She was the eleventh child. She was born in the lap of plenty— "constantly more carest than fathers generally do their children." She says that when she was in her ninth year she was even then the family plaything, indulged by her father. She married Aaron Bancroft. "How happy I was when I had a half douzen children. . .

I learned many cheap dishes and made them satisfactory to my family. I was grateful for the bright prospect of the children as they advanced for their readiness to learn and the very great love they show their mother"—thus she wrote in a letter in 1828. She had thirteen children.

Susan B. Anthony was born into a staid and quiet but very comfortable home where there was great respect and affection between father and mother. She was welcome. She had an insatiable ambition, especially for learning the things considered beyond a girl's capacity. The children liked to go and feast at both grandmothers. When Mr. Anthony failed in business Susan and Hannah taught for next to nothing and gave their father all they could spare to help pay interest on the mortgage on factory, mills, and home. Years after, he paid them back. At school at eighteen Susan continually expressed pain at separation from the dear home.

A suggestion of the spirit that was possible in family relations with the advent of democracy appeared in the *Memoir of Hon. Wm. Appleton* whose second son died in 1843. He and his father had been chums. "We were more nearly brought together than most fathers and sons. We had entire confidence in each other." The son would tell his father the latter's faults. "I heard them from him with a better spirit than I should from any other." Louisa Alcott's father romped with the children. He was their chum. The family was never conquered by poverty and penury. It was a romping, boisterous family. They gave half their scant stock of wood to a family whose head was on a spree with all his wages.

With the abolition of imprisonment for debt the

home became more secure. Additional laws were passed for its protection. In 1820 a speaker at the Massachusetts Constitutional Convention argued that the household furniture exempt by law from attachment was nearly enough to give the right to vote. The constitution of the new state of Texas authorized the legislature to exempt from taxation two hundred fifty dollars' worth of household furniture or other property belonging to each family in the state. The homestead of a family, not exceeding two hundred acres, or town or city lots not over two thousand dollars in value were not to be subject to forced sale for debt. The legislature might by law exempt from forced sale a portion of the property of all heads of families. According to the California Constitution of 1849 laws were to be enacted exempting from forced sale a certain portion of the homestead and other property of all heads of families.

Familism was a marked element in early American affairs. According to De Tocqueville it was hard to find an American that did not plume himself on belonging to one of the original families. In the first half of the nineteenth century occur numerous hints of kinship solidarity. One hundred years ago the family "was still the microcosm of the state" and accepted responsibility toward poor and incapacitated members. Well-to-do families had many dependent members, chiefly women, but also old and worthless men; the law could be invoked in order to compel families to look after their own. "The different members of the family," wrote an observer of 1833-1834, "are firmly united together." "When a brother or sister dies leaving orphan children," wrote another person, "they are readily adopted into the families of their uncles and other kindred, who treat them entirely as their own."

Democracy divides the children's "inheritance but allows their hearts and minds to unite," said De Tocqueville. On the frontier, there was even some development of clan spirit. In many of the colonists this was a fixed quality to begin with; but isolation, breeding aloofness and independence, would tend to hold the expanding family of the frontiersman together, thus forming the nucleus of a new-world clan life. Such a development of kin-consciousness was possible even along with the disposition of children to leave as soon as possible the paternal roof.

Family ties constituted an important factor in politics and business. A study of political manoeuvres and economic frauds perpetrated in the early days and entailing a lasting legacy of corruption and exploitation upon the country will show how largely the family motive was operative and the family tie accessory. A few conspicuous instances may be given. Beard in his *Economic Interpretation of the Constitution* has shown the significance of family connection and family wealth in the formative days of the nation. Thus according to Maclay, Hamilton imparted important official secrets to a financier who was engaged in dealing in securities for Hamilton's brother-in-law, Church, under Hamilton's orders. Myers in his *History of the Supreme Court* continues the tale of family cohesion and incentive in big deals. In spite of America's technical freedom from hereditary nobility and a privileged caste, the substance of this anachronism has been ever present. John Jay was allied by birth, marriage, and interest with some of the greatest manorial lords in the United States. He was "descended from an intermingled line of landed families," and "married into another mighty landed family, which . . . had its alliance of family and interests with powerful British nobles." This was the Livingston family, members of which held high federal, state, and city offices.

> The political motto of the Livingston family was direct and concise: the family should always derive benefit, and nothing of any degree of value was to escape it. . . For a century, the Livingston family, beginning with nothing, and becoming one of the richest in the colonies, had assiduously pushed themselves, their ties and connections into every office and scheme promising profit and assuring power. . . The Livingstons again proved their political skill and great power by having Jay installed as Chief Justice of the Supreme Court of the United States.

After the Revolution the courts "were filled with judges who had been attorneys for, or were relatives of, families whose estates had been confiscated." Hammond related that he was informed that the Livingston family "one evening had a meeting . . . and that the result of their deliberation was such, that the next morning every member of it took a position in the ranks of the Republican party," except some Livingstons in Columbia County.

> They did not neglect to have their able representatives and connections on both sides, so that whichever party won, the family would be in a position to draw benefit. . . From the time of the organization of the Supreme Court of the United States, [till the twenties of the nineteenth century] the Livingston family had four direct or related representatives on that bench, in the persons of John Jay, William Paterson, Brockholst Livingston and Smith Thompson. It was virtually a succession of the Livingston dynasty.

This is but one instance of familism in public affairs. Justice Curtis wrote from Washington in 1852: "Wayne and Daniel dissent, on account of an interest, in some way, which some of their relatives have." In one case Taney did not sit, as a near family relative was involved.

Democracy introduced a new complication into American family life – the servant problem. While white servitude lasted, a supply of menials was obtainable. But as this atrocity dwindled in the first part of the nineteenth century the servant problem became acute. Mistresses were troubled by the disobedience, carelessness, faithlessness, inefficiency, and independence of their hirelings. Mrs. Graves in 1841 said:

> Domestics are very exacting; they repeatedly threaten to leave, and on the slightest pretext execute their threats; so that the mistress is afraid to reprove her menials. Servants no longer consider their time at their mistress' disposal but after doing the specified work claim the rest of the time for themselves. They are beginning to demand the right to receive visitors.

The influx of immigrants relieved, in a measure, the dearth of servants; but the newcomers were not always above learning American independence. Mistresses were largely to blame for the unsatisfactory state of affairs. "Christian" women were almost wholly inattentive to the spiritual needs of their help. In many families no duty was recognized toward the domestics save the payment of wages. Such negligence sometimes led to seduction by some sympathetic man and then the girl had almost no recourse save prostitution. Even such a girl as Louisa Alcott, having gone impulsively as companion for two old folks in a family, was treated with great indignity "by a family in which no one would have feared to place her." What must have been the lot of the obscure, unfriended girl?

A girl of seventeen in 1840 did the entire housework of a family including cooking and care of a new baby for one dollar per week. This was average pay of her neighborhood in Massachusetts. This case suggests that the inertia of domestic wages handed down from the days of unpaid drudgery by spinster relatives was a cause of the difficulty over servants. The unsavory status of the problem may have worked toward an increase of wages for household service. Naumann in 1848 said that a sixteen year old German girl received, if only moderately usable, more than the stoutest fellow did for the hardest work.

Besides the general independence of girls in America and the feeling that menial service was unworthy of a native American there were the attractions of factory industry with its better pay and freer life. If American matrons had been willing to meet this competition they could have had servants. As it was, one Englishwoman of the mid-century said: "So far as the observations and enquiries of sixteen months could elicit such facts, I have not discovered that the servants in the United States are of a worse description than the same class of persons in England." The relatives of the help were not usually in such abject poverty as to tempt the servants to steal for them — a happy contrast, it would seem, to England.

The fact that women of some means had to attend to housekeeping was regarded by some as a blessed constraint and indeed as a possible boon to health; but dissatisfaction with the trials of housekeeping promoted resort to hotel life — an untoward phenomenon that receives due attention in a later chapter.

It will, of course, be necessary to treat separately the unique phenomenon of the Slave States family. It was more conservative and intense, more careful of the old values and less open to the new, than was the family in North and West, where diffusion of economic opportunity and the resultant democratic dignity held promise of an exalted type of democratic family life based not on economic necessity but on spiritual values.

VII. SEX MORALS IN THE OPENING CONTINENT

New world conditions save as marred by slavery were relatively favorable to chastity. So long as economic conditions facilitated early marriage and large fecundity; so long as mercenary marriage remained largely in abeyance; life, while crude or even coarse, remained measurably pure. Democratic freedom of choice contributed to raise the moral tone and the improving status of woman worked in the same direction. Moreover conditions in the early days of the nation were such as to give public opinion great force; for life conditions were not complex, the ordinary community was small, and relations were personal. A man was very greatly dependent on his neighbors and his life was under their observation more than in older, more densely settled regions. Public opinion was on the side of purity, though it seems to have weighed more heavily on women than on men. Schoepf is probably putting it over strongly when he says: "Conjugal disloyalties, on either side, are punished by ineffaceable infamy." Doddridge in his western *Notes* says of the early days that seduction "could not then take place without great personal danger from the brothers or other relations of the victims of seduction, family honor being then estimated at a high rate." In settled communities legal process could also be invoked.

The relative absence of fixed class distinctions in the free states served as a certain protection to the chastity of women. In Europe the victims of lordly lust were chosen from classes that could not secure redress, while in America justice was perhaps less biased. The fact, too, of the general American preoccupation with industry or business helped to avert evils that attend on the goings of a leisure class. There may have been something in the climate, also, to curb excess. Gurowski in 1857 advanced an interesting theory as to the superior chastity of the American woman.

> The American woman has the appearance of coldness, founded in notions, principles, as well as in the temperament; she seems not to be exposed to the ebullitions of blood, to those violent emotions common to the women of the Old World. . . The climate affects the senses differently, it is supposed, in the New and in the Old World. . . The American woman is not often thus exalted passionately to that extent as to overstep the limits traced by the social comprehension of morality. In general she is, therefore, a surer guardian of the domestic hearth and of its purity, than is, in many cases, the European, surrounded by inner and outer urgings and temptations.

It was only with the development of feverish luxury and conspicuous consumption that depravity began to threaten seriously the integrity of women of the "better" class.

Chastellux, who visited the country toward the close of the Revolution, said: "There is no licentiousness in America." Social scandals at the end of the colonial period related mostly to the "mishaps of love-making." Crèvecoeur said: "A general decency everywhere prevails; the reason, I believe, is that almost everybody here is married, for they get wives very young and the pleasure of returning to their families overrules every other desire." Mazzei wrote: "In America . . . girls have a good time with the young men, but married women are reserved, and their husbands are not so familiar with young girls as before they were married."

Bundling lingered long in Pennsylvania among the Dutch and German settlers and their descendants. It was a matter of court record as late as 1845. In New England it prevailed longest in the Connecticut Valley where there was Dutch influence. Holmes in his *Account of the United States* says that among the Dutch in the Middle States bundling is a custom. Parties of men and girls spend the night together at inns, both sexes sleeping together.

> Such great command have the females acquired, that several who have bundled for years, it is said, have never permitted any improper liberties. Indeed, it is considered as not in the least indelicate . . . the females say, that the Dutch boys would never think of acting improperly.[72]

In general as regards pioneer life it is probably safe to say as Cooley does of Michigan: "Domestic scandals were exceedingly rare, and divorces almost unknown. Society was very primitive and there was little courtesy and less polish, but there was no social corruption and parents had faith in each other and little fear for the morals of their children." Of course Arcadian simplicity did not imply delicacy. In general we may assume for the frontier what has been said of early Tennessee, that "a broad humor that enjoyed obscene jests was dominant . . . among the males." Nor were the vices of a sophisticated society slow to arise with town life.

One hundred years ago there were many unfaithful husbands but very few unfaithful wives. Colonial penalties had weakened. For the first half of the nineteenth century we can affirm that in spite of (or perhaps by reason of) the great freedom of contact between the sexes, offenses against the seventh command-

---

[72] Earle. *Customs and Fashions in old New England,* 63-64; Holmes. *Account of the United States,* 347.

ment were remarkably rare. Infidelity on the part of
the wife was almost unknown and a liaison was well
nigh out of the question; successful intrigue meant
odium. For a married lady to receive attentions from
a man not her husband would have made her the scandal of the community, and adultery spelled for her
ostracism. The seducer risked death or heavy atone-
ment. Country life particularly was pure. On the
whole, the free section of America contrasted favor-
ably with the Old World in point of purity. Marryat
was indeed of the opinion that conjugal disloyalty was
invariably hushed up and he implies that the number
of illegitimate births may not have been an adequate
measure of illicit intercourse. Miss Martineau was
rather of the opinion

> That married life is immeasurably purer in America than in
> England: but that there is not otherwise much superiority to
> boast of. I can only say, that I unavoidably knew of more
> cases of lapse in highly respectable families in one state than
> ever came to my knowledge at home; and that they were got
> over with a disgrace far more temporary and superficial than
> they could have been visited with in England.

She recognizes, however, the facilities afforded in Europe for concealment owing to social stratification.

There was a specific connection between religious
excitement and sex morals. James D. Davis, a pioneer
lawyer of Memphis, writing as late as 1873 of a camp-
meeting held between Raleigh and Memphis prior to
1830, when the country for miles was depopulated,
said:

> There may be some who think that a camp-meeting is no place
> for love-making; if so they are very much mistaken. When
> the mind becomes bewildered and confused, the moral restraints
> give way, and the passions are quickened and less controllable.
> For a mile or more around a camp-meeting the woods seem
> alive with people; every tree or bush has its group or couple

while hundreds of others in pairs are seen prowling around in search of some cosy spot.[73]

The reverend John Brooks wrote:

All denominations of Christians except the Cumberland Presbyterian, opposed them with all their power. . . There was a great many who thought it would have disgraced their wife or daughter forever if they stayed on the camp ground all night. Sometimes their wives or daughters would be so convicted that they would go up to be prayed for – they would come into the altar in great haste to get them out. Those who were praying for them would reason with them and entreat them to let them get religion, but to no purpose; out they would have them, right or wrong. Then in great rage cursing the straw pen, as they called the altar; and off home they would take them. . . If the children of other denominations would get religion among us, they would rather that they would be anywhere else than in the Methodist church. They would do all in their power to keep them out, and, if they had joined, to get them out again. . . It was dangerous for a Methodist preacher to walk out of the encampment unless he had a respectable company with him, for there were some, it would seem, always watching for some opportunity to tell a slanderous tale upon them; and as there were more or less women of ill fame lurking about, they only wanted suitable circumstances to give coloring to their hellish designs.[74]

It is scarcely necessary to take up the various sects that specialized in peculiar doctrines as to marriage; in most cases they have had little permanent influence. The Mormons constitute the most conspicuous exception. Just what interpretation is to be put upon the rise of their communion the viewpoint of this book does not make it easy to say. To attribute so great an achievement to mere animalism is the cheap recourse of the idler or the fanatic.

Clearly one of the main factors to be counted was the

---

[73] Hale and Merritt. *History of Tennessee and Tennesseeans*, vol. i, 225.
[74] — *Idem*, 225-226.

call of the empty continent for prolific propagation, and this need set a sanction upon "the most sacred duty man can owe to God and the human race." "In the world, it takes two sets of parents to produce five children while in Mormondom this number is produced by one set." That polygamy and rapid increase were fruits of pioneer possibilities is suggested positively by the fact that of late it has become incumbent on Mormons to frown upon untrue "saints" and to fight Malthusian tendencies in the midst of the church. President Smith with his forty-two children and Lorin Farr with his forty are not likely to be duplicated in the present era of capitalist control of natural resources, universal adoption of "prolonged infancy," emancipation of woman, and inflated standards of living.

Another element in determining the rise and success of Mormonism was the excess of women in the East. "Mormon plural marriage was never a menace to monogamy. . . It took up the old maids . . . now accumulating . . . ; it arrested that contingent which now directly, or through marital failures, finds its way to gilded palaces of sin." If hosts of men eschewed matrimony and buried themselves in remote pioneer activities or in urban irresponsibility how could every fit woman be a mother and fulfil her normal desire save by polygamy? The institution, however, could never be very widespread; for it is impossible to marry more women than there are.

Polygamy was interlocked, also, with the need for economic exertion in a difficult region. The priests permitted plural marriages only to such as had means to support several families, "and so used the satisfaction of polygamous instincts as a reward for unusual economic" prowess.

It can not be seriously argued that Mormonism meant degeneracy in any fundamental sense; it was merely a reversion produced by the recurrence of an earlier phase of racial experience. "The real growth of the Mormon ideal in family life began with their exodus" and pioneer struggles close to nature. The new system "permitted such a choice of sires as prevented the thriftless and vicious from perpetuating their undesirable progeny" or at least from swamping the more competent strains of heredity. Economic prosperity attested the practicability of the Mormon cult. "But the primitive moral virility of the pioneers did not survive in the polygamy of the second generation. The younger generation was in danger of being utterly debauched by it;" and naturally so, inasmuch as it was normal only so long as the peculiar conditions that evoked it persisted. Disappearance of free land; pressure of organized exploitation; the opening of careers for detached women; the development of wealth and ease – all conspire to alter the merits of the whole situation.

Opposition to Mormonism had the advantage of cloaking itself in the pretext of outraged decency. But base factors were in play. In the Mormon War in Missouri a mob outraged fifteen or twenty Mormon girls and drove the Saints out. It would seem that the Mormons had fertile land that they would not sell to the "mobocrats" at their own price.[75]

Certain elements in the Mormon theory of the family tend to corroborate the preceding interpretation of the movement. When it is asserted that the natural use of copulation is procreation, and that any other use, at least in so far as it interferes, is against nature, we

---

[75] American Anti-slavery Society. *American Slavery as it is*, 191-192.

envisage forthwith an environment that puts a premium on fecundity and effort rather than on leisure and conspicuous consumption. When it is alleged that to refuse to procreate is to block the path of a soul we call up to a view a situation in which the coming of a new child meant a larger total of life, rather than a reduced total by reason of economic stringency. (The argument for propagation had not the same background as the identical command of the Catholic hierarchy who urge fecundity for the laity while practicing sterility themselves.) When we are told that hereafter the Mormon family idea requires to be sustained by hope of salvation and exaltation in the life to come and that fitness for authority in heaven must be developed by experience here, we are reminded that supernatural sanctions once developed as a justification for forms of conduct tend to persist as unnatural sanctions after the conditions that evoked them have passed away. The Mormon leaders need not expect to maintain the patriarchal ethic in the new régime of capitalism. The claim that "the Bible Family" as upheld by Mormons will be the dominant type of the future is made in forgetfulness of the fact that the recedence of the Mormon forbears to the tribal type of the Hebrew patriarchs could last only so long as economic isolation and group solidarity consequent on the desert struggle lasted.[76]

In view of the furor that has raged over Mormonism it is of interest to remember a contemporaneous pronouncement from reputable sources. In 1846 the American Board of Commissioners for Foreign Missions voted unanimously against instructing missionaries to exclude polygamists. The reverend Doctor

[76] On the Mormons, see the "Bibliography," item *The Mormon Family*; Münsterberg. *Americans*, 516.

Allen, missionary in India for twenty-five years said:

> If polygamy was unlawful, then Leah was the only wife of
> Jacob and none but her children were legitimate. . . And
> yet there is no intimation of any such views and feelings in
> Laban's family, or in Jacob's family, or in Jewish history. . .
> God honored the sons of Rachel, Bilhah, and Zilpah equally
> with the sons of Leah.[77]

The early Mormon could make out a plausible case
for the superior morality of his system as compared
with the pernicious promiscuity that tended to spring
up in the growing centers of population. *DeBow's
Review* of March, 1857, contained this indictment:

> In eighty years, the social system of the North has developed
> to a point in morals only reached by that of Rome in six cen-
> turies from the building of the city. . . Already married
> women, moving in the fashionable circles of the North, forego
> the duties of domestic life, bestow their minds upon dress and
> equipage, and refuse to no inconsiderable extent to undergo the
> pains of child-bearing. . . Already the priceless gem of
> chastity in woman has been despoiled of its talismanic charm
> with men. [The moral rule is], so long as exposure is avoided,
> no wrong is done.

DeBow idealized the society of the South though
he very well knew that it was rotten to the core with
illicit miscegenation. Moreover ordinary sexual
pathology was early important there as is witnessed by
such an advertisement as the following from the *Times*
of Alexandria, Virginia, January 1, 1801: "The Cor-
dial Balm of Gilead, an immediate restorative and
corroborant, a most powerful remedy in female ob-
structions and suppression, and in cases of retention at
maturity." There is advertised also a restorative
counteractant of masturbation. Also "A Guide to
Health" with essay on the "Venerial Disease and Sem-
inal Weakness" recommended to men and boys.

[77] Gage. *Woman, Church, and State*, 406.

Sex sin in its ordinary forms was early prevalent. Congressman Rutledge of South Carolina shot a man in intrigue with his wife. Two theatrical men at Charleston fought over the woman kept by one. The lover was beaten in the duel. The victor ejected the woman, who went and lived with the wounded lover. The other man married. Hodgson who in 1824 published *Letters from North America* thought that Mobile seemed to be characterized by profaneness, licentiousness, and ferocity. Arfwedson in 1834 recorded that opposite Columbus, Georgia, "on the Alabama shore, a number of dissolute people had founded a village, for which their lawless pursuits and notorious misdeeds had procured the name of Sodom." They were in Indian territory. Virtue and beauty they regarded as proper prey. Abdy, who was in the United States in 1833-1834, found influences ruinous to unprotected youth. "Two boys, about twelve or fourteen . . . stationed themselves in front of us, and one . . . exhibited a drawing . . . the most indecent . . . possible to imagine. . . I remonstrated . . . he burst out into a laugh." Abdy's companion, a North Carolina slave buyer, seemed to think very little of the incident. "There is a greater regard for decency even in Paris."

The reverend R. I. Mallard in *Plantation Life before Emancipation* says: "In our county . . . the most frequent cause of suspension from church fellowship and even excommunication was offences against" the seventh commandment. The pastor of a colored church in the South said in a letter that "the violation of chastity . . . among my congregation is the besetting sin. Of the three hundred seventeen persons excluded during a certain period . . . two hundred were for adultery." The congregation contained an unusual proportion of free blacks.

North and South were fond of bandying back and forth charges of immorality. Slavery, the exploitation of the poor whites, and the feverish city life of New Orleans marred the South with impurity. Capitalism, urban industrialism, and the rise of luxury in the North bred comparable evil. The influence of these factors upon the standards of sex morals observed in the rural simplicity of the new world will be touched in other chapters. The North had at least one moral advantage – a more normal and wholesome rural life which held back the tide of demoralization.

At a "Free Convention" in Rutland, Vermont, in 1858, the platform was used for a vigorous advocacy of free love. An attractive woman recommended it to her audience. The speech was so well received that the meeting "went forth to the world as a free-love convention. . . But the almost unanimous northern sentiment in regard to this convention, and the haste with which some participators in it rushed into print to clear themselves from any accusation of sympathy with free-love, are an indication of the severity of opinion touching sexual relations." [78] Such evidence is, however, far from conclusive. The public is notoriously antagonistic to a public theoretical justification of evils whose practice is patiently tolerated.

Prudery was an interesting phenomenon of the social life of nineteenth century America. The mother of Susan B. Anthony was very timid. Before the birth of every child she was overwhelmed with embarrassment and lived in seclusion and would not speak of the expected event even to her mother. Harper relates:

---

[78] Rhodes. *History of the United States*, vol. iii, 98-99.

That mother would assist her overburdened daughter by making the necessary garments, take them to her house and lay them carefully away in a drawer, but no word of acknowledgement ever passed between them. This was characteristic of those olden times, when there were seldom any confidences between mothers and daughters in regard to the deepest and most sacred concerns of life, which were looked upon as subjects to be rigidly tabooed.

Marryat, who was in America in 1837-1838, spoke of prudery: American girls would not say "leg." Some even referred to the "limb of a table." An English lady keeping a boarding-house in an Atlantic city said some girls showed hysterical agitation at meeting a man or boy unexpectedly. Grattan in his *Civilized America* said:

The newspapers . . . abstain, on a point of delicacy, from ever announcing the birth of a child; while marriages and deaths occupy their columns without reserve.   No lady allows herself to be seen publicly while she is visibly enceinte. A rigid confinement to her house, and even to her "chamber" is observed for a considerable time preceding her confinement. . . It has frequently happened to me to miss ladies from . . . parties . . . and on enquiring . . . to be told they were "in the country" or "visiting" and on meeting them, in probably a year or more, to find them [with a new child].

Buckingham in the *Slave States of America* has a comment, made at Athens, on American prudery. "Hip" and "thigh" are, he says, tabooed. They alter prayerbook and Bible by the elimination of "womb," "belly," "cock." He speaks in contrast of the demoralization wrought upon young New Englanders, many of whom return from the South dissipated rakes.

VIII. THE STRUGGLE FOR THE WEST

The project of building a homestead West encountered five large obstacles: the opposition of the Indians, the stubbornness of distance and environment, the expansionist projects of the plantation South, the unscrupulousness of voracious land speculators, and the selfish obstructionism of the eastern capitalist jealous of his cheap labor. All these were positive enemies of the homestead family and handicaps to the western home. All save the first require brief attention.

In 1786 William Cooper, father of James Fenimore Cooper, opened the sales of forty thousand acres "which, in sixteen days, were all taken up by the poorest order of men."

The greatest discouragement was in the extreme poverty of the people, none of whom had the means of clearing more than a small spot in the midst of the thick and lofty woods, so that their grain grew chiefly in the shade; their maize did not ripen; their wheat was blasted, and the little they did gather they had no mill to grind within twenty miles distance; not one in twenty had a horse, and the way lay through rapid streams, across swamps, or over bogs. They had neither provisions to take with them, nor money to purchase them; nor if they had, were any to be found on their way. If the father of a family went abroad to labor for bread, it cost him three times its value before he could bring it home, and all the business on his farm stood still till his return. [Cooper came in one April with several loads of provisions. Soon it was all snapped up, for people were living on roots and on maple water.] Judge of my feelings at this epoch, with two hundred families about me, and not a morsel of bread. . . I . . . obtained from the Legislature . . . seventeen hundred bushels of corn.

This we packed on horses' backs, and on our arrival made a distribution among the families, in proportion to the number of individuals of which each was composed.

This settlement was at the foot of Otsego Lake (Cooperstown, New York). The extract is from Cooper's *Guide in the Wilderness*, published in Ireland in 1810 to promote migration to Otsego. He says further:

If the poor man who comes to purchase land has a cow and a yoke of cattle to bring with him, he is of the most fortunate class, but as he will probably have no money to hire a laborer, he must do all his clearing with his own hands. Having no pasture for his cow and oxen, they must range the woods for subsistence; he must find his cow before he can have his breakfast, and his oxen before he can begin his work. Much of the day is sometimes wasted, and his strength uselessly exhausted. Under all these disadvantages, if in three years he attains a comfortable livelihood, he is pretty well off: he will then require a barn, as great losses accrue from the want of shelter for his cattle and his grain; his children, yet too young to afford him any aid, require a school, and are a burden upon him; his wife bearing children, and living poorly in an open house, is liable to sickness and doctors' bills will be to pay.

John Bradbury (author of *Travels in the Interior of America in the Years 1809, 1810, and 1811*), noticed that emigrants lacking the stamina for clearing the wilderness always found opportunity to buy out the backwoodsman's clearing. The latter preferred the harsh frontier to the encroaching civilization. The clearing that he sold generally consisted of a log house, an orchard, and from ten to forty acres enclosed and partly cleared. Poverty on the sea-board pushed people westward. Bradbury observed many farms abandoned in Virginia. A traveller in Pennsylvania about the same time mentions a "singular party of travellers— a man with his wife and ten children. The eldest of the progeny had the youngest tied on his back; and the father pushed a wheelbarrow, containing the movables of the family." They were leaving New Jersey and making for Ohio. Farther on a young woman was passed, "carrying a sucking child in her arms, and leading a very little one by the hand."

An Irish traveller giving advice to his fellow countrymen drew an interesting picture of the possibilities for an immigrant on the cheap western land as contrasted with ugly city conditions. A man and wife without children could get employment in the same family. She could earn four or five dollars a month—sufficient in a year to stock a farm. In one year or thereabouts, tho they landed penniless, they could be ready to start to the West where the land was cheap and good. A couple with small children, under ten or twelve years, would have difficulty in getting a start. Older children could get work in families or factories. But with small children the wife would have to have a home, where she must stay earning nothing. Thousands of Irish, reared on farms and unacquainted with the vicious life of cities, had, on coming to America, settled in filthy cellars and garrets, and worked in the nasty labor allotted to friendless strangers. When they have earned a little money, instead of moving out in search of a wholesome farm they married and started a family in the midst of poverty, vice, and sin; the family, subject to the countless evil influences of city life, and often disgracing the parent and the fatherland. "But when you get the farm, Patrick, the more children you have the happier you will be." Thus even in the first half of the nineteenth century the contest between city and country was on; and their contrasting influence on the family noted.

The opening of California led to a mad rush toward the Pacific.

Mothers might be seen wading through the deep dust or heavy

sand of the deserts, or climbing mountain steeps, leading their poor children by the hand; or the once strong man, pale, emaciated by hunger and fatigue, carrying upon his back his feeble infant, crying for water and nourishment, and appeasing a ravenous appetite from the carcass of a dead horse or mule.

A traveller of 1854 wrote of Chicago:

A family of Germans going by the hotel one morning . . . struck me as the most remarkable show I had seen in the West – the coming in of European immigrants to take possession of our western plains.

The father strode down the middle of the street. Unaccustomed to the convenience of sidewalks in his own country, he shared the way with the beasts of burden, no less heavily laden than they. . . By one hand he held his pack, and in the other he carried a large tea-kettle. His gude-wife followed in his tracks, at barely speaking distance behind. A babe at the breast was her only burden. Both looked straight forward, intent only upon putting one foot before the other. In a direct line, but still further behind, trudged on, with unequal footsteps, and eyes staring on either side, their first-born son, or one who seemed such. There were well towards a dozen summers glowing in his face. A big tin pail, containing, probably, the day's provisions, and slung to his young shoulders, did not seem to weigh too heavily upon his spirit. He travelled on bravely, and was evidently trained to bear his load. A younger brother brought up, at a few paces distant, the rear, carrying, astride his neck . . . a sister.

. . . They would not stop or turn aside, save for needful food and shelter, until they crossed the Mississippi. On the rolling prairies beyond, the foot-worn travellers would reach their journey's end, and, throwing their weary limbs upon the flowery grass, would rest in their new home, roofed by the sky of Iowa.

As if the vast distances of the continent and the hardships that the environment imposed upon the pioneer were not enough, the history of settlement has been a continual record of the exactions of rapacious land speculators[79] whose slimy trail reaches from the Atlan-

[79] Myers. *History of the Supreme Court*, 304-354, 372-388, 403-469.

tic to the Mississippi, to the Great Plains, to California and Oregon, and now finally to the ultimate continental frontier in Alaska. Early, the Supreme Court heard cases "revealing that thousands of families had been peremptorily driven from their homes, and reduced to destitution, by the claims and exactions of land jobbers." The Court had validated these claims. A Senate Committee in 1836 reported that land speculation was looking to a land monopoly.

> The poor but industrious occupant generally attends the land sales, having no more money than a sum sufficient to buy the land he occupies at the minimum price; a speculator bids a few cents over him, and becomes the purchaser of the land and the owner of an improved farm, paying not one cent for the value of the improvements. In other cases, where the settler has collected something more than the money sufficient to pay for the land he occupies, at the minimum price, and bids that sum, the speculator, by some secret agent . . . overbids the settler, the land is struck off to this agent, and the settler leaves the sale in disgust, to mourn over the injustice of the government of the Union, and to prepare for the removal of himself and family from the little farm which he has improved and expected to have purchased from a paternal government. After the departure of the settler, the tract is forfeited for non-payment, and the speculator purchases in his own name the forfeited tract, probably at the minimum price per acre.
>
> The scenes ensuing at many of our land sales are scenes of the deepest distress and misery. They are scenes in which many families are driven forth from their homes to seek some other spot in the wilderness, where keen-eyed avarice and sordid monopoly may not overtake them. But another land sale comes on, the same scene is repeated, till all hope is extinguished, and nothing is left to the settler but despair and ruin . . . taking all the sales of the public lands, from the adoption of the cash system, in July, 1820, down to the present period, the average price received by the government upon these sales, has been less than six cents an acre over the minimum price.[80]

[80] Myers. *History of the Supreme Court*, 386-387.

The committee proposed the sale and entry of all of the public lands in forty-acre lots – "a whimsical suggestion to make to a Congress a large number of the members of which were interested in the land companies."

Garesche wrote from Louisiana to the Secretary of the Treasury on June 9, 1836:

> It is folly to talk of the poor squatter – the laws have never been made for him; he gets but a very small fraction of the whole; all the benefits of the speculation fall into the hands of the intriguer; it is for him that the bill is introduced; it is for him alone that the voice of our orators is heard on the floor of Congress.[81]

The New England Protective Union declared: "We must proceed from combined stores to combined shops, from combined shops to combined houses, to joint ownership in God's earth, the foundation that our edifice must stand upon." The first Industrial Congress of the United States (New York, 1845) declared "it is a well-known fact that rich men, capitalists and non-producers associate to devise means for securing to themselves the fruits of other men's labors"; therefore farmers, mechanics, and workingmen ought to organize. It was declared that further traffic in land by the government should stop and that the public lands should be made free to actual settlers so that every person might have a home.

The Laborers' Union memorialized Congress to end traffic in public lands. "This system . . . is fast debasing us to the condition of dependent tenants, of which condition a rapid increase of inequality, misery, pauperism, vice, and crime are necessary consequences."[82]

[81] Myers. *History of the Supreme Court*, 387.
[82] — *Idem*, 444-446.

Before the close of 1852, bills, resolutions, and memorials for grants of land to actual settlers were introduced in Congress. A homestead bill passed the House in 1852 but the Senate did not pass it. Hammond of South Carolina in 1858 said in the Senate: "Your people are awaking; they are coming here. They are thundering at our doors for homesteads, one hundred and sixty acres of land for nothing, and Southern Senators are supporting them." In 1862 Congress passed the Homestead Bill presenting one hundred and sixty acres to every settler on condition that he built a home and proceeded to cultivate and improve the soil.

The consequences of the struggle for the soil have been far reaching. On the whole, even the well intended homestead acts have not safeguarded general welfare but have grown or been twisted into agencies of special privilege in the form of unearned increments to the undeserving successors of the pioneers or to their speculative exploiters. "Our efforts to give land to the landless have bred an immense amount of corruption, fostered speculation, endowed private monopoly with public wealth, and pauperized whole communities." [83] The far reaching fact is that originally through the ignorance, carelessness, or corruption of the government the people's heritage of land was dissipated and the vast stores of natural wealth not created by any man were made into a lever by which most of the created wealth has been separated from its producers so that decent home life has been for millions pushed far beyond the bounds of possibility.

It is important to note how the self-interest of the eastern labor exploiters opposed the opening up of the West for settlement for fear that the homesteads of the new country would reduce their supply of labor and

[83] Ely. *Outlines of Economics*, 593-594.

advance its price.	It was urged, indeed, that "instead of giving homes to the homeless, the bill will unsettle the homes of many honest persons who have bought their farms with hard earnings by bringing them into competition with other farms received as an alms by men too indolent and improvident to acquire them as others have."[84]	It is not generally known that Daniel Webster's "Liberty and Union" oration found its occasion in the conspiracy against the free home of the West as a refuge from exploitation in the East.	It was delivered in support of a resolution by Senator Foote of Connecticut to stop the survey of public lands and limit sales.[85]	One would suppose that the West and the laborers of the East might have awakened to the real situation and if necessary sought alliance with the South against what was to prove the deadly foe of all of them—the capitalist power of the financial centers.	There were indeed signs of such a rapprochement of West and South; but the attempted expansion of the plantation system to the West and Northwest was regarded as an encroachment on the pioneer home and as a possible curb to the spread of the small farmstead by the sons of the pioneers.	The danger was in reality insignificant; for, inasmuch as one can not repeal the laws of nature, the slave system could never have been a serious menace to the upper West.	But Westerners and would-be pioneers thought it was and gave their sons to crush the fancied foe, the South, while under cover of the War their nominal allies, the monied men of the East, were forging a new conspiracy and fastening on the neck of the whole nation a new and lasting slavery, a practicable, workable sort of bondage.	Thus

[84] *National Intelligencer*, June 1, 1852, cited in McMaster's *History of the People of the United States* (1913), vol. viii, 107-109.

[85] Simons. *Social Forces in American History*, 203.

the homes of the West and the proletarian homes of
the East have suffered immeasurably for their faulty
sense of proportion, their failure to size up the real
enemy. The Civil War was in a sense a war for a
specific type of family and a specific type of home. Its
sequel was not merely the reconstruction of the system
of the South but the reconstruction of the West likewise at the hands of the money lender of the East.

The liberalizing influences of new-world life were
largely a function of the frontier and tended to become
conservatized as fast as the frontier receded before the
advance of urbanization. Meanwhile migration westward factored in the shaping of family conditions in the
more settled East. To the settlement of the Great West
went the young and vigorous leaving the elderly, the
invalids, the orphans to the care of some widowed or
unmarried sister or daughter. Throughout the older
states there were countless such broken families. The
guardian of the household "stood in her lot strengthen-
ing the things that remained." In consequence of the
young men's migrating westward in great numbers,
many eastern young women, who normally would have
been their wives, married widowers old enough to be
their fathers. Such conditions contributed to the de-
crepitude of the old New England stock. Even after
the Civil War the westward drain of men continued,
leaving an excess of women in New England.

It was not the "best people" from New England that
moved to the Western Reserves. It was not the "successful" families at home that pioneered Ohio. But the
West "has been fed all along by the prolific stocks of
New England. It was the families with large numbers
of children that moved west. If the prolific stocks migrate to the west they leave the unprolific stocks."

Hence (perhaps) some of the modern sterility of the North Atlantic Americans.

The West constituted a refuge for the hard-pressed and bankrupt of the seaboard states. By 1817 some eastern cities ceased to grow, so great was the exodus of the poor from the coastal states. Hard times in the Middle States in the thirties pushed people West. Prior to 1840 some one remarked that "our fashionable women . . . do more for the settlement of the western country than the soil, climate, and cheapness of land." Competition in the East was too sharp for some merchants, and professional men were too numerous, even before the War. Some such, having married early, and having expensive habits could not keep pace with the demands of an increasing family. In such cases the West offered an escape. In that crude country one might live more simply and cheaply without losing social position. Often the wife consented to removal only because she could not help herself. Such women were likely to be ill-suited to roughing it. In some instances families were driven back by the wife's discontent. But sometimes fashionable women, settling in the West, became, from example or from necessity, splendid housewives. "That is to say," observed the Bostonian, "they scrub their own floors, clean their door handles, wash the windows . . . walk about with children in their arms; all which . . . is done by the women of the best society in the western states without destroying either their health or good looks." Thus the hinterland served as a safety valve to the developing East. This relation must be kept in mind, for it retained in the older country something of the pioneer flavor and retarded the growth of the family phenomena that more recently mark our industrial civilization.

IX. THE NEW INDUSTRIAL ORDER

At the close of the Revolution, wages were low and the price of necessities was high. Only by strictest economy could a mechanic keep his children from starvation and himself from vile imprisonment. The home of the workman was plain and unattractive. "He rarely tasted fresh meat as often as once a week." The pinch of poverty, North and South, guaranteed a welcome for anything that would make possible a completer utilization of the labor force, including women and children, reduce dependence and charity, and add to the wealth of the community. Home production for the market developed to some extent but was a fleeting stage in America. Some more efficient system was indispensable.

At the beginning of the nineteenth century many children of agriculture were just preparing to leave the farm for the factory. Household industry lingered long in country districts. In Indiana, for instance, in 1816 there were 2512 looms and 2700 spinning wheels, most of them in private cabins "whose mistresses . . . converted the wool which their own hands had often sheared, and the flax which their own fingers had pulled, into cloth." Before 1836 in New England nearly every article of domestic use that is now made with the use of machinery was "done by hand;" the population was mainly rural and the material for clothing was grown on the home farm and fabricated by the women. Even the sons of comparatively prosperous families went to college in homespun.

In the infancy of the factory system a frequent argument in its favor was that it could utilize the labor of women and children who would otherwise be idle. Washington in a letter to Lafayette said: "Though I would not force the introduction of manufactures by extravagant encouragements, and to the prejudice of agriculture, yet I conceive much might be done in the way of women, children, and others, without taking one really necessary hand from tilling the earth." [86] Hamilton observed that one advantage of the extensive introduction of machinery would be

> The employment of persons who would otherwise be idle, and in many cases a burthen on the community, either from bias of temper, habit, infirmity of body, or some other cause indisposing or disqualifying them for the toils of the country. It is worthy of remark, that, in general, women and children are rendered more useful, and the latter more early useful, by manufacturing establishments, than they would otherwise be.

He seems to have had in mind principally the gain to the heads of families, for he said: "The husbandman himself experiences a new source of profit and support, from the increased industry of his wife and daughters, invited and stimulated by the demands of the neighboring manufactories." [87] Such philanthropists as Matthew Carey pointed out the extra value to be got from girls between the ages of ten and sixteen "most of whom are too young or too delicate for agriculture" and by way of contrast directed attention to the "vice and immorality to which children are exposed by a career of idleness." [88]

Manufacture was early contemplated as the salvation of the South. The exercises incident to the lay-

[86] McVey. *Modern Industrialism*, 45.

[87] Beard. *Economic Interpretation of the Constitution*, 26.

[88] Abbot, *Early History of Child Labor in America* should be consulted as a general reference.

ing of the corner-stone of "The South Carolina Home-spun Company of Charleston" in 1808 brought a gathering of three thousand people. Mr. Lloyd, head of the Masonic order of South Carolina, "said in a most memorable address about the prospective cotton mills:"

> Here will be found a never-failing asylum for the friendless orphans and the bereft widows, the distribution of labor and the improvements in machinery happily combining to call into profitable employment the tender services of those who have just sprung from the cradle, as well as those who are tottering to the grave, thus training up the little innocents to early and wholesome habits of honest industry, and smoothing the wrinkled front of decrepitude with the smiles of competency and protection.[89]

Many instances might be given of the employment of children in the early factories. They became a more and more profitable mechanism and their labor was looked upon as a valuable asset in view of the scarcity and cost of male labor. (Jay complained in 1784 of the "wages of mechanics and labourers, which are very extravagant.") At Slater's first establishment in Rhode Island the operatives were described as between seven and twelve years. Manufacturing no longer required able-bodied men but was "better done by little girls from six to twelve years old." A New Hampshire act of 1791 empowered overseers to bind out the poor and the idle. By means of such acts the factory capitalists obtained a cheap supply of woman and child labor. Before the close of the eighteenth century, manufacturing with child labor was so far developed that, as a French traveller put it, "men congratulate themselves upon making early martyrs of these innocent creatures, for is it not a torment to these poor little beings . . . to be a whole day and almost every day of their lives employed at the same work, in an

---

[89] Wetherell. *Among the cotton Mills*, 416.

obscure and infected prison?"[90] Josiah Quincy in 1801 found a Rhode Island factory employing over a hundred children at twelve to twenty-five cents a day.

> One attendant was very eloquent on the usefulness of this manufacture, and the employment it supplied for so many poor children.   But an eloquence was exerted on the other side of the question more commanding than his, which called us to pity these little creatures, plying in a contracted room, among flyers and coggs, at an age when nature requires for them air, space, and sports.   There was a dull dejection in the countenances of all of them.[91]

The early American factories were "manned" largely by women and children. It was maintained that social as well as economic gains came from the employment of women in industry. Young women who had been "with their parents in a state of poverty and idleness, bare-footed and living in wretched hovels . . . are comfortably fed and clothed, their habits and manners and dwellings greatly improved and they have become useful members of society," while the women in villages remote from manufactures are "doomed to idleness and its inseparable attendants vice and guilt." A village where "free independent and happy workmen with their wives and children were employed" was an emblem of prosperity. Manufactures educated women in habits of honest industry and gave added encouragement to labor and population. "They become eligible partners for life for young men, to whom they will be able to afford substantial aid in the support of families. Thus the inducement to early marriages . . . is greatly increased . . . and immensely important effects produced on the welfare of society." "To deprive the wives as well as the children of the farmers and country laborers of profitable

[90] Oneal. *Workers in American History*, 128-129.

[91] Massachusetts Historical Society, *Proceedings*, second ser., vol. iv, 124.

employment in manufacturing establishments would be most injurious." [92]

Women formed, roughly speaking, two-thirds to three-fourths, and in some places as much as nine-tenths, of the total number of factory operatives in the first half of the century. Many of the early mill-workers were country girls who simply came in for a time in order to earn a little money, often for their wedding outfits. Mrs. Robinson, who went to work in the Lowell mills at the age of ten, has said:

> The most prevailing incentive to our labor was to secure the means of education for some male member of the family. To make a gentleman of a brother or a son, to give him a college education, was the dominant thought in the minds of a great many of these provident mill girls.

In such towns as Waltham and Lowell the hands were almost all farmers' daughters, who lived in corporation boarding-houses. Since the board cost more than a child could earn, the employment of children was unprofitable. But children were often employed very young, even in "model" places like Lowell and Waltham. Most of the women operatives in the early days were in the lower twenties. Of a thousand women employed by the Lawrence corporation only thirty were married or widowed. To Lowell came widows to open boarding-house or store, and sometimes married women came and worked in the mills in order to assist their husbands to pay for farms. Women with a past came to hide their identity. In New York, female operatives were enabled to support dependent families.

Samuel Slater transplanted to Providence and the neighborhood the family-system which he had known in England. The Rhode Island type of factory vil-

---

[92] Abbot's articles cited in the bibliography should be consulted as general reference on woman labor.

lage was, therefore, made up of families entirely dependent on their labor in the mills, and the mill children lived at home with their parents. Connecticut and southern and western Massachusetts resembled Rhode Island with its tendency toward the family system. The following memorandum of January 27, 1815, illustrates the family system:

> Dennis Rier . . . has this day engaged to come with his family to work in our factory on the following conditions. He . . . is to have the following wages per week:

Himself . . .	$5.00	Sister . . .	$2.33
Son, 10 yrs. . .	.83	Her daughter, 8 yrs.	.75
Daughter, 12 yrs. .	1.25	Son, 13 . .	1.50
Son, 13 yrs. .	1.50		———
Son, 16 yrs. .	2.00		4.58

10.58

Smith Wilkinson wrote from Pomfret, Connecticut:

> We usually hire poor families from the farming business of from four to six children, and from a knowledge of their former income, being only the labor of the man say $180-200, the wages of the family is usually increased by the addition of the children to from $450-600. [Again] In collecting our help, we are obliged to employ poor families, and generally those having the greatest number of children.

The company's real estate investments are explained as an attempt "to give the men employment on the lands while the children are employed in factory." A writer in *Niles' Register* in 1816 calculated the gain to the parents of employing the whole population of children in cotton factories. Miss Martineau noted that more parents were bringing their children to the factories. Before 1835 "whole families (not one of whom can read or write)" were finding "an asylum" in Maryland factories.[93] An advertisement in the *Federal Union*

[93] Abdy. *Journal of a Residence and Tour in the United States*, vol. i, 383.

of Milledgeville, Georgia, 1834, showed that a textile company wished

> To hire twenty to thirty suitable laborers to work in the factory. White women, girls and boys are such as will be wanted, aged ten years or upwards. Entire families may find it to their interest to engage in our service. A good house of entertainment will be kept near the Factory.[94]

About 1850 J. H. Taylor of Charleston, favoring manufactures as a relief to poor whites, represented that:

> The active industry of a father, the careful housewifery of the mother, and the daily cash earnings of four or five children, will very soon enable each family to own a servant; thus increasing the demand for this species of property to an immense extent.[95]

During the period in which the factory system was fastening itself upon the country, labor experienced no golden age. Of about 1816, Carey said:

> Thousands of our laboring people travel hundreds of miles in quest of employment on canals at 62½, 75, and 87½ cents per day, paying $1.50 to $2.00 a week for board, leaving families behind, depending upon them for support. They labor frequently in marshy grounds, where they inhale pestiferous miasmata, which destroy their health, often irrecoverably. They return to their poor families broken-hearted, and with ruined constitutions, with a sorry pittance, most laboriously earned, and to take their beds sick and unable to work. Hundreds are swept off annually, many of them leaving numerous and helpless families. . . There is no employment whatever, how disagreeable or loathsome or deleterious soever it may be, or however reduced the wages, that does not find persons willing to follow it rather than beg or steal.[96]

In 1820 Flint wrote of having seen upwards of one thousand five hundred men out of employment during the previous eleven months. Wages at Philadelphia and elsewhere had dropped to twenty cents per day

---

[94] *Documentary History of American Industrial Society*, vol. ii, 334.

[95] Tower. *Slavery Unmasked*, 347-348.

[96] Simons. *Social Forces in American History*, 174.

and board. A Cincinnati paper advertised a place for receiving old clothes for the poor and cast-off shoes for children. Of the period 1825-1829 McMaster says that "Nothing but perfect health, steady work, sobriety, the strictest economy, and the help of his wife could enable a married man to live on such wages" as laborers received.

Northern capitalists did not need to repine over the passing of the profitless negro slavery. Gustavus Myers says:

> A system allowing the unrestricted exploitation of white men, women and children for fourteen hours every working day in the mills, and paying from $1.75 to $2.00 a week to women, and less to children, presented its superior advantages over the chattel slavery system. That many of the workers were swept to premature death by disease contracted in the factories, or in foul habitations, or by accidents while plying their trade, entailed no economic loss to the mill owners.[97]

Southern enthusiasts were fond of boasting of the greater cheapness of labor in their section. An anti-slavery writer reported that while in Lowell men got eighty cents a day and women two dollars a week, in Tennessee the rate was not over fifty cents a day for men and on the average a dollar and a quarter a week for women. A Mr. Gregg said on one occasion: "It is only necessary to build a manufacturing village of shanties, in a healthy location, in any part of the state [of South Carolina], to have crowds . . . around you seeking employment at half the compensation given to operatives at the north." He shows that slavery is a club whereby in the South capital can control labor. But in spite of the fact that the races could be induced to work side by side, "the white girls working in the same room and at the same loom with the black girls;

⁹⁷ Myers. *History of the Supreme Court,* 301.

and boys of each color, as well as men and women, working together without apparent repugnance or objection," [98] and in spite of the need to find remunerative employment for indigent persons and to relieve distress, industry could scarcely be said to flourish in the South.

Early factory labor was almost incredibly severe: twelve to fifteen hours a day. By 1830 some of the factories became chambers of horrors. Women and children were frequently beaten with cowhides and otherwise abused. Wages, too, were miserably low and tended downward. By 1835 chiefly the poorer sort of workers filled the mills but even skilled labor complained constantly of cruelties and injustice. There were sad cases of cruelty to children, and outrage of every sort among the women, whose pay had dropped almost to the subsistence point. Parents gave false returns of age and grasped eagerly at the chance of their children's earning something.

Harriet Robinson, one of the early mill girls of Lowell, has said:

> Except in rare instances, the rights of the early mill-girls were secure. They were subject to no extortion, if they did extra work they were always paid in full, and their own account of labor done by the piece was always accepted. They kept the figures and were paid accordingly. This was notably the case with the weavers and drawing-in girls. Though the hours of labor were long, they were not overworked . . . and they had plenty of time to sit and rest. . . Help was too valuable to be ill-treated. . . After a time, as the wages became more and more reduced, the best portion of the girls left.

Humane employers deplored "the policy which confines and constrains small children during the working hours of a long day, and consequently excludes them from the benefits of school." But the "benefits of

---

[98] On this paragraph see *Documentary History of American Industrial Society*, vol. ii, 339, 357; Tower, *Slavery Unmasked*, 350-357.

school" were likely to be nominal.[99] School-teachers of 1835 were prone to cruelty. "The day of children's rights had not yet dawned." In 1836 the Massachusetts House Committee on Education declared that since

> Human labor . . . must inevitably be dearer in a country like our own than it is in any other with which we are brought in competition in manufacturing, this operates as a constant inducement to manufacturers to employ female labor and the labor of children, to the exclusion of men's labor, because they can be had cheaper. [The factory families are near the poverty line.] Of course when such families numerous and indigent as they usually are, begin to increase, and when their wants begin to press hard upon their scanty means of comfort, or perhaps even of necessary subsistence, there is a strong interest and an urgent motive to seek constant employment for their children at an early age, if the wage obtained can aid them even but little in bearing the burden of their support. . . [Causes] are operating, silently perhaps but steadily and powerfully, to deprive young females particularly, and young children of both sexes in a large and increasing class in the community, of those means and opportunities of mental and moral improvement . . . essential to their becoming . . . good citizens.

The committee called attention to the fact that in four of the largest manufacturing cities (excluding Lowell) with a population of a little less than twenty-five thousand, there appear to be "1895 children between the ages of four and sixteen who do not attend the common schools any portion of the year."

In the *Voice of Industry*, a labor paper published at Fitchburg, Massachusetts, in 1845, a typical instance of labor conditions is given in the statement of a frail girl of eight or nine years: "I go to work before daylight in the morning and never leave it until it is dark,

[99] McMaster. *History of the People of the United States* (1910), vol. vii, 157-161; Robinson. *Loom and Spindle*, 19-20.

and don't make enough to support mother and baby." The paper refers to the increase of two hundred per cent in the cotton mill dividends in a single year, and a corresponding decrease of twelve and one-half per cent in the wages of women and children.

Early labor organizations opposed child labor partly on account of its effects upon the wage-scale and partly out of regard for the physical, mental, and moral welfare of the children. In the forties and fifties some minor gains were made in the way of legislation – sufficient to stir the enthusiasm of well-wishers but not always sufficient to escape the scorn of Horace Greeley and the *Tribune*. A Massachusetts Legislature Committee of 1850 reported with reference to long hours that left almost no time for amusement or betterment that so long as the operatives were the children of New England trained in good homes and at school the menace was not so great. But foreigners were rapidly replacing the New England mill hands. Untaught at home and having no leisure for education here they would remain steeped in ignorance, and morals and physical condition would be low. The committee accordingly urged a limitation of the hours of labor and more time for meals, and reported a bill, which was not passed. "The real precursors of adequate child labor legislation were the two Massachusetts acts of 1866 and 1867."

Under the old apprenticeship system children were supposed to receive certain education. Franklin wrote in 1784 with reference to apprenticeship contracts:

[They] are made before a magistrate, who regulates the agreement according to reason and justice; and having in view the formation of a future useful citizen, oblige the master to engage by written indenture, not only that during the time of service stipulated, the apprentice shall be duly provided with

meat, drink, apparel, washing, and lodging, and at its expira-
tion with a complete new suit of clothes, but also that he shall
be taught to read, write, and cast accounts; and that he shall
be well instructed in the art or profession of his master, or
some other, by which he may afterwards gain a livelihood, and
be able in his turn to raise a family.

The factory system might possibly have been required
(as was suggested by a writer in *Niles' Weekly Register* in 1815) to assume responsibility for some instruction; but one of the conspicuous demands of organized
labor was for a system of free public schools.   Some
even favored a plan to remove the children from
their parents lest they acquire the foolish ways of the
old society, and to clothe, feed, shelter, and teach them
alike.   On this communism of education the New
York labor movement split.   But final victory for democratic facilities of education was secured over the opposition of aristocracy and intellectual fossildom.

The question of woman in industry raised similarly
urgent issues.   The much-quoted statement of Harriet
Martineau that in 1836 only seven occupations were
open to women (teaching, needlework, keeping board-
ers, working in cotton mills, book-binding, type-setting,
house service) is erroneous.   Before 1837 women were
employed in over a hundred different industrial occupations.   It is true, however, that prior to 1850 there
was no field for educated women; and there were practically no opportunities for training.

At the beginning of the second quarter of the century
the earnings of women were lower than even the starvation wages of men.   Many occupations now open to
women had not then arisen or were confined to men.
Women in need of work might bind shoes, sew rags,
fold and stitch books, become spoolers, or make coarse
sheets and duck trousers at eight or ten cents apiece.

Shirt making was much desired because the work could be done at home, the seamstress being often the mother of a family and perhaps a widow. The most expert could not finish more than nine shirts a week, for which the stipend would be seventy-two or ninety cents. Fifty cents seems to have been the average.

A Boston paper of 1832 contains reference to tables showing the gain to the community from having women spin and weave in factories instead of at home. In the factories they may earn perhaps one hundred twenty-five dollars each per year. But the strain of factory labor, of a different nature from old-fashioned home industry, however trying that may be, coupled with unsanitary surroundings and unhygienic habits raised a serious problem with regard to the health of the future mothers of the race, a problem that is still unsettled. In this way factory industry has an additional bearing on the family. In the early factory with its long working-day the ventilation and lighting were poor, and the corporation boarding-houses were overcrowded and insanitary. (The Lowell Manufacturing Company's rules, 1830-1840, provided that all employees must board at the company house and observe its minute regulations.) Factory girls often slept six to eight in a room and even three in a bed. A delegate to the first National Trades' Union Convention (1834) asserted that the cotton factories were "the present abode of wretchedness, disease, and misery."

Mr. D. entered into a description of the effects of the present factory system upon the health and morals of the unhappy inmates, and depicted in a strong light the increase of disease and deformity from an excess of labor, want of outdoor exercise, and of good air – of the prevalence of depravity from their exposed situation, and their want of education, having no time or opportunity for schooling, and observed, that the decrepid, sickly, and

184 *The American Family*

debilitated inmates of these prison houses were marrying and propagating a race of beings more miserable if possible than themselves. . . "We talk," said Mr. D., "of the rising generation! What must that generation be, coming from such a stock of disease and deformity!"

Charles Dickens visited several Lowell factories in 1842 and found the girls well dressed and cleanly as they thronged from the mills.

They were healthy in appearance . . . and had the manner and deportment of young women; not of degraded brutes. . . The rooms in which they worked were as well ordered as themselves. . . There was as much fresh air, cleanliness and comfort, as the nature of the occupation would possibly admit of. . . The owners of the mills are particularly careful to allow no persons to enter upon the possession of [the boarding-houses], whose characters have not undergone the most searching and thorough inquiry. . . There is a joint-stock piano in a great many of the boarding-houses. . . The girls labor in these mills upon an average, twelve hours a day; these girls (often the daughters of small farmers) come from other states, remain a few years in the mills, and then go home for good.

There were, indeed, in the life of the Lowell mill girls, in the early days, certain opportunities for improvement and cultivation that must have been of importance to the communities to which they returned.

One of the most interesting features of the situation arising from the presence of women in industry was a recognition on the part of workingmen, in spite of the irritation felt at female competition, that the women were, so to speak, in their trust. In the thirties organized labor took a serious interest in the problems incident to woman's entry of industry, and if, as earlier, the concern was stimulated by resentment at the consequences of female competition in the way of lower wage levels and the elimination of men, still the discussion evidences serious concern for the health and morals of women and their economic rights. Frederick Robinson in a July Fourth oration to Boston trades unionists, said:

> All legislative power is in our hands . . . we are the natural guardians of the other, the weaker and the better half of our own species. . . However much we have borne from the aristocracy in every age, our mothers, our wives, our sisters, our daughters have been still more abused. Their suffering calls for our immediate interposition and we ought never to rest until we regulate the hours of their labor in factories by direct legislation, until we make it a crime to work . . . more than six hours a day.

Being subjected to like treatment, the man and the woman worker tended to draw together. A new chivalry was in process of formation inasmuch as woman lacked the right to political self-expression. The pressure of the new industrial conditions began to forge a bond of fellowship between the sexes that furnished, in a sense, a substitute for the old industrial bond of family union that had been broken by the decadence of domestic industry. But the new unity was broader than the family and more communal.

The wrongs of working women received marked publicity, partly in connection with the woman's rights movement, as we have seen in a previous chapter, and partly in labor publications, but also in the general press. The *Ladies' Magazine* (Boston) of 1830 contained an appeal for relief for orphans and widows. A writer said that inquiry showed that in New York, Baltimore, and Philadelphia earnings of females were inadequate for their support. In Philadelphia a number of the most respectable ladies said that expert seamstresses, if fully employed, and unencumbered with children could not make over one dollar twelve and one-half cents a week.   They had to pay fifty cents for lodgings, leaving nine cents a day for all other expenses. Moreover there were cases where piece rates were as low as half the above.   These women were frequently unemployed.   Many were widows who formerly lived in affluence.   Various other species of female labor were as badly paid.   The reverend Mr. Tuckerman said there were numerous cases of mothers doing their utmost for the education of their children, with little assistance from their husbands, and requiring aid.   It was hard, however, to arouse enthusiasm in the cause of this oppressed labor.

The *Man* of March 3, 1834, quoted the *Trades Union* on Lowell girls.

> The price of female labor is already too low, and the amount of labor that females have to perform too great.   Many of these young women have poor and aged parents depending on the earnings of their children for support.   Others who are not obliged to assist their parents, can receive no assistance from them, and must, out of their small earning, which rarely exceeds two dollars and fifty cents a week, provide board and clothing, and lay by something to support themselves when they are sick or unemployed.

The *Man* of March 7, 1834, reports that six hundred factory girls at Dover, New Hampshire, met and protested against a wage cut.   "Resolutions evincing on the part of the girls a thorough knowledge of their rights and interests were passed unanimously."   These resolutions set forth that many of them were far from home, parents and friends, and that it was only by strict economy and untiring industry that any of them had been able to lay up anything.   The *Man* of March 15, 1834, quoted the *Sun* as follows:

> The low rate of female labor is a grievance of the very first magnitude, and pregnant with the most mighty ills to society. . . This unjust arrangement of remuneration for ser-

vices performed diminishes the importance of women in society — renders them more helpless and dependent — destroys in the lower walks of life much of the inducement to marriage — and of course in the same degree increases the temptations to licentiousness. It is difficult to conceive why, even in those branches, wherein both sexes are engaged, there should be such an extreme degree of disparity in the recompense of labor.

The *Man* of March 20, 1834, quoted a Lowell girl thus:

> If the proprietors and agents are not satisfied with alluring us from our homes — from the peaceful abodes of our childhood, under the false promises of a great reward, and then casting us upon the world, far from our friends and our homes and merely because we would not be slaves.

In the *Man* of March 26, 1834, there is an account of working girls at Lowell being insulted at a labor meeting. The instigation of the outrage was attributed to members of the aristocracy.

Susan B. Anthony as a young woman was indignant at the "custom everywhere to pay men four times the wages of women for exactly the same amount of work, often not so well done." Even the government was an exploiter of women. Mrs. Bodichon shortly before the war declared:

> In the mint in Philadelphia, I saw twenty or thirty young ladies who received half, sometimes less than half, the wages given to men for the same work. They were working ten hours a day for a dollar. This proportion shows the lamentable amount of competition among women, even in the United States, for any work which is open to them.

To a certain extent women found courage to stand for their rights. In New York City in 1845 several hundred women constituting the Female Industry Association, tailoresses, shirt-makers, book-folders, cap-makers, representatives of all trades then open to women, met in the Superior Court room to assert their rights against oppressive employers. The president said that in her trade wages were from ten to eighteen cents a day. Only the most capable received twenty-five cents. On such pay it was not possible to live decently and honestly. A committee was therefore appointed to prepare an appeal to the public.

In 1845 and 1846 great meetings of workers in Lowell, Chicopee, Manchester, New York, Philadelphia, demanded a ten hour day. In these agitations girls and women were as aggressive as the men. To supply the place of these agitators the Chicopee mill-owners sent a wagon on regular trips through New England, paying the man in charge a dollar or more for every girl secured. It was charged that farm girls were enticed on the representation that the work "was very neat, wages high, and that they could dress in silks and spend half the time in reading."

Vicious conditions developed early. McMaster, writing of the period of 1825-1829, says:

> To the desperate poverty produced by such [starvation] wages [of women] many evils were attributed. . . Children were sent into the streets to beg and pilfer, and young girls were driven to lives of shame to an extent which but for the report of the Magdalen Society in New York and the action of the people elsewhere would be incredible.

Newspapers of 1825 report that at Portland the people on three occasions pulled down houses of ill fame, and that a similar riot occurred in Boston. Horrible prison conditions had contributed to immorality.

Miss Martineau thought that the morals of the female factory population might be expected to be good considering of what class it was composed. Many of the girls, she said, were in factories because too proud for domestic service. Such could hardly be low enough for gross immorality, it seemed to her. Chevalier in the thirties quoted a director of a factory at Lowell as saying: "There have been in our establishment only three cases of illicit connections, and in all three instances the parties were married immediately, several months before the birth of the child." His statement seems very shallow.

The Lowell *Offering*, however, in December, 1840 had an interesting article signed by a "Factory Girl" in vigorous rebuttal to the editor of the Boston *Quarterly Review* who had said: "'She has worked in a factory' is sufficient to damn to infamy the most worthy and virtuous girl." The writer asserted that the editor slandered

A class of girls who in this city alone are numbered by thousands, and who collect in many of our smaller towns by hundreds; girls who generally come from quiet country homes, where their minds and manners have been formed under the eyes of the worthy sons of the Pilgrims and their virtuous partners, and who return again to become the wives of the free, intelligent yeomen of New England, and the mothers of quite a proportion of our future republicans.

Wyse, in his *America,* wrote:

[The daughters of shopkeepers and mechanics, the working girls] the moment they are enabled to work . . . are sent abroad to seek employment, in some of the numerous trades to which the American females are usually accustomed; and are from thenceforth only entitled to a place within the domestic circle, as they are able to contribute to a proportionate share of its expenses. . . When a female arrives at an age that enables her to exert herself after this mode, she ceases, to be an object of parental anxiety, or consideration, is no longer considered entitled as of course to any indulgence, or those other advantages she might reasonably expect to derive from her parents, circumstances, or position in the world. When with this is considered the difficulty of realizing by female industry and labor the merest necessaries of life, the thoughtlessness and love of dress, which is almost inherent in every young

person, with the infectious and demoralizing influence of bad
example – the many temptations to spend money, with the few
guards and restraints to which females are subject in the United
States, it is scarcely surprising that morality should be at a very
low ebb, and female impropriety (to speak in milder phrasel-
ogy) amongst this class, unfortunately of frequent and very
general occurrence.

The reverend A. Stevens, writing in 1849 on woman,
said: "Female vice does exist among us, but it is less
common than in any European community: it prevails
almost exclusively among our denser populations, and
is chiefly the result there of poverty and miseducation."

Southerners found satisfaction in assailing the industrial system of the North and sometimes impugned the
virtue of its working women. The northern factory
girl was represented as a great slave, and the "misery,
and poverty, and hunger, which is to be met with among
the poor widows, and orphans, and free negroes of the
north" was compared disadvantageously with slave
conditions in the South. In truth, the wretched sewing
girls who toiled incessantly for bare sustenance and
broke down or died in misery, while benevolent cus-
tomers beat down prices and neglected payment might
have envied the slaves on many a southern plantation.
Conditions were of course worst in the East.

A book of the fifties entitled the *North and South, or
Slavery and its Contrast* asserted that there was just as
real slavery in the North. Children were torn from
bosoms that loved and nurtured them and exposed to
every cruelty. In a recent case a so-called lady whipped severely a little bound girl and shut her up till she
died of starvation. "Let the thousands of slender,
fragile, children, in each of our great cities, children
covered with the coarsest garments; their little feet
bare; their backs bowed . . . their features sharp

and pinched . . . let their sorrows plead." The binding of apprentices to the employer's service by hard and fast indenture fell into disuse before the middle of the century; but for a long while after this change, in small towns the apprentice often lived with and drudged for his employer's family.

The Industrial Revolution brought urbanization. In 1790, three per cent of our population lived in cities of eight thousand or over; in 1800, four per cent; in 1830, six and seven-tenths; on the eve of the Civil War, sixteen per cent were urban dwellers. By the early twenties: "In many of the cities, the high price of fuel and rent is severely felt by the lower classes. This causes several families to live in one house. There are even instances of two families living in one room; the consequences of which are highly injurious to the health of the inhabitants." The tenement house was a problem before 1830. The cities were growing with great rapidity. In New York, houses could not be found for all. Buildings were put up cheaply. Some collapsed. Others were torn down by order of authorities.

The winter of 1837-1838 was mild and open far into January but it was one of pervading destitution and suffering in New York City owing to paralysis of business. Tens of thousands were in danger of starvation. Horace Greeley wrote:

> I saw two families, including six or eight children, burrowing in one cellar under a stable – a prey to famine [vermin, and disease]. I saw men who each, somehow, supported his family on an income of five dollars per week or less, yet who cheerfully gave something to mitigate the sufferings of those who were really poor. I saw three widows, with as many children, living in an attic on the profits of an applestand which yielded less than three dollars per week, and the landlord came in for a full third of that.

Again in 1850 he took up the indictment of society:

> While Labor builds far more sumptuous mansions in our day
> than of old, furnishing them far more gorgeously and luxuri-
> ously, the laborer who builds those mansions lives oftenest in a
> squalid lodging, than which the builders of palaces in the fif-
> teenth century can hardly have dwelt in more wretched . . .
> while the demands for labor, the uses of labor, the efficiency of
> labor, are multiplied and extended on every side by the rush of
> invention and the growth of luxury around us, yet . . .
> labor is a drug on the market . . . the temperate, efficient,
> upright worker often finds the comfortable maintenance and
> proper education of his children beyond his ability.

By 1852, gold flow had resulted in depreciation and steady rise in prices. "Rents and the cost of clothing, meats, flour, butter, provisions of all sorts went higher and higher till the workingman forgot all other grievances and cried out for higher wages." Hammond of South Carolina, in the Senate in 1858, said: "Your people . . . are assembling . . . with arms in their hands, and demanding work at one thousand dollars a year for six hours a day."

In view of conditions disclosed, it would seem probable that some of those citizens that were so greatly perturbed lest higher education for women should "break up the home" might have found in the industrial system a real danger to attack. The reverend R. B. Thurston wrote well when he said:

> All progress in domestic felicity and in religious culture de-
> pends on property, and also on the equitable distribution of pos-
> session of property, as one of its essential conditions. Property
> lies in the foundation of every happy home, however humble;
> and property gilds the pinnacle of every consecrated temple.

The nascent capitalism of the North when put to this test did not compare too well with the chatteldom of the South.

When Southerners, assailed by the abolitionists,

learned of negroes in Philadelphia living in houses and
cellars with hardly any furniture they were excusable
if they remarked: "And this is nigger freedom!"
Forrest in *Historical and Descriptive Sketches of Norfolk, Virginia*, gave vivid information that was certainly of interest to Southerners.   He quoted from the New
York *Express* a description of "Cow Bay," a negro
quarter of New York:

A small narrow, and exceedingly dirty court, about one hundred twenty or one hundred thirty feet deep, with a row of
shabby three story brick houses on one side, and dilapidated
brick and wooden hovels on the other. Pigs, cats, dogs, rats,
and children black and white, wallowing in the mud, or taking
their initiatory lessons in rascality together – a labyrinth of
alley ways, bordered on all sides with dirty and filthy houses –
a hive, sweltering full of human brutes – a small city in itself,
teeming with a population altogether of a different nature from
those who live but a few blocks from them. [Here] is the
principal dwelling place of the negroes   .   .   .   here they live
and die like pigs, and their carcasses are stowed away in some
corner of the Potter's field with about as much respect as would
be paid to the carrion of an old horse.

The houses have generally eight or ten rooms, including the
attics and cellars, and in these are crowded not infrequently
two or three hundred souls. The cellars are so arranged that
the sidewalk comes up to within eighteen inches or a foot of
the wall of the houses and, looking down, one may perceive a
deep, dark, nasty trap, into which all kinds of refuse are thrown,
and into which, not infrequently, the inebriated inmates of the
courts themselves meet their end. At intervals, reaching from
the sidewalk to the bottom of this gutter, are placed ladders or
steps, to give ingress and egress to the animals who burrow in
the cellars. The front cellar is usually eight or ten by six
feet   .   .   .   with a ceiling so low that an ordinary sized
man must look out for his hat on entering. One end of this
apartment is fitted up with a bar, stocked with villainous com-
pounds called liquors, which are sold to the wretched inhabitants for three cents a glass each, as long as they have money,
and four cents credit, as long as they have any personal prop-

erty that the landlord can levy upon for his pay when their money is gone. Back of the "bar-room" appears another apartment, perhaps a little larger, perhaps a little smaller, according to the size of the house, and in this kennel are often crowded together fifteen or twenty persons, negroes and whites, male and female, adults and children, without any more light and air than what can come in through the door. These sleep together on the same rags—beds there are none—or on the same straw, and rarely or never do the inhabitants of these cellars retire to their rest until they are too much inebriated to remain longer awake, when they lay themselves down, in the clothes which probably they have not taken off for months, and sleep off the fumes of their drunkenness in the midst of the most revolting filth.

Not infrequently, in the larger houses, one or two apartments are not all that are to be found in a cellar; sometimes these sinks are two stories deep, or have side branches extending under the courts, and these all, of course, worse than the first. With no floors, or with such as were originally laid, long ago rotten and worn out, so out of repair that whenever it rains the filth of the gutter and courts is washed down to make part and parcel of the heap the wretches sleep upon; never cleaned out from one year's end to the other—these noisome holes are not fit habitations even for the vermin which swarm in them; and yet here these creatures, who call themselves men and women, and who would feel insulted were a white man to call them "niggers," drag out their miserable existence.

During the day, the inhabitants of "Cow Bay" and its "courts" and "alleys" keep themselves pretty quiet; they only step out to get their three or four cents worth of gin, and then burrow themselves in their dens again. [By day they loaf or steal, or beg. By night they drink and dance and gamble—male and female. The law discriminates against negroes. They are not citizens till they own (unencumbered) five hundred dollars' worth of real estate. They can't get licenses to do certain jobs till they are citizens.]

We have ourselves seen, in a six by eight attic room of a house in Thomas Street . . . two entire negro families containing thirteen individuals, male, female, young and old, who in that small kennel, with only one window of six panes of glass, ate, drank, slept – indiscriminately, men and women to-gether – cooked, washed, and ironed (for the women generally help to support the family, by taking in washing), and in fact transacted all the business of a household. . . Not only did they cover the floor, but moveable shelves, which during the day time were let down parallel with the wall by a hinge, were at night time, when the negroes wished to "turn in," propped up, and, having a raised edge to keep the inmates from tumbling out – with the clothes worn by the sleeper during the day thrown on the shelf to make it a little softer . . . they declared they had capital accommodations. Table they had none, chairs they had none, but the sleeping shelves, when a table was wanted for eating or ironing, answered every purpose, and the floor, or half a dozen camp stools, that could be shut up and stowed in a small space, answered for the seats.

Such were conditions ten years before the War. The author of the book in which the extract was reprinted said, doubtless with a contented smile at the contrast to the South: "We withhold the darkest part of the frightful picture." In the *Planter: or Thirteen Years in the South* (1853) it is stated that in the North "among the millions of working people, the number is . . . miserably small, in proportion to the whole, who get for their labor more than the necessary food, clothing, and shelter for themselves and families; and innumerable is the host that fall very far short of the commonest needful comforts of life." Hundley (a southern man that had lived north) in *Social Relations in our Southern States* (1860) said: "We do not entertain the least doubt but there are fully one hundred thousand respectable families in the North, who are out of employment, and who consequently will have to live for the next three months . . . in a state of semi-starvation." The tenement class of New York City was living in 1863 in "hives of sickness, vice, misery, and wretchedness."

As in more recent times there was before the War positive mistrust of the tendencies away from the land and from home. Condy Raguet argued in the *Free Trade Advocate* "that farm work was better for both boys and girls than factory work, and that girls were more likely to become good wives if they worked in kitchens instead of factories." As early as 1834 a speaker at the Trades Union National Convention deplored the drawing of the farmer's

> Sons and daughters from the farm to the factories. For a few years past, the sons of our farmers, as soon as they are of sufficient age, have been induced to hasten off to the factory, where for a few pence more than they could get at home, they are taught to become the willing servants, the servile instruments of their employer's oppression and extortion! The daughters, too, must quit the farm house, the scene of ruddy health and former content, for a confined and baneful workshop, where, to be sure, she earns a little more money, for a short time; but as surely loses health, if not her good character, her happiness!

In 1836 a committee of the Massachusetts House enlarged upon the fact that the industries of Massachusetts were rapidly changing from agriculture to manufactures; that the population was shifting from rural to urban; and expressed the conviction that in view of this change

> It becomes the solemn and indispensable duty of the representatives of the people to provide seasonably and effectually that those institutions which have given New England her peculiar character for general intelligence and virtue be not changed with the changing employment of her people . . . [for it] requires no spirit of prophecy to foresee and to know that the collection of large masses of children, youth, and middle-aged persons of both sexes, into compact villages, is not a circumstance favorable to virtue.

As manufactures and commerce took precedence over agriculture, New England lost her young men while the young women were held by industry.   Competition of Irish girls depressed the standard of labor. Catherine Beecher wrote in 1851:

> The power-loom and spinning-jenny have banished household manufactures. . .   Conveniences and luxuries have attracted the gentler sex, and artificial wants have rendered female labor more solicitous of employment. . .   Wages of men have been reduced; and half of the unmarried females have few means of obtaining support, or of gratifying their artificial wants, by labor appropriate to their sex.

The significant feature of the economic transformation detailed in this chapter is that the economic ground of family unity was slipping.   Family bonds were being weakened.   Woman seemed to be coming dangerously into competition with man, as when organized labor attempted to better itself by strikes.   In the waiters' strike at the Broadway House in the fifties women were used as strike-breakers; girls were similarly employed on newspapers.   The openings that woman secured in the industrial system were menial rather than uplifting. Long hours of factory labor abolished family life.   Insufficient wages forced parents to set children prematurely to work.   In short the transition had begun that has resulted in so many vexed questions of family integrity to-day.   Especially significant is the fact that with the passing of home industry woman had to go out into public work or remain a dangerous parasite.   The man might go to the works without upsetting the home center, though his constant absence could not but weaken old ties; likewise the children; but when woman ceased to be "housekeeper" the reality of the home came in question.   Evidently the sweat-shop conditions that introduced into the home the infection of outside industrialism were not preferable to the menace of the factory.   One notes with interest such an item as occurs in the *Man* of March 17, 1834, to the effect that the *Dover Gazette* expects silk culture at home to be a pleasant alternative to factory labor by women. But no expedients could retain the old basis of family stability.

A transition glimpse is gained in the case of Daniel Anthony (father of Susan B.), who in 1826 moved to New York State to manage a factory. His wife was almost heartbroken at leaving her aged father and mother. (The distance was forty-four miles.) Tenements were built for the operatives. Every man had a little garden around his house. Mr. Anthony looked on the employes as his family. But in the long run patriarchism had to go. It could not expand or otherwise adapt itself sufficiently to save the day. The stage of domestic industry had been favorable to the unity of the patriarchal family. As the business head, the father's will was the criterion of family interests. But when the family passed into the factory they could not be kept under his eye. They came to be treated, not as a family, but as units. The members of the family were no longer directly dependent on him for a livelihood. Moreover if he could not find work where the family lived he would have to leave in search of employment. A new basis of family integrity was in order.

The movement described has had a large place in the democratization of the family. Whittier, who recognized many evils in connection with the early cotton industry, saw compensation for the hardships of the mills in the fact that there, more than in any other mechanical employment, woman's labor was substantially on an equality with man's. He said:

Here at least, one of the many social disabilities under which woman, as a distinct individual unconnected with the other

sex, has labored in all times is removed; the work of her hands
is adequately rewarded; and she goes to her daily task with the
consciousness that she is not spending her strength for naught.

We may question the adequacy of her reward but it is
true that the day of woman's economic independence of
man had dawned – the day of unsettled marriage relations that force a readjustment of marital institutions
on a new basis.

To one class of women in particular, the new opening came as a boon. Mrs. Robinson has said:

> In almost every New England home could be found one or
> more [spinsters or widows], sometimes welcome, more often un-
> welcome, and leading joyless, and in many instances unsatisfac-
> tory, lives. The cotton-factory was a great opening to these
> lonely and dependent women. . . For the first time in this
> country woman's labor had a money value.

It should be noted, too, in connection with woman's
access to industry that public works constituted a new
prophylactic against inbreeding. They drew people
from various communities and widened the range for
choice of life-partners. This fact was wholesome in
the long run, both in the enhancement of opportunity
for family happiness and in the dynamic effects of the
mixing of cultures. Though according to Mrs. Robinson the early mill workers were not deemed capable
of education into something more than mere work
people, the most favored of the girls were sometimes
invited to the homes of the dignitaries of the mills and
some Lowell mill girls married into the "best families."
"At one time the fame of *The Lowell Offering* caused
the mill-girls to be considered very desirable for wives;
and that young men came from near and far to pick
and choose for themselves, and generally with good
success."

X. THE REIGN OF SELF-INDULGENCE

Even in the colony days there were signs of aristocracy in the midst of the new life. Schouler says in his
Americans of 1776 that in some centers like Philadelphia, feasting among the fashionable (at weddings) was
prodigal. De Rochambeau, one of the French allies,
said that the wives of American merchants and bankers
were clad to the top of French fashions. Brissot de
Warville, who visited America in 1788, wrote:

> At Mr. Griffin's house at dinner, I saw seven or eight women
> all dressed in great hats, plumes, etc. It was with pain that I
> marked much of pretension in some of these women; one acted
> giddy, vivacious, another the woman of sentiment. This last
> had many pruderies and grimaces. Two among them had
> their bosoms very naked; I was scandalized at this indecency
> among republicans.

A Hessian captured at Saratoga wrote: "The daughters keep up their stylish dressing because the mothers
desire it. Should the mother die, her last words are to
the effect that the daughter must retain control of the
money-bags." Chastellux wrote:

> The salary of a workingman must not only provide subsistence
> for his family, but also comfortable furniture for his home,
> tea and coffee for his wife, and a silk dress to put on every time
> she goes out.

Bayard said:

> In vain Citizen Livingston, of venerable memory, recalled his
> fair compatriots to their spinning wheels and to conservative
> simplicity of manners and fortune, for he was not listened
> to. . . The rage for luxury has reached such a point that

the wife of the laboring man wishes to vie with the merchant's wife, and she in turn will not yield to the richest woman in Europe.[100]

So much for the eighteenth century. But on through the era of nationalization a well-marked type of "swell" life continued to rise counter to democracy. This new development influenced markedly the family and the home.

One of its most important consequences was a decline in marriage. In Pennsylvania even before the national government came into existence there was a "Batchelor's tax." Schoepf wrote:

> Every male person twenty-one years old and still unprovided with a wife pays from that time on 12s. 6d. . . . a year. . . It effects the desired purpose, because young men will not long expose themselves to mockery of this sort in a country where working hands can so easily find support for a family.

The existence of such a law implied a reluctance to marry. Both Brissot and Mazzei attacked vigorously the hard-hearted bachelors, the former conceding, however, that luxury is to blame "for the extravagance of the women makes them fear marriage." Mazzei added: "As for bachelors, who should be rarer here than in Europe (and for well-known reasons), they are more numerous in Philadelphia than in any other American city, while in other parts of Pennsylvania they are no rarer than elsewhere." He thought the bachelors ran small risk, because they were treated so frankly. Imlay noted that the sea-faring life of New England kept the sexes apart there, but he observed also that slavery caused contempt for labor; amusements were invented;

---

[100] Schouler. *Americans of 1776*, 36-37; Hale and Merritt. *History of Tennessee and Tennesseeans*, vol. ii, 417-418; Sherrill. *French Memories of Eighteenth Century America*, 55-56.

dissipation followed. "The fair sex were neglected; marriages were less early and less frequent."[101]

In the early years of the nineteenth century fast-women of fashion were not numerous enough to form a considerable class in any part of the land; but in the *Ladies' Magazine* (Savannah) of 1819 occurred an item from the (New York) *National Advocate*, on the falling off in marriages.

> Why don't people marry? Why are there so many antiquated damsels and superannuated bachelors? . . . The errors of education, and the extravagance of fashion, for which young ladies are celebrated, frighten the young men from making advances – and the follies and personal expenses of young men, render them insensible of all the joys and comforts of matrimony; faults thus on both sides, have a tendency to keep them separate, 'till young ladies become old, and old bachelors marry to get nurses. . . I see, with regret, mothers dragging their daughters of twelve and thirteen years to parties and balls, under an erroneous impression, that it gives them an air of ease and confidence . . . boys are very apt to be equally spoilt.

The New York *Cabinet* of 1829 made note of "increasing extravagance of the modern fair" and that "the really prudent and somewhat home-bred man feels obliged" to relinquish or postpone marriage by reason of the cost of living.

Writers of the forties and fifties call attention to the repression of marriage by the luxury and rivalry of fashion and by the indolence and extravagance of young ladies. Artificial standards of consumption were deterring many from assuming the risks of matrimony. "We see marriages in fashionable life every day becoming fewer; thus leaving in our cities a numerous class of finely dressed, pretty and accomplished young ladies,

---

[101] Schoepf. *Travels in the Confederation*, vol. i, 129; Sherrill. *French Memories of Eighteenth Century America*, 64-65; Imlay. *Topographical Description of the western Territory of North America*, 57-58.

doomed to become disappointed 'establishment seekers' and to fade into fretful and repining 'old-maids'." Men took refuge in clubs; if unscrupulous they not infrequently tried their hand at peculation or speculation; vice was promoted.[102]

Tower (a formerly proslavery preacher) wrote of New Orleans: "As no young man ordinarily dare think of marriage until he has made a fortune to support the extravagant style of housekeeping, and gratify the expensive tastes of young women, as fashion is now educating them, many are obliged to make up their minds never to marry." A mistress would suffice. According to this author there were hundreds of the lowest grade brothels all through the city; and adultery, fornication, and prostitution seemed to be unknown categories. A record for their practice made one a beau ideal. Hundreds of pairs lived like man and wife but unmarried. Some had private marriages performed in order to enable children to inherit property. A gentleman found in a clergyman's private book of marriage records that he had within two years married thirty-three heads of families many of whom were parents of married children. Business men and others from the North kept here a second family. Such men were quite respectable. The concubine might be as faithful as a wife; otherwise she would be discarded. Such differences were fewer, Tower said, than if the pair had been really married.

It was a sort of honor to be able to support two families; but

There is still another class of individuals here who have not the means to support two families. They are for the most

---

[102] Compare for instance, "Family Circle," in *Democratic Review*, vol. xliii, 243; Olmsted, *Journey in the Seaboard Slave States*, 600; Bodichon. *Women and Work*, "Introduction," by Catherine M. Sidgwick, 5-6.

part, men engaged in the same business with others, and required to be absent from the city nearly half the time. These
men also have mistresses, either white or colored. . . While
the man is in the city, the house which the woman occupies is
their home, jointly and as distinctly as if they were married;
and when he is absent, the woman seeks another companion,
for the time being, and in doing this does not in the least
hazard the displeasure of . . . "her husband" as she calls
him. [Thus] she is able to support herself in great style, and
with as much ease and comfort around her as can be desired.
They usually occupy a room, or suite of rooms, a parlor and
bedroom, furnished with as much elegance and splendor as
money can purchase. Most of [these females] have been flat-
tered and seduced, poor things, away from their home and
friends by glowing descriptions and representations of the pleasures, and gaieties, and unceasing enjoyments, which go to make
up life in New Orleans. Connections of this character are as
much a matter of contract, and the terms and conditions by
which each shall be governed are as definite, as any other business transaction can be, and thus they live for years, and in
many instances an attachment for each other is the result, and
they finally settle down as man and wife, and sooner or later
are married, and become respectable, for New Orleans at least.

The extent of licentiousness and prostitution here is truly
appalling, and doubtless without a parallel, and probably double
that of any other place in the whole civilized world. The indulgence and practice is so general and common that men seldom seek to cover up their acts, or go in disguise; but in all
these things keeping their mistresses or frequenting bad houses
and having women come to their rooms at night, they do it as
openly, and as much before the eyes of the world, as any other
act among the common civilities of the social circle. . .
Three-fifths at least of the dwellings and rooms in a large portion of the city are occupied by prostitutes or by one or the
other class of kept mistresses. Those women who are the
companions of one man, and hold that position under a pledge
of confidence not to seek intercourse with others, hold themselves very much above the character of common prostitutes,
and regard themselves as respectable; and as such many of them
move in society with some degree of favor and consequence.

The regular prostitutes . . . are composed of a crowd —
nay an army of broken down females so large that they can
scarcely be numbered.

One day in my tour of observation I came pat upon whole
streets and squares of these localities occupied by these poor
creatures. There, said I to myself, are thousands of ruined,
fallen immortal beings, once fair and beautiful, of elevated
moral caste, the pride and center of some distant family and
social circle: perhaps a wife or daughter, the adored of her husband and parents. . .

Many of these poor, abandoned things, I am informed, come
here at the opening of business in the fall, and return to the
North in the spring as business closes, as regular as mechanics
and other business men; quite a number of them come from
New York and other northern cities under the protection of
young men, a certain class of gamblers and blacklegs who have
long made this their field of operations during the winter
months. The prostitutes of this migratory class form the great
mass of the inmates of the regular kept brothels, of which
their number here is legion.

The character of these houses cannot be misjudged, as the
females who occupy them are constantly making voluptuous ex-
hibition of themselves at the doors and windows and very unceremoniously inviting men as they pass by to come in. And in
some of the principal streets . . . just at evening, it is no
unusual sight to see the windows and doors of almost every
house as far as the eye can recognize them, filled with these
women. As bad as New Orleans is, its municipal regulations
are such that these creatures are prohibited from publicly prom-
enading the streets; hence they are obliged to resort to other
measures to make themselves known. In view of all these
abominations, doubtless the main cause of so much licentiousness, and the immense number of prostitutes, of every class,
grade and color that is human, is the overwhelming number of
loose irresponsible men who frequent this place. Under such
circumstances as men meet here, they almost lose their identity
as responsible beings, having no checks around them, and under no obligation to society, consequently no pride of character,
they soon become as bold and reckless in licentiousness and
crime as though the pall of night perpetually shrouded their

deeds. And yet men, and some women too, will come here, and mingle in rounds of dissipation and pollution, who before and while at home and in other associations, would shudder at the sight, and even at the very thought of deeds they have unhappily been lured into. Such persons I daily meet. . . Another cause that aids in promoting these evils, is the small portion of men who have families here. Probably not one in twenty is married, and if so, leaves a family at the North, and while here entirely forgets that at home he has left a wife, who is little dreaming of the rounds of licentiousness and dissipation, that constitutes the almost daily track of her truant husband. [Good men] are "few and far between," [so that] the sins of licentiousness, adultery and prostitution [come] to be regarded as the proper elements of society.

A large number of men with their wives, who visit New Orleans to spend the winter . . . to support themselves take the round of the gay and fashionable throng, and . . . the wife, with a perfect understanding of the matter with her husband, suffers herself to become seduced, and thus falls into the arms of some wealthy, wild, dashing young southern blood, who is proud of his conquest. He lavishes upon her costly presents and money, and in fact will bestow upon her anything that she may demand, within the compass of his purse. And when he ceases to give large sums, the husband contrives to make the accidental discovery of their intimacy, and in the fearless rage of an injured husband, threatens to come down upon the seducer with all the heated vengeance of southern chivalry. And to save himself the man will pay almost any sum the injured husband may demand. Thus the wife will go on, for months, making conquest after conquest, and being seduced at least by half a dozen different men she has victimized, and with all of them, practicing the most cunning and deceptive arts, charging each one to be exceedingly circumspect and cautious, so as to avoid the least suspicion in the eyes of the world and her husband especially. During all this time her hands are filled with costly and magnificent presents and money, and in fact, anything she may desire, while each one of her victims regards himself as the sole possessor of the stolen fruit. She is enabled to pursue this course, and avoid suspicion among her favorites of being intimate with more than one, by meeting them at houses of assignation. . . They usually go in disguise, I am informed, and often in mask, and very frequently are unknown to the men who see them there, and their name is never inquired for, as it is generally understood, that none but respectable ladies, both married and unmarried, frequent these houses. And yet during all these love scenes . . . the lady and her husband are in the foremost rank of the fashionable circle, supporting a style and splendor of equipage that few can surpass or even imitate. . . Into this circle are thrown the virtuous and unsuspecting visitors who come into this city for pleasure, pastime or business, and if they can pass through and come out unsullied and as pure in mind and as chaste in their sense of propriety and as virtuous in feeling as when they entered, they are equal to the three Hebrew children at the fiery furnace.[103]

In the South the extreme facility of promiscuity, or concubinage, with negro women encouraged some men to remain bachelors. Similarly in the North the development of vice went along with celibacy. St. Victor wrote in 1832 of terrible prostitution and debauchery. A little later Miss Martineau wrote:

Even in America, where every young man may, if he chooses, marry at twenty-one, and appropriate all the best comforts of domestic life, even here there is vice. Men do not choose to marry early, because they have learned to think other things of more importance than the best comforts of domestic life. A gentleman of Massachusetts, who knows life . . . spoke to me with deep concern of the alteration in manners which is going on: of the increase of bachelors [etc.].[104]

In 1834 a New York grand jury indicted a paper run by a minister for presenting "odious and revolting details" of vice. Marryat notes the case of a man in New York who, having murdered his mistress in a brothel, was acquitted and allowed to depart for Texas. One man at New Orleans, conceding that quadroon concubinage was not right, declared it "much better than

[103] Tower. *Slavery Unmasked*, 319, 321, 335-342.
[104] Martineau. *Society in America*, vol. iii, 127.

the way . . . most young men live who depend on salaries in New York."

American fecundity, at least in some regions or classes, suffered diminution even in the colonial period and the decline continued in the nineteenth century. Centers of population were most likely to be affected.[105] In the early days and in country life the family had been an asset. With the rise of the standard and cost of living and the growth of cities it became an expense. The difference in cost of living between city and country districts early became great. Life in provincial cities is pleasanter and cheaper than in the great centers, wrote Sidons in 1826. He said:

> With seven to eight hundred dollars a family of six to eight members can, if they have their own house, live very decently, and keep three horses and as many black servants, which in Philadelphia would cost four thousand, in New York five thousand, and in New Orleans six thousand dollars.[106]

In the decade of the thirties immigration greatly increased, yet the population of 1840 was about what would have been expected had no increase in foreign influx occurred. In 1843 Professor George Tucker predicted a decline in birth-rate by reason of prudence or pride, and increasing with the increase of cities and of the wealthy classes, so that the population in 1890 would be sixty-three million. In the forties, arrivals from Ireland and Germany were enormous, but the population increased during the decade at a lower rate than when foreign arrivals were relatively negligible. Mansfield said in 1845:

> The progress of population, wealth, and fashion in our country has made [the crime of criminal abortion] quite common. In

---

[105] Englemann. *Education not the Cause of Race Decline*, 178-180; Thorndike. *Professor Pearson on the Distribution of Fertility*; Dwight. *Travels in New England and New York*, vol. ii, 270-272.
[106] Sidons. *Die Vereinigten Staaten*, vol. i, 98.

the large cities it is, we fear, practised frequently, as it has been in the large cities of the old world. Indeed, public advertisements, shameless as they are, have been published in the newspapers. directing the child of fashion or of vice, where she might find a woman to perform that service.

A leading medical professor said in 1854:

> The evil affects educated, refined, and fashionable women; yea in many instances women whose moral character is in other respects without reproach. The contagion has reached mothers who are devoted with an ardent and self-denying affection to the children who already constitute their family.

In 1858, Professor H. R. Storer read before the American Academy of Arts and Sciences a paper on the "Decrease of the Rate of Increase of Population now obtaining in Europe and America." He attributed the declining birth-rate in America almost wholly to prudential checks, tho he did not think that passion had cooled or come more generally under control; nor was the infecundity to be attributed to abstinence from marriage. "Prevention of pregnancy, to whatever extent existing, can not account for the decrease of living births; actual pregnancies being proved fully as frequent as ever." In New York City while the population had increased but sixfold since 1805, the annual number of still and premature births had multiplied over twenty-seven times. Dr. Storer gave a table intended to show the increase in foetal death-rate in New York. The figures indicate an almost uninterrupted rise from one in 1633 of the population in 1805 to one in 341 of the population in 1849. He added, however: "It is evident that but a small proportion of the abortions and miscarriages occurring are ever reported," and one may raise the question whether part of the contrast of figures may not be due to improvement in accuracy of data. The New York ratio of foetal to general mortality in 1804-1809 was given as one to 37.6 and in 1856 as one to 11.1. The foreign population of Massachusetts had a much higher proportion of living births to pregnancies than did the native Protestant, and this fact the doctor attributed to the attitude of the Catholic church, whereas "we find infanticide and criminal abortion . . . justified, rendered common, and almost legitimated [by political economy]."[107] This phenomenon is not hard to account for. The encroachments of luxury demanded retrenchment somewhere. So long as women are not mistresses of their own persons, abortion is the logical outcome.

During the generation preceding the war material conditions were becoming more favorable in some ways to normal increase of population. The old deadly medicine was being banished from civilized communities; houses were becoming larger; food and clothing were improving. The changes, however, did not suffice to counteract the influence of the more ambitious standards of city life and the custom of boarding.

Doubtless infecundity was not all intentional. There may be significance in the fact recorded by Schouler in his *Americans of 1776* that "no advertiser figured more constantly in the local wants . . . than the wet nurse with a good breast of milk." This prominence of hired lactation suggests functional (or social) defect. A book appearing in 1807 informs us, too, that "venereal doctors . . . rise up in print like mushrooms."[108]

Female fragility was a considerable factor in the

---

[107] Mansfield. *Legal Rights, Liabilities, and Duties of Women*, 136; Hodge. *On criminal Abortion*, cited by Carlier, in *Marriage in the United States*, 157-159. Storer's article was printed in 1867 in the *American Journal of Science and Arts*, second ser., vol. xliii, 141-155.

[108] Janson. *The Stranger in America*, 349.

question of racial integrity. Girls still married too
young—were cheated out of their youth. As late as
1850 a girl was rather old at twenty, an old maid at
twenty-five.[109] This early marriage and the consequent undue cares were very injurious to the health of
women. Many writers of the first third or so of the
nineteenth century comment on the early fading of
American women. Works of the forties continue the
plaint of woman's frailty. Wyse said that married women very soon faded and that offspring were seldom so
numerous as in England. Von Raumer said: "I have
seen in no country in the world, among handsome women, so many pale, sickly faces. . . Many professional men complain of the great number of still-born
children and premature births." The reverend George
W. Burnap wrote that women did not take enough care
of their health; there was a great falling off in one generation; the women then passing off were a very different race from their successors. "When I see the fragile and diminutive forms of the women of our times,
and compare them with the women whom I recollect as
the partners of the men of the revolution, it seems to me
that if the men of that age had had such mothers, we
never should have had any revolution at all." Luxury
had loaded the tables of the affluent with the delicacies
of all lands. This rich living to women sitting in warm
rooms reading or doing needle-work while almost totally neglecting active exercise was absolute destruction. Add to this late hours and improper clothing.
When European woman is at meridian, said Burnap,
American woman is withered.[110]

The delicacy of American women during the first
half of the nineteenth century was to some degree the

[109] Blackwell. *The Laws of Life*, 143.
[110] Burnap. *The Health of American Women*, 185-188.

realization of an ideal. Woman was supposed to be of
finer clay; and this "finer-clay," fragility, futility ideal
was already pretty well established at the end of the
eighteenth century. In American periodical literature of the early part of the nineteenth century, girls
languishing of broken hearts or dying of flower-like
nature were an immensely popular theme, especially in
ladies' magazines. Women up to the War and beyond
were nourished in the cult of female delicacy and refinement. Of course this theory was capable of complete application only in leisure-class circles; but it
helps us to understand the neglect of physical training
for girls and also to appreciate the remark of a physician of the first quarter of the nineteenth century who
said that not one woman in ten enjoyed perfect health.
At a much later date Catherine E. Beecher "made
enquiries into physical health of American females
and . . . among her immense circle of friends and
acquaintances all over the union, is unable to recall ten
married ladies in this century and country who are perfectly sound, healthy, and vigorous."[111]

With increasing prominence of wealth and luxury
went an increase in sordid economic marriage. From
the very beginning of the nineteenth century repeated
evidences of shamefully mercenary matches obtrude.
Various writers of the first half of the century treat
emphatically of this evil, sometimes with reference to
parents' abuse of their daughters' deeper welfare and
again in condemnation of the procedure of ambitious
young folks of either sex. Robert Owen attacked marriage resting on a property basis.

A magazine of 1805 informs us that "advantageous
settlement" for their daughters is the universal aim of

[111] Reed. *Female Delicacy in the Sixties*, 855-862; Dixon. *White Conquest*, vol. ii, 309.

parents and the major object of female instruction. A review of Miss Martineau's work affirms that "many of our fairest are sacrificed at the expense of their affections, and that this is an increasing evil." In a periodical of the early forties occurs reprobation of the numerous mercenary marriages forced by parents – often with deadly consequence to the victim.

Fortune-hunting males were at large. A book of 1807 cited a lottery advertisement in New York papers which urged people to become rich since "the question now asked concerning a lady is not, Is she handsome? Is she accomplished? or, Is she amiable? but, Is she rich?" A Broadway clerk thought he might "pick up a fortune in the way of marriage." A New York paper of 1829 remarked the "ridiculous rage among gentlemen for rich sweethearts. . . The first enquiry that our young men make now, when a woman is proposed for a wife is, 'Is she rich?' and for variety, or a salvo, 'is she handsome?' Let a husband die and leave a rich widow or heiress . . . and . . . how the beaux scamper." A periodical of the forties referred to the many females of character and merit "sacrificed to the machinations of a fortune hunter!" Marryat said:

However much the Americans may wish to deny it, I am inclined to think that there are more marriages of convenance in the United States than in most other countries. The men begin to calculate long before they are of an age to marry, and it is not very likely that they would calculate so well upon all other points, and not upon the value of a dowry; moreover the old people "calculate some," and the girls accept an offer, without their hearts being seriously compromised. Of course there are exceptions: but I do not think that there are many love matches made in America, and one reason for my holding this opinion is, my having discovered how quietly matches are broken off and new engagements entered into; and it is, perhaps, from a knowledge of this fact, arising from the calculating spirit of the gentlemen, who are apt to consider twenty thousand dollars as preferable to ten thousand dollars, that the American girls are not too hasty in surrendering their hearts. . . On the whole, I hold it very fortunate that in American marriages there is, generally speaking, more prudence than love on both sides, for from the peculiar habits and customs of the country, a woman who loved without prudence would not feel very happy as a wife [the men are so little at home].

That the feminine feelings often had a mercantile turn is corroborated by other writers. Mrs. Houstoun extenuates this failing by the consideration that American young ladies see so little of their husbands that the amount of money they can secure from their mates is the prime concern. Thus matrimony is a business venture. "A partner at a ball, who has chanced to receive encouragement as the owner of a pair of horses is speedily discarded for one with four, and he, in like manner, must stand aside if the possessor of a still larger stud should chance to present himself." The reverend F. A. Ross of Alabama in *Slavery Ordained of God* wrote:

Do you say the slave is sold and bought? So is the wife, the world over . . . the New England man, the New Yorker — especially the upper ten — buy the wife — in many, very many cases. She is seldom bought in the South, and never among the slaves themselves; for they always marry for love. . . Old ugly brute, with gray goatee — how fragrant — bids one, two, five, ten hundred thousand dollars, and she is knocked off to him — that beautiful young girl asleep up there, amid flowers, and innocent that she is sold and bought. Sir, that young girl would as soon permit a baboon to embrace her, as that old, ignorant, gross, disgusting wretch to approach her. Ah, has she not been sold and bought for money? But — But what? But, you say, she freely, and without parental authority accepted him. Then she sold herself for money, and was guilty of that which is nothing better than legal prostitution. I know what I say; you know what I say. Up there in the gallery

you know: You nod to one another. Ah! you know the parties. Yes, you say — All true, true, true.

Breach of promise cases were a normal accompaniment of mercenary marriage. In a magazine of 1819
was an account of a verdict of five thousand dollars in
New York against a man who seems to have been lured
away by the wealth of another woman. Naumann remarks in his *Nordamerika* that it behooves well-to-do
young men to be very careful in their language to girls.
Golovin said that "the most vulgar flirtation is often
times considered as a matrimonial declaration" and
told of a Pole who was forced to marry his washerwo-
man. It would seem that juries were ready to decide
in behalf of victimized women; and shrewd females,
taking advantage of the readiness to accept circumstan-
tial evidence of engagement, lured on elderly men of
wealth until they thought sufficient evidence was accumulated and then demanded marriage or indemnity.
Sometimes the man yielded; sometimes the case came
to trial and the man was heavily assessed. This business went on until the New York *Semi-Weekly Times*
of April 6, 1860, remarked that "it has become absolutely dangerous for wealthy men to be polite towards
an unmarried woman."

As in every property civilization, marriage in the
Old South was largely a mode of conveying possessions.
It involved the economic dependence of woman and
mercenary marriage. In *Letters from Virginia* published in 1816, it was said:

The fair damsels of Virginia show no disposition, that I can
see, to declare themselves independent of the men. So far
from it, I overhear frequent complaints of the scarcity of beaux
and husbands. . . The embargo and other restrictive measures . . . have fallen very heavily upon the ladies by im-
poverishing their lovers at home, and cutting off supplies from
abroad.

It is maintained that in the first half of the nineteenth century "the female portion of Tennessee's population . . . had an eye to the money bags." The author of "Singleton's" *Letters from the South and West* (1824) wrote of New Orleans: "It is common to ask a young gallant, who is about to marry – 'how much?' rather than – 'whom?' And too frequently do insolvent libertines come from the North to the South, to speculate into a lady's heritage."

Buckingham was impelled to say:

From all the observations I have been enabled to make . . . and from the facts I heard from others, I should think that the wealth of the respective parties about to form a matrimonial alliance, was much more frequently an object of consideration in the Southern States of America, at least, than in England, [although] no one need be deterred from marriage from a fear of being able to support themselves. There are two causes, which appear to me to lead to this state of pecuniary consideration in the marriages of the South. . . First . . . the chief, if not the only certain method, of ensuring homage or consideration from the mass of the community is the acquisition of wealth. To this, therefore, all attention is directed, and in this almost every other passion is swallowed up and absorbed. Marriage is one of the modes by which this object of universal desire may be most easily achieved; and it is therefore planned and pursued as an affair of business: and a fortunate alliance of this description is talked of as a matter of skill and good management on the part of the husband, just as a successful issue of some well-planned speculation in a commercial undertaking. Many are the instances in which a man marries two sisters, in succession, each of them very wealthy, and sometimes even a third, so rapidly do they give place to each other. A second cause of pecuniary marriages, I think, is this – that the passion of love is not felt with the same intensity by either sex . . . as even in France; still less so than in England.

A writer in the Louisville *Examiner* prior to 1850 said that the worst slaveholders were men that came from the North and married plantations and gangs of

slaves, with wives annexed.   An English traveller said
that women in South Carolina looked more to a prospective husband's means than to the probability of living happily with him.   The North Carolina University *Magazine* of 1857-1858, in an article on "Husband
Hunting" proclaimed that women were keen anglers.

Let him but waltz once or twice and his fate is sealed. A
touch of her soft hand — a glance of her bright eye smiling in
voluptuous languor — the gentle trembling pressure of her
rounded arm, resting in such innocent confidence upon his
shoulders as they whirl around the room. [But she won't
marry you unless you have money.] It requires no gift of
prophecy to foresee what must be the ultimate effect of a system of education, which sets out with the *datum* that to obtain
a rich husband is the *summum bonum* of a girl's existence —
the great end to which she is born. To bring about this consummation so devoutly wished for, she is taught from her earliest infancy that no sacrifice is too great. It is to purchase this
that she is endowed with beauty — it is for this that neither
trouble nor expense has been spared to teach her the fashionable accomplishments; it is for this that mamma is so particular
about her dress — so careful of her complexion — so anxious
about her health. She is early taught that her smiles and
glances are too precious to be wasted, and she measures them
out by rules of proportion, which, by the way, is nearly all the
arithmetic she is ever taught — as your income, so shall my af-
fability be. . . Her creed is: "I believe in elder sons, a
house in town and a house in the country, I believe in a coach
and six, diamonds, a box at the opera, *point de Bruxelles* lace,
crinoline, etc." . . No natural emotions, none of the finer
feelings find a place in such a system, neither would they flourish in such arid soil. . . Thanks to this cramping process,
to which they are subjected day by day and year by year, the
minds of most young ladies lose their elasticity altogether, and
by the time they arrive at the age for turning out as the phrase
goes (it should be trotted out), they are quite as artificial as
the most exacting parents could desire. Like the Chinese
women, whose feet are so cramped from infancy, that they become utterly useless for walking, — the minds of most of our

young ladies are so contracted, that it would be a difficult matter to determine whether they ever had any. [How would such a woman] be a help to any man – unless to help him spend his money, for which most of them show a very decided talent, and for which, indeed, their previous training peculiarly fits them. [Our woman-culture is like that of the Turks. The rest of a Trans-caucasian family eat coarse food, bathe in the river, and wear old clothes in order that a handsome daughter may be groomed for the Sultan. Similarly in America.] Have you not seen the heads of families pinching themselves and the other children to give some favored one an education beyond their means that she may marry well as they call it? Have you not been witness in your own country to a bargain and sale quite as flagrant, as any that was ever transacted in the slave market of Constantinople? My innocent friend without going fifty miles from the place where I now sit, I could cite you an instance . . . where the lovely bride was forced into the arms of a man whom she loathed – where the agonizing screams of the helpless victim were unheard amidst the musical chink of the bridegroom's dollars. . . In most cases the victim is anything but unwilling . . . it is by no means uncommon for the lady to conclude the bargain for herself – indeed I believe it is usually the case. . . "Charity covereth a multitude of sins" but money hideth them much more effectually. Dissipation of the very worst kind and an empty head – aye even disease itself is considered no drawback, if the bridegroom elect has metallic attractions sufficient.

Such is the manner in which most of our young ladies are brought up. . . Like the deadly Upas tree, its influence poisons and withers every natural emotion – dries up the very purest feelings of our nature . . . and makes the victim a mere machine, capable of moving (aye, and gracefully too), of singing divinely, of smiling sweetly, of thinking – never.

It extends to the marriage relation, and brings into contempt that which ought to be regarded as the most solemn compact into which a man can enter. . . Of this levity with which men look upon marriage, we have abundant proof in the "elopements in high life," and the numerous applications for divorce, and the readiness with which they are granted. . . Marriages of convenience, a term fit for the mouth of a liber-

tine or a fool, are the legitimate result of the art of which we
are speaking. . . As matters now stand, marriage is a luxury which is of necessity·confined to those who are comparatively rich.   And if the present state of things continues, we
may look for a large and continually increasing stock of old
bachelors and old maids, in the upper classes of society. . .

In the next volume of the same magazine an author
told that some men counted a girl's father's "niggers";
nothing counted with them but gold.

Americans prized rank as well as wealth. Sidons,
pseudonym of Sealsfield, in 1826 remarked about girls
being on the lookout for attractive foreigners. Sealsfield
in 1828 said that the ladies are prone to set off their
attractions, particularly if a foreigner of supposed rank
should appear. St. Victor in 1832 commented on the
passion of the American ladies for titles of nobility.
Macay said, near the middle of the century:

The social position of the husband is not carried, in all its extent, into the social relations of his family. . . Equality
without, exclusiveness within – such seems to be the contrasts
of American life.   The professional man may be on the very
best of terms with the blacksmith, but ten chances to one if the
daughters of the professional man know the blacksmith's daughters, or if they would acknowledge it if they did.

Carlier held that the greatest ambition of the young
American girl was to wed a title; an European of title,
however doubtful his character, could be sure of a rich
wife. "Place before her two men, one of whom has
but his noble title; and the other a man distinguished in
science, in letters, or in business, – there will be no doubt
of the young American's choice."   In his *Legalized
Prostitution*, published in 1862, Charles S. Woodruff,
M.D., asserted that when two young people contemplate matrimony

The social world looks on, with its long list of form and ceremony, warning them continually that they must be of equal

rank, as established by social order, or else public opinion will frown upon them so terribly that one or the other shall lose caste, and be banished from all intercourse in certain cliques or grades of life.

Woodruff went on to say that in the case of two young people of equal rank they put the best on the surface and were able to hide under a pleasing exterior the shallowness and hollowness of their hearts. Many alliances were contracted by the power of wealth alone — the soul being bartered for gold and the mismated couple held together in an unholy union entailing curses on the offspring. The lives of many were no better than prostitution.

> We observe, in the daily walks of life, young and fair maidenhood withering and pining away under the curse of hereditary blight, the product of disunited souls, who, living in disobedience to nature's commands, have brought forth "buds of promise" only to find, for earthly hopes, a premature grave; and on the other hand, imbecile young manhood stares us in the face at almost every turn of the street-corner having depicted upon the countenance the brand of that transgression of nature's laws which has been committed by parents and of which he remains a living witness, though entirely innocent himself.

With the rise of economic surplus and complex city life, old moral criteria lost influence. Even as early as the twenties in the nineteenth century in club-cellars of New York were found the sons of high and low enjoying oysters, drams, tobacco, and low revelry. "Thousands become morally rotten before they are ripe. The number of tippling shops is prodigious; and there is perhaps no part of the world where [it is so cheap to get drunk as in the United States]." Boys of twelve or under drink in liquor shops. The *Man* in 1834 notes that a fashionable hostess at a small party is drunk. Parents in the forties are warned against allowing children to run wild in the temptations of the streets and to loiter at night around some coffee house.[112]

The cityward drift was early a menace. Before 1820 remonstrance was made against the sending of children to the city. "Most of our small retail stores are filled thus with the sons of farmers, who, eager to escape salutary labor, and partake of the delusive pleasures of a city, are crowding to New York."[113] The old folks back home were likely to be more and more neglected. In the fifties this subject received magazine attention: a young man in the city was reluctant to visit his "old folks" in the country; it was too dull; they wanted him to stay too long; he did not go as often as he could.

The current of life was setting away from the home. New conditions augmented the new world tendency to coolness of family affection. At least as early as 1840 many husbands and sons seemed to consider home as a mere place of boarding and lodging; to provide for the physical wants of one's family was the sum of duty. "Shows, convivialities, plays, entertainments . . . do their part in turning men loose from home and breaking those hallowed social bonds which are the strong guards of virtue and the firmest barriers to vice." A thousand interests were crowding on the minds and stirring the blood of the vigorous and the young; hence home influences and restraints suffered and home contacts were circumscribed. A magazine article of the fifties presents the opinion that too many wives burn the midnight oil waiting for their husbands and alleges that many men allow societies or clubs to

[112] *Literary and Scientific Repository*, vol. i, 525-526; Cobbett. *Year's Residence in the United States*, 212; *Man*, April 30, 1834, 241; *Dwight's American Magazine*, vol. i, 268.

[113] *Ladies' Magazine* (Savannah), vol. i, 182-183, quoting New York *National Advocate*.

crowd out their wives.[114] Carlier saw in summer jaunts
a weakening of the family; the husband could visit his
wife only at intervals; the children lost home restraints.

Women of 1840 often received men that had forfeited the approval of right thinking people. "Such
ladies . . . are strong in the faith that 'a reformed
rake makes a good husband';" (but they found in
course of time that the charm was a failure). European looseness tended to creep into American society.
In the *Ladies Repository* (Cincinnati) of 1844 we learn
that Bulwer and his type were diffusing in America
ideas of European high life – sacredness of marriage
betrayed; the seducer commonly the hero, And Sue's
enormity "has been deemed a meet offering to the youth
of America!" In the same periodical in 1849 appeared
this stricture:

> That fashionable and decorated vice, which exists among the
> more pretending classes in all European communities, has not
> yet dared to obtrude itself among the American people, how-
> ever frequently instances of it may be detected under the deep
> concealments in which it is here compelled to shroud itself.
> [Yet] the almost universal aping of European fashion and gay-
> ety among us, and, above all, the imported literature and scenic
> drama, which have of late years overspread the land, threaten to
> break down the hallowed barriers that have circled the do-
> mestic purity of American life.

There was surely point to a story in *Graham's Magazine* of 1845 of a husband's neglecting his wife and
going with a scheming coquette; the wife pines and
dies. Said Milburn in the *Pioneer Preacher*:

> Mamma suggests that all young men are a little wild, but mar-
> riage cures them of that; and our young ladies think him only
> the more interesting because he is esteemed a "fast young

[114] Graves. *Woman in America*, 65, 160-164; *Arthur's Home Magazine*,
vol. vii, 123.

man." . . . You permit the seducer to lead your daughter to the altar, and give him your paternal blessing.

The domesticity of women in certain circles seemed to suffer decline. In the *Literary Focus* of 1827-1828 a man expressed a desire to marry but declared that instead of the former beautiful domestic creatures he found a set of giggling triflers, who thought chiefly of balls, carriages, and novels. They never entered the kitchen and were ignorant of domestic affairs. Husband and father were simply old fashioned furniture — in the way. Fashionable females had nothing to do but harass servants and gouge money out of husband and father.

A woman answering the indictment acknowledged the prevalence of the evils in every part of the country but blamed the men: nine times out of ten they paid more attention to the giggling nondescripts than to worthy, unassuming females. In order to get a train of admirers a girl needed to play a little, and sing affectedly, pretend to study French, have a name for having a fortune, take a journey on pretext of ill health. Most gentlemen were attracted by these things, said this lady, while qualifications of greater use were treated with ridicule.

Fanny Kemble in her *Journal of a Residence on a Georgian plantation* said:

> The democratic daughters of America . . . are, for the most part so ignorant of [sewing] that I have heard the most eloquent preacher of the city of New York advert to their incapacity in this respect as an impediment to their assistance of the poor, and ascribe to the fact that the daughters of his own parishioners did not know how to sew, the impossibility of their giving the most valuable species of help to the women of the needier classes. . . I have known young American school girls, duly instructed in the nature of the parallaxes of the stars, but, as a rule, they do not know how to darn their stockings.

In Grund's *Aristocracy in America* it was alleged that a fashionable young wife is no use save as a stimulus to industry.

Mrs. Graves charged women with overlooking home responsibilities and enjoyments or wantonly deserting them "for those of a more ostentatious character that are to be found abroad. Thus comparatively few women at the present day are content to be simply useful, and to shine in the domestic circle alone." The decline of female domesticity was attributable to the "flood of European follies" that was sweeping in; to the new ideas of woman's sphere; to the "fatal notion that there is something servile in labor;" to the desire for the "luxury of indolent leisure."

> It is not avarice that crowds our cities with those who are "making haste to be rich;" it is the desire to be lifted above the necessity of labor. . . Many of our females in their ambition to be considered "ladies" refuse to aid their toiling mothers, lest their fair hands should lose their softness and delicacy, and while using these useless appendages in playing with their ringlets, or touching the piano or guitar, they will speak with contempt of the household drudge, and boast of their lady-like ignorance of domestic employments. Many a woman of intellect, on becoming a housekeeper, finds herself . . . unprepared. . . Want of practical knowledge and the unskillfulness of inexperience cause what little strength she possesses to be ineffectually expended. . . Our women are generally less fitted for active household duties than in some countries are those even of the higher classes who are never placed under the necessity of performing them. . . [Few mothers teach their daughters how to be happy and useful at home.]

Thus idleness, the toilet, men, were displacing housekeeping. A writer in the *Ladies' Repository* (Cincinnati) of 1841 complained that mothers often entrusted their children to coarse, vulgar servants; that there was too much violent angry thrashing and sentimental indulgence.

Works of the fifties corroborate the charge against
women. Mothers do not keep their girls within bounds
and "romping giddy girls . . . become dressy, un-
companionable wives, and negligent and careless
mothers." Ladies go shopping and lunch down town
and are not good company at dinner, even if their husbands are lucky enough to find dinner ready.

> In no saloon throughout America, did I ever see any female
> even momentarily employed with children, with books, or with
> needlework. . . When an Englishwoman of whatever class,
> would have had her embroidery frame or her crochet work or
> even her novel, the American woman whether rich or poor, had
> her rocking-chair and her fan; her simper and her sigh, her
> whine and her finery.

Mrs. Bodichon said:

> I believe there is in America as strong a public opinion against
> women working for a livelihood as in England. No father in
> a "respectable class" thinks of giving his daughter a professional
> education. If he can live in some "style" he counts on his
> daughters marrying, and if he cannot, he probably sends them
> to some relative in a city, who receives them for a long visit,
> with the hope of "getting them off." Many thousands of young
> girls come to the cities to stay with brothers, uncles, or friends
> for this purpose. A worse preparation for any serious life can-
> not be conceived. Years of idleness are often passed in this
> way, years spent in nothing but driving and dissipation – and
> what does it lead to? Marriage probably: but what sort of
> marriage can be formed by young girls looking at the world
> from such a false position. . . Unless a woman can earn
> her own livelihood or has a certain income, she has little chance
> of forming an equal union.

Another said: "Can it be denied that the toilet and the
men are the two influences of absorbing interest to the
mass of young American women between the ages of
sixteen and twenty?" Catharine Sidgwick wrote:

> [Our forefathers' wives] were helpmeets. If they could not
> earn bread, they could make it. If they did not comprehend

the "rights of women" they practised her duties. If they did not study political economy and algebra, they knew the calculation by which the penny saved is the penny gained. Instead of waiting to be served by costly and wasteful Milesians they "looked well to the ways of their household, and ate not the bread of idleness." The Puritan wife did not ask her husband to be decked in French gauds.

The fact of the matter was that the new world was developing Orientalism and among the "better classes" woman was developing into a parasite. From being regarded as drudges, women "came to be admired as dolls. The first decades of the nineteenth century record this transformation." The tendency has already been affirmed for the South in connection with economic marriage and will receive explicit treatment in connection with the discussion of the southern family, but the aristocracy of the North were involving themselves in the same evil. Concerning this Mrs. Graves wrote in 1841:

"The tendency to Orientalism" is visible, too, in the false position in which woman is placed, as a being formed for no higher purpose than to be decorated, admired, and valued for her personal charm. Do we not see females in every fashionable circle who fill no loftier station in social life, and who live as idly and as uselessly as the gorgeously attired inmates of the harem. . . When we hear it said that woman should be kept "like a jewel in a casket," and listen to the soft flatteries . . . we can not help feeling the injustice that is done her. [Women thus become feeble useless things. They can not bear the trouble of taking care of children. A hired nurse or school will do. How many women fail of their full duty to their husbands!] They seem to look upon their own interests, or those of the family, as being something separate from the interests of its head. Thus they consider whatever is added to the furniture or wardrobe as so much gained, without reflecting that every superfluous expense is a sum withdrawn from the general fund to which they must all look for support. And if their husband

becomes embarrassed in business they regard these domestic ac-
quisitions as a clear saving, forgetting that the money thus laid
out may have been one of the causes of their embarrassments.
[This is natural] since so many husbands do but little to make
their wives feel their responsibility as partners. . . Men are
losers in every way by not charging their wives with the responsibility of managing the family expenditures, and by keeping
them ignorant of the limits within which they must be confined. . . Do not experience and observation ordinarily show
that the character of the wife depends more upon that of the
husband that does the husband's upon that of the wife? Man
usually does not enter into the married state until after his
character has become fixt, but woman most frequently in all
the tender pliancy of youth. . . We condemn the Chinese
for barbarously crippling the feet of their women, while we
with scarcely more humanity, and with deeper injury, cripple
in ours the growth of all that is vigorous in thought or energetic in action, by keeping them bound from infancy to maturity in habits of indolence and of helpless dependence. We
despise . . . the folly of the Turkish despot, who ab-
surdly supposes that guards and imprisonment are required to
keep women virtuous, while we, instead of relying upon the
cultivation of virtuous principles and of moral strength, adopt
the scarcely less preposterous maxims of the world, which teach
that woman's safety is in the social restrictions by which she is
surrounded.

Mrs. Bodichon in the later fifties wrote:

In no country have I been so much struck by the utter idleness of the lady class, except perhaps in the East, among the
Turks and Moors. There is in America, a large class of ladies who do absolutely nothing. . . In America – in that
noble, free, new country, it is grievous to see the old false snob-
bish idea of "respectability" eating at the heart of society, making generations of women idle and corrupt, and retarding the
onward progress of the great Republic. [In this respect, society presented great contrasts.] A great proportion of American women live indoors and do nothing; the others, again, live
indoors and do too much. There are thousands who have to
do household work, bear and nurse children, cook and wash, and

live continually indoors, often in badly built, undrained, unhealthy wooden houses, and suffer terribly. The beginning of civilization falls hard on American women. As a pendant to this, side by side, may be seen a sister, living in the midst of luxuries, which many an English lady of rank would refuse as superfluous.

The proletariat naturally was adept at imitation. Burn who spent three years among the working-classes during the war said:

> In the towns, many of the young women are ruined by vanity and false notions of personal independence. Pride of dress is rampant in all ranks, a masterly self-will sets them above advice, and there are few who will bend to paternal authority. . . Think of a workingman's partner being obliged to decorate her head with four different styles of bonnets in the course of twelve months! In the country, young women are instructed in all the household duties; but in the towns it is difficult to find a girl who can darn a pair of stockings, much less do the duties of a domestic establishment. . . I was in the company of a woman a short time ago who had left her husband because, among other things, he did not allow her more than thirteen dollars a week, out of which she had to provide food for themselves and a baby; the husband paying rent, coals, and clothing. This model wife was .the partner of a sober, hard-working man. The father has the child, and she is performing in the character of a young widow in a boarding-house in another state, two hundred miles from all her woman's heart should hold dear.

Female parasitism was in part due to man's propensity for admiring futility when he can afford to subsidize it. If American ladies became "very fond of show, adornment rather than culture," man was primarily responsible. Candler wrote prior to 1825: "If it be true, as I was several times assured, that the ladies prefer Europeans to their own countrymen, may it not be in part attributed to the superior respect paid to their understandings by the former? What sensible

young lady admires being treated as if she were only a
dressed doll?" In a ladies' magazine of 1833 occurred
a comment on "Hiring a Cook." A man found that a
cook demanded four dollars a week. He paid a boy
and a chambermaid each one dollar and twenty-five
cents. Each would cost at least two dollars a week
for board – twelve dollars and fifty cents a week in all.
His income was only fifteen hundred dollars at most.
Something was wrong. An educated man might work,

> But women who are educated must not put their hand to house-
> hold employment; tho that is all the task we assign to our fe-
> males. It would degrade a lady to be seen in her kitchen at
> work. O, how many are now sitting at ease in their parlors,
> while their husbands, fathers, brothers, or sons, are toiling like
> slaves! – and what is worse than toil, anxiously bearing a load
> of care, lest their exertions should not meet the expenses of
> their families. . . It may be the folly and pride of us men,
> after all. We want the whole command of business, the whole
> credit of management. We do not communicate to our wives
> and daughters the embarrassments we suffer, or the need we
> have of their assistance, at least, coöperation.

So he put his daughters to cooking and found it worked
like a charm. Not all men, however, were guilty of
folly. The *Ladies' Wreath* of 1848-1849 has an article
by Professor Alden of Williams College on *Gentility
and Industry* – a story of two would-be ladies, girls that
thought housework ungenteel. The hero passed them
by and married a farmer's daughter of cultivated mind.

It should be kept in mind that the status of women
in general was by no means revolutionized. Mrs.
Graves spoke of the opinion "still so current, even
among men of intellect, that a wife was intended to be
nothing higher than the obsequious ministering servant
of man – a menial without wages." Speaking of American wives Mrs. Houstoun in 1850 said: "When (as
too frequently happens) their husbands are reduced by

one unfortunate speculation from wealth and ease, to poverty and privation, then it is that their fortitude smooths the path of misfortune, and their courageous exertions lessen the force of the blow." McIntosh in 1850 remarked:

An increasing family brings increased expenditure; [retrenchment must come where the world will least see. The wife must work! The superintendent of an insane asylum in Hartford, Connecticut reports that] in many cases, not having received in early life a judicious physical or moral training for her new and arduous station, the young wife, impelled by affection and an honest pride to her utmost efforts soon finds that, with her increasing family, the burden of care and duties increases; while her physical strength and capacity for endurance diminish in even greater ratio. An economy sometimes deemed necessary, more often ill-judged and cruel, leads the husband to refrain from supplying the necessary domestic assistance; the nurse is discharged too soon and sometimes no suitable one is provided. . . Thus it must naturally follow, that between child-bearing, nursing, and the accumulation of household duties and drudgery, the poor heart-broken and disappointed wife loses, in turn, her appetite, her rest, and her strength; her nervous system is prostrated, and sinking under her burden, she seeks refuge in a lunatic hospital. This process of inducing insanity is by no means limited to the above-mentioned classes; the same thing, differing more in degree than in manner, is often seen elsewhere.

Evidently the age of conspicuous consumption was on. In his *Personal Narrative*, 1817-1818, Fordham noted that Virginia "women are pretty, languishing, made-up misses. Their chief pleasures seem to be in dressing well and in combing their long fair hair. They have most beautiful hair." In Tennessee at the same period "in the summer the girls wore Leghorn hats . . . sometimes . . . costing fifty dollars."[115] The Methodists had occasion to condemn

---

[115] Hale and Merritt. *History of Tennessee and Tennesseeans*, vol. ii, 419.

garish apparel. The desire to remain among the relatively 'luxurious scenes of the East began to lead to
various inconveniences and even to pauperism. City
stores lured women to spend lavishly. In a periodical
of 1819 occurred a quotation from a New York paper
inquiring why ladies of character and delicacy should
attire themselves in the trappings of luxury. A pros-
titute goes along Broadway with several hundred dollars of attire on her person. A New York merchant is
said to have sold a cashmere shawl to a lady in that city
for eleven hundred dollars.[116] In 1834 in Tennessee
some capes cost one hundred dollars.[117]

McMaster describes picturesquely the New York
City of 1840. Broadway of an afternoon presented "a
sight such as no other American city could show."
Barefoot girls swept the crossings and ragged urchins
vended matches and newspapers; but young beaux appeared "with Byron collars and whiskers under their
chins" and women displayed bright attire. "Heaven
save the ladies," wrote Boz, "how they dress. We have
seen more colors in these ten minutes than we could
have seen elsewhere in as many days. What various
parasols, what rainbow silks and satins, what pinching
of thin shoes, and fluttering of ribbons and silk tassels,
and display of rich cloaks with gaudy hoods and lin-
ings!" Another traveller asserted that the finery worn
by the women was astounding, "That the show of
shawls, bonnets, feathers, furs, and waists pinched almost to nothing was astonishing, and that any fine day
you could see enough velvet at four dollars a yard to
cover Broadway from one end to the other." Mc-
Master says that "Fashion and luxury were running
riot, and there were now a Ladies' Oyster Shop, a

[116] *Ladies' Magazine* (Savannah), vol. i, 14.
[117] Hale and Merritt. *History of Tennessee and Tennesseeans*, vol. ii, 420.

Ladies' Reading Room, and a Ladies' Bowling Alley with luxurious carpets and ottomans, and dressing rooms, and girls to set up the pins." [118]

The number of servants employed was continually growing. People that used to do their work often hired help. In Atlantic cities and villages "we find the wives of journeymen mechanics and laborers following . . . pernicious example set by the wealthy or those who are making a show of being such." [119]

In the absence of proper intellectual interests, fashion received inordinate attention. There was conspicuous consumption in the house. The wife made drudges of the servants. Thackeray wrote in New York: "It suffices that a man should keep a fine house, give parties, and have a daughter, to get all the world to him." Olmsted wrote in 1859:

A woman may have spent a year in learning how a loaf of bread and a dish of soup can be made, a steak broiled, and a potato boiled, in a perfectly wholesome and yet palatable manner; things which it is certain that not one American man or woman among a thousand has ever seen. . . She may have spent ten years in the study of beauty, of taste and domestic fine art, and thus possess an unfailing power of self-cheering and of elevating the lives of all in her house, and it will command for her, if her husband is a bookkeeper, or an editor, or an actor, on a small salary, less respect and less influence – for her children, less exterior social advantages – than the woman with no solid acquirements will possess, if her husband is able to pay one thousand dollars rent for a stone veneered dwelling, and furnish a stylish carriage for her to send cards from.

Perhaps I am wrong in saying that this is so. I believe in New York it is not so. But such is the general opinion, and by this unfortunate opinion the mass of young minds are ruled. . . There are . . . so few houses built in our towns with prime regard to health and simple convenience, and

[118] McMaster. *History of the People of the United States* (1910), vol. vii, 75-77.
[119] Graves. *Woman in America*, 84.

there are so few of us sufficiently educated as purveyors and cooks, to provide a palatable variety of good food, except at a wasteful expense, that a large income is really made necessary for a merely wholesome and comfortable family life.

Stirling in his *Letters from the Slave States* declared:

The dresses of American women generally, at least of the new rich class, are something fabulous in expense. . . The dresses of ladies in New Orleans, I am told (and by New Orleans people) are often equal [to] those of your crowned heads. . . Ladies [in that city] think nothing of expending a large proportion of the profits of a year's trade on a few dresses. . . [Husband] works, or speculates, and his wife wears the *spolia opima*. [Land in America is too cheap to create adequate social distinction. Your wife's back is the only place to display your wealth.]

As has already been indicated, reckless expenditure brought many families to disaster. A magazine of 1819 cited the New York *National Advocate* to the effect that New York merchants were failing. Some of their houses had been furnished equal to those of the British nobility. Several of the bankrupts had spent ten thousand dollars per year for ten years in houses, carriages, and wines. A merchant would rent a house for one thousand or twelve hundred dollars.

Why will families plunge themselves in ruin, merely to live a few years in luxury? . . . While . . . amiable wives are . . . anxiously struggling to get rid of their husbands' money, their husbands . . . are toiling in the sun, borrowing, at large premiums, in Wall St., and doing all to preserve their credit, while their unthinking companions are plunging them into deeper difficulties. . . Why buy a plated soup tureen for forty dollars? – will not one of china for five dollars do full as well – [other things likewise]. The eccentricities of fashion are ruining families by wholesale.

In the same magazine was this statement:

I was told that several bankruptcies occurred lately in Baltimore, among merchants who had foolishly lived like nabobs –

and I also heard, that their wives and daughter behaved
well . . . and resigned their luxuries and extravagancies
without a sigh.[120]

The New York *Literary Gazette* in 1825 contained
warning against wifely expensiveness. In the *Ladies'
Magazine* (Boston) of 1830 fortune was said to be precarious in America. "Family wealth" was relatively
unknown. "Marriage settlements, properly speaking,
are almost unknown." People were reckless. Extravagant women, lavishing large sums on foolish finery or
extravagant housekeeping, were exhorted to remember
this. In Grund's *Aristocracy in America* it was said:

> With us, where young men without fortunes marry, at the age
> of twenty-one, girls of eighteen that have no money either,
> where the husband relies solely on his wits for supporting his
> wife and children, but few men can indulge themselves in reck-
> less expenditure without growing indifferent as to the ways
> and means of paying their debts. . . With all the morality,
> virtue, and beauty of our women, they are but helpless crea-
> tures. The wife of one of our young "merchants of respect-
> ability" requires more waiting than, in proportion to her rank,
> an English peeress; and, ten chances to one, does not even un-
> derstand superintending her servants. The husband has to
> take care of his household.

Craving for finery resulted in reckless speculation
and ruin. "Witness the innumerable instances," said
Mrs. Graves, "of families by these causes plunged from
affluence into the depths of poverty." *Graham's Magazine* of 1843 gave a story of a "Decayed Family."
The father demanded retrenchment. The family was
extravagant; he as bad as they. They did, however,
cut down expenses. Finally failure came. In the
Ladies' Repository (Cincinnati) of 1845, a minister
wrote: "Many a husband and father is being made

[120] *Ladies' Magazine* (Savannah), vol. i, 137, 138, 156.

bankrupt by female extravagance. [Some ladies even boast ignorance of domestic science.]" Greeley in 1850 said:

> Half the men who are loathed as dragging down their families to shame and destitution are really themselves dragged down by those families – driven to bankruptcy, shame, and crime by the thoughtless and basely selfish extravagance of wife and children. Let a man be in the way of receiving considerable money, and having property in his hands, and his family can rarely be made to comprehend and realize that there is any limit to his ability to give and spend. . . The man of means or of business is too often regarded by his family as a sponge to be squeezed, a goose to be plucked, an orange to be sucked. . . Not one of them could bear to disgrace him by earning a dollar; they couldn't go out shabbily drest, for fear his credit would suffer.

The husband was often to blame nevertheless in that he did not make his wife acquainted with his affairs. One writer had said: "Her husband's hair stands on end at the idea of her working, and he toils to indulge her with money." Another wrote in a magazine of 1852:

> [She] knows nothing – has not even an idea of her husband's fortune. . . She spends, as a matter of course, all he gives her to spend with the full confidence that when that is gone, and she asks for it, he will give her more. . . Many a wife who is plunging her husband deeper and deeper into debt through ignorance, would, if she knew his embarrassment be the first to retrench [and] help . . . reinstate his falling fortunes.

It is easy to imagine how children were reared in the circles of economic surplus. Timothy Dwight as early as 1821 asserted that

> People of fashion in Boston and elsewhere often try to make their children objects of admiration. Children are brought into the presence of guests for praise and show off. Children learn that the end of their efforts and existence is appearance

only. Girls are taught to regard dress as a momentous concern. Girls are reared in romance and unreality.

Children came to be neglected. Grund said: "The education of the children is only at the extreme North and South . . . superintended personally by the mother."

According to Mrs. Graves, an oft-repeated American maxim was: "Girls should enjoy themselves while single, because, poor things, they will have trouble enough when they are married." A young lady remarked: "I do not know how some of my acquaintances find time to do their own sewing; mine is wholly taken up in dressing myself, paying morning calls, and sitting on the sofa to receive my visitors." Through the eyes of Mrs. Graves:

> We see mothers toiling on from day to day; overwhelmed with the pressure of domestic cares; wearing out their life and shortening its natural period by exertions to which their age and failing strength are wholly inadequate; and who still permit their daughters to waste their hours in idleness or in trifling occupations, and neglect to call upon them for that assistance they so much need. . . We often see aged fathers, whose few remaining locks are whitened by the many years that have passed over them, still treading with trembling steps the same fatiguing round of business duties, while their sons are, perhaps, rioting in dissipation or living in indolence, on the means thus painfully accumulated; and many, many a toil-spent. "time-worn mother," too, still hastening with anxious solicitude to answer every call for every member of the family, as if her part in the duties of life was not only to have waited upon her children in infancy but to conduct them to an easy and luxurious old age; in short to spare their feet from walking, their hands from labor, and their heads from thought. . . Look around upon the groups of young females who crowd our private parties or public balls; who lounge upon the sofa receiving visits, or throng the city promenades to exhibit their decorated persons or to make morning

calls, and how many can you point out among them who have fulfilled one useful purpose of existence to themselves to their families or to society. And all this waste of time and energy in the pursuit of folly is in the hope of becoming thereby candidates for matrimony, while by this very means they are unfitting themselves for the situation they are seeking to attain.

Coxe said in 1842:

I apprehend great and almost incalculable evil has been produced by this ambitious feeling, so prevalent among the mothers of America. If we look around on every side, we behold innumerable examples of women, who are practicing self-denial and enduring privation, not in reality to train their children for the stations to which God has appointed them, but to educate them above the place which they will probably be called on to fill; and who have thus, strictly speaking, been the enemies and not the true friends of the objects of their affections.

Probably in this last instance we must blame the inadequacy of means for real education. Parents themselves had been poorly educated and according to Duncan (1852), at an examination of their children often exhibited weariness when the subjects of investigation were solid.

In no country shall we find more lovely examples of cheerful domestic union, or more honorable and self-denying exertion on the part of the parents, in sharing and lightening the studies of their children . . . but, in the ever-changing mass of people in the maritime and commercial cities, such steadfast and enlightened characters are far from being the majority.

Hotel and boarding-house life constituted a striking phenomenon of the generation before the Civil War.[121] Numerous causes contributed to this abandonment of

[121] Holmes. *Account of the United States*, 355; Martineau. *Society in America*, vol. iii, 132-135; Grund. *Aristocracy in America*, vol. i, 125; Arfwedson. *The United States and Canada*, vol. i, 33-34; Von Raumer. *America and the American People*, 500; Maury. *Englishwoman in America*, part i, 193, 196-197; Mackay. *Western World*, vol. i, 220-221; Duncan. *America as I found it*, 161-174; Bunn. *Old England and New England*, 37-42; Milburn. *Pioneer Preacher*, 165; Bodichon. *Women and Work*, 16-20; Grattan. *Civil-*

the home: boys and girls marrying before they were ready for the cares and troubles of housekeeping took to boarding; the possibility of this course encouraged early marriage. Young married people constituted a large part of the clientele of the boarding establishments. The life was livelier than could be found in the seclusion of a home, and attracted young women still in giddy girlhood. It was a comfort to have no housework or other duties; plenty of time was available for amusements. In addition, boarding was thought to be more economical than housekeeping; it was sometimes hard to get houses, and rents were in some cases excessive. The high standard of living of the "better" class made housekeeping too expensive for persons of limited means. "I know many an American that is now living in Europe merely because he does not wish to board, and is not rich enough to keep house according to our expensive fashion," said one person before 1840. The scarcity, uncertainty, and difficulty of managing servants was another contributing factor. Almost any city family, even the wealthiest, might, at some time, try this manner of life. Probably the responsibility lay chiefly with the wives. This careless public existence often continued from a couple's youth to their maturity and might even be resumed after a period of housekeeping. Even in the South the usage found entry. Stirling in *Letters from the Slave States* wrote from New Orleans that "the St. Charles Hotel . . . is a characteristic picture of American life." Owing to the scarcity and unsatisfactory quality of servants, he said, it was natural for the American girl-wife to seek refuge in a hotel. Another contribu-

ized America, vol. i, 109-113; Oldmixon. *Transatlantic Wanderings*, 37; Mackay. *Life and Liberty in America*, 30-34.

tory factor was the feebleness of the domestic tie between parents and children in America. According to Stirling, the young American on reaching self-support left home for a neighboring hotel. In summer, northern hotels were full of planters and their families; in the winter, the reverse occurred. Planters spent one or more weeks or months in winter with their families at New Orleans. "In every large town in the United States," said Mrs. Bodichon, "There are five or six (in some places twenty or more) large hotels or boarding-houses containing several hundred inhabitants each. This hotel population mainly consists of families who live altogether in hotels."

It goes without saying that in hotels and boarding-houses real family life was impossible. The women were free to gossip, and having nothing else to do, were prone to enjoy this freedom. Conditions were highly unfavorable to the character and happiness of young couples; there was little of the essential privacy; what should have been family secrets became public property, and differences between husband and wife were complicated by the "sympathy" of meddlesome onlookers. The life ministered to selfishness, laziness, and vanity in the women or to positive vice; it offered no training for home-making, but rather tended to beget carelessness and want of forethought. Mrs. Bodichon said:

These [hotel] "ladies" have not the cultivation which glosses over the lives of so many women in Europe, and does give them some solid value in society as upholders of the arts and literature, but are generally very ignorant and full of the strangest affectations and pretentions. The young ladies, especially, reminded me of certain women I have seen in Seraglios, whose whole time was taken up in dressing and painting their faces; with this difference, the ladies of the East spend their days in adorning themselves to please one lord and master – the ladies of the West to please all the lords of creation.

Especially was the homeless life pernicious for the children on account of unsuitable food, excitement, and the promiscuous associations of life in public.

The dangers of female parasitism even outside of hotel life were arousing discussion. In the period before the War the importance of giving women a means of livelihood independent of marriage was discussed by the press. The necessity of greater activity among women was urged vehemently by the newspapers in the belief that "the health of the mothers of men . . . is deteriorating in America in consequence of the extreme idleness and luxury in which the ladies live." Women were menials or idlers in too many cases. For want of discipline of the mind "large numbers of our married women degenerate into housekeeping drudges or drones, with scarce a thought above cooking and dusting, fall into scandalmongering, or what is worse into the wretched and painful boarding-house life of towns and cities, sink into intrigue, wantonness, and destruction." Professions for the idle hotel-women "are necessary to save their souls from the devil, and to save their husbands, too, from that terrible treadmill, that 'everlasting grind' in which American men live."

It must be remembered in retrospect of the ground so far covered in this volume that new world influences, the rise of industrialism, and the development of urban luxury were contemporaneous. The first factor was, indeed, soonest in the field, and the last was largely a matter of the generation before the Civil War, but in order to understand that generation the three factors must be thought together. In a sense the latter two were different phases of the same thing; exploitation and parasitism at opposite poles, but alike wrecking the family. During the period so far covered, the special advantages of the new continent began to be of less significance in shaping institutions, and the artificial processes of commercialism and industrialism came to play an increasing rôle. In some particulars the three factors tended in the same direction, e. g., in the matter of unsettling family traditions. On the whole, however, the influence exerted directly by the conditions of the developing continent was wholesome while the earlier manifestations of the new economic forces of industrialism, though not without their redeeming features, were ominous. By the time of the Civil War, the problem of the family had assumed, at least in outline, the character that it wears to-day. Before studying the consequences of that struggle upon the family, it is necessary to examine in some detail the distinctive features of the family in the old South.

XI. NEGRO SEX AND FAMILY RELATIONS IN THE ANTE-BELLUM SOUTH

During the period covered in this volume the South was becoming more unlike the North. The senescence of chatteldom expressed itself in institutions markedly different from those that nascent capitalism bestowed upon the North; different also from the usages of the new West. How much the new world movement and the counter-trend of industrial exploitation affected the civilization of the Slave States may be better estimated after a specific survey of the old South.

Of family life in the old South, as indeed of all the social institutions, the suzerain was Slavery. The chattel system avenged by its pollutions the exploitation embodied in it. The threshold to our study of the vaunted family life of the South must be a study of the sex and family relations of the slave race. These were extramoral phenomena – the behavior of irresponsible cattle. If the blacks were gross and bestial, so would our race be under a like bondage; so it is now when driven by capitalism to the lower levels of misery. The allegedly superior morality of the master race or class is not an inherent trait but merely a function of economic ease and ethical tradition.

In some cases, negro-breeding was carried on like that of animals. A Charleston advertisement of negroes for sale stated "they were purchased for stock and breeding negroes, and to any planter who particularly wanted them for that purpose, they are a very choice and desirable gang." Another notice read: "For Sale—a Girl about twenty-nine years of age, raised, in Virginia, and her two female children. . . She is very prolific in her generating qualities, and affords a magnificent opportunity to any man who wishes to raise a family of healthy niggers for his own use."[122]

When a young man had a fine family the planter very often forced him to serve as a stallion. A gentleman interrogated a fine-looking fugitive slave as to why he had run away. The man was slow to reply: said he was not cruelly treated but did not like his work. When pressed to explain he reluctantly said that he had been kept "as a breeding man, in order to improve the stock of little niggers for the market. . . Similar statements are whispered from other quarters."[123]

A "Stranger in America" wrote in 1807 that the negresses were valued for their fecundity. "The infant slave is generally valued at a year's service of the mother, and as she is compelled to work, three parts of the time she is breeding and nursing, planters are very attentive to this mode of enhancing the value of their estates." In Virginia it was common for planters to command girls and women to have children. On a Carolina plantation of about one hundred slaves the owner threatened to flog all of the women to death because they didn't breed. "They told him they could not while they had to work in rice ditches (in one or two feet of water). After swearing and threatening he told them to tell the overseer's wife, when they got in that way, and he would put them on the land to work."

In 1832 ex-governor Randolph of Virginia protested against the state's being made a slave breeding menag-

---

[122] *Documentary History of American Industrial Society*, vol. ii, 57-58; *Suppressed Book about Slavery*, 175.

[123] Noel. *Freedom and Slavery in the United States*, 87; Newman. *Character of the Southern States of America*, 8-9.

erie.[124]   Olmsted found that most gentlemen of character in Virginia objected to discussing the slave-trade and that it was denied warmly that slaves are often bred for sale.   But "that a slave woman is commonly esteemed . . . most for those qualities which give value to a brood-mare is . . . constantly made apparent."   A slave-holder wrote him:

> In . . . Maryland, Virginia, North Carolina, Kentucky, Tennessee, and Missouri as much attention is paid to the breeding and growth of negroes as to that of horses and mules.   Further South we raise them both for use and for market.   Planters command their girls and women (married or unmarried) to have children; and I have known a great many negro girls to be sold off because they did not have children.   A breeding woman is worth from one-sixth to one-fourth more than one that does not breed.[125]

An admixture of white blood tended to improve the breed.   About the end of the eighteenth century in Virginia an orphan white girl was indentured to a man who died insolvent and left her thus in the hands of a creditor.   He treated her as a slave and compelled her to cohabit with a negro, by whom she had several children.   After long litigation she and her children were declared free.   Obviously profit-seeking abetted sensuality; for, said Ferrall in 1832 "if the offspring . . . be a handsome female, from eight hundred to one thousand dollars may be obtained for her in the Orleans market.   It is an occurrence of no uncommon nature to see the Christian father sell his own daughter, and the brother his own sister."   One planter offered a white man twenty dollars for every impregnation of a female slave—his purpose being to improve the breed.   Elliott remarked that

Great solicitude is often manifested that the breeding wenches,

---

[124] Wyse. *America, its Realities and Resources*, vol. ii, 8-9.
[125] Olmsted. *Cotton Kingdom*, vol. i, 57-58.

as they call them, should be the mothers of mulatto children, as the nearer the young slaves approach to white the higher will their price be, especially if they are females. . . Some affirm that rewards are sometimes given to white males, who will consent to be the fathers of mulattoes.

Newman remarked that "the master's licentiousness does but breed for him a peculiarly valuable stock of cattle."[126] Tradition still lingers of the importation of college boys from the North to spend a profitable summer improving the slave breed.

There seem, however, to have been circumstances (probably altered market conditions) that sometimes worked against such miscegenation. Marryat in 1837-1838 recorded that planters of Virginia and other eastern states did not encourage intercourse with negresses.

[Young men visitors] cannot affront them more than to take notice of their slaves, particularly the lighter colored, who are retained in the house and attend upon their wives and daughters. Independent of the moral feeling which really guides them (as they naturally do not wish that the attendants of their daughters should be degraded) it is against their interest in case they should wish to sell; as a mulatto or light male will not fetch as high a price as a full-blooded negro; the cross between the European and the negro, especially the first cross . . . is of a sickly constitution, and quite unable to bear up against the fatigue of field labor in the West. As the race becomes whiter, the stamina is said to improve.

Slave conditions furnished facilities for spontaneous sensuality. Mr. Jefferson said that the negroes "are more ardent after their females," but an anonymous commentator added: "If they appear so (though I am by no means satisfied of the fact) I think it may be

126 Abdy. *Journal of a Residence and Tour in the United States*, vol. iii, 9-10; Ferrall. *Ramble of Six Thousand Miles through the United States*, 195; American Anti-slavery Society. *American Slavery as it is*, 16; Elliott. *Sinfulness of American Slavery*, vol. i, 154; Newman. *Character of the Southern States of America*, 7.

fairly ascribed to the greater facilities of indulging a criminal intercourse which their manners, morals, and mode of living impose upon the violence of their passions." Yet "love seems with them to be more an eager desire, than a tender, delicate mixture of sentiment and sensation." Carolinians said: "Oh, there is no danger of a *nigger* being at a loss for a wife, or a *wench* in finding a husband upon any estate." Slaves paired at discretion and the more children the better for the master. In 1834 Mr. Seabrook of South Carolina said:

> In general, the intercourse between servants is as unrestrained as the most unbounded ambition could desire. The daily business of the plantation having been finished . . . the master . . . knows not, and apparently cares not, in what way the hours of the night are passed by his people.

A man who spent some time in the South in 1837-1838 said: "I have seen from forty to sixty, male and female, at work in a field, many of both sexes . . . entirely naked—who did not exhibit signs of shame more than cattle." Many slaves worked, especially in summer, with only a breech-clout. Clothes were often so torn as not to serve common decency. Women worked in warm weather clad in a short petticoat with some covering for their breasts. Slave huts were ordinarily small and cramped. Men, women, and children often lay down together. Sometimes persons of both sexes were thrown together without regard to family relations. Görling said that when a negress became a mother, the father generally treated her as wife; the master would "set them up."

The promiscuities of chatteldom must have spread disease among both races. A Georgia overseer wrote to his employer that two negroes

> Are down with the venereal disease, Die and Sary. Doctor Jenkins has been attending Die four weeks and very little al-

teration as I can learn. It is very hard to get the truth but from what I can learn Sary got it from Friday. I have got Mr. Broughton now to doctor those that are yet to take it as I have been informed he is a very good hand.

At the bottom is a note, probably by the owner: "Friday is the house servant sent to Retreat every summer. I have all the servants examined before they leave Savannah." In view of the miscegenation detailed in the following chapter, one is prompted to surmise that the proverbial "delicacy" of the ladies of the South may have been, at least in some measure, the result of venereal disease contracted from their self-indulgent husbands.

It should not be supposed, however, that negro sex relations went entirely uncensored. Some masters restrained sex relations in order to prevent irregularities that might hurt male labor or female fecundity. Large owners often refused to allow marriage off the place. An essay on management of slaves written by Robert Collins of Macon, Georgia and printed in many southern papers, says that marriage abroad should be avoided as it tends to trouble.

They cannot live together as they ought, and are constantly liable to separation. . . Many of them look upon their obligation to each other very lightly; but in others, again, is found a degree of faithfulness, fidelity, and affection, which owners admire; and hence they always dislike to separate those manifesting such traits.

Sentiment was a precarious safeguard however. The St. Louis *Republican* in 1854 reported the complaint of a free negress that her husband has taken another wife. "As the subject of the second marriage is a slave, and some fears being entertained that he might take her out of the state to the injury of the master, the City Marshall sent some police officers . . . and had him arrested."

Slave marriage was likely to involve the master's consent. Maryland forbade ministers to marry slaves without the owner's consent, under penalty of a heavy fine. In North Carolina free negroes were forbidden to cohabit with slaves without the written consent of the master and in 1830 even the master's consent was made ineffectual. Of course slaves could have no legal marriage and often there was not even a marriage form. The reverend Mr. Long, a Maryland man, said just before the War: "Masters seldom attach any importance to the marriage of their slaves. This is shown by refusing to give the slave money to pay his marriage fee."

Favorite house servants might be honored with a pompous ceremony in the great house under the auspices of the white folks. Often there was a negro wedding at the holidays. The master might officiate, or a colored preacher might perform the ceremony in the quarters. "It was a gay occasion, and the dusky bride's trousseau had been arranged by her young mistress, and the family was on hand to get fun out of the entertainment, and to recognize by their presence the solemnity of the tie." In some cases proper ceremony was a requirement of the master, who provided the partners.

The tie was as easily undone as formed. Unless the master enforced the bond a slave could leave his wife when he tired of her. There was little to emphasize the sanctity of the marital relation. Yet Hildreth asserts that "more husbands and wives among the slaves are separated by the hammer of the auctioneer, than by the united influence of infidelity, disgust, or the desire of change." Yet a

Gay carpenter's wife was a woman of serious sentiments. . . They did not agree very well. . . She had informed her owner that, if he would like to take her into the country with him, she had no particular objections to being separated from her husband . . . he was "so gay."

A mother of thirteen children left their father and went with another man. A maid in South Carolina preferred to go to Alabama with her mistress who married, rather than stay with her husband. She got a new man. On the occasion of a contemplated visit to the old place she laughed as she spoke of probably meeting her old husband. An overseer when asked whether marital partners were true to each other laughed heartily and "described a disgusting state of things. Women were almost common property, though sometimes the men were not all inclined to acknowledge it; for when I asked: 'Do you not try to discourage this?' the overseer answered: 'No, not unless they quarrel.'" The wife of an Alabama pastor says that a certain Colly could not be made to see the guilt of forsaking his lawful wife and taking another. She was too extravagant he said and he left her for some better-off nigger. He was distressed at offending his master but his conscience was clear.

> Not one in a thousand, I suppose, of these poor creatures have any conception whatever of the sanctity of marriage; nor can they be made to have; yet, strange to say, they are perfect models of conjugal fidelity and devotion while the temporary bondage lasts. I have known them to walk miles after a hard day's work, not only occasionally, but every night, to see the old woman, and cut her wood for her, etc. But to see the coolness with which they throw off the yoke is diverting in the extreme.

This lady was amused at an attempt of a negro woman to discard her husband. The reverend Doctor Mallard, however, writing on plantation life says: "There were as many faithful husbands and wives, we believe, as are to be found among the working white population in any land." Jealousy was operative. A mulatto child was born to a black cook in Tennessee. Her husband hated the child and threatened her life so that she had to be sent away. Such facts were frequent.

Of course slaves could have no guarantee of family ties. There was no such thing as legitimacy of children. The attorney-general of Maryland declared: "A slave has never maintained an action against the violation of his bed. A slave is not admonished for incontinence, or punished for fornication or adultery—never prosecuted for bigamy. . ." Marriage was a temporary contract dissoluable at any time at the caprice of the master. Booker Washington wrote:

> In the days of slavery not very much attention was given to . . . family records – that is, black family records. . . Of my father I know even less than of my mother. I do not even know his name. I have heard reports to the effect that he was a white man who lived on one of the near-by plantations. . . I never heard of his taking . . . interest in me or providing in any way for my rearing.

The full property right of the master involved, of course, the right to break up families and sell the members apart, and this right was frequently exercised. When Miss Martineau asked a southern lady, "Is it possible that you pair and part these people like brutes?" the lady looked surprised and asked what else could be done. When slave mothers wished to keep their children quiet they threatened them with the negro buyer. One woman had three husbands sold from her in three years by reason of the straightened circumstances of the master. A fugitive slave from Kentucky complained that his "wife was sold at a great price to a French profligate for vile purposes." There was related the case of a quinteroon daughter of a Scotchman who thought himself legally married. Nine children were kept in slavery. Delia, in sight of brother and mother, was brutally whipped because she would not submit to a new master's lust. When he could not prevail he sold her to a New Orleans brothel. Her beauty attracted a Frenchman who took her to Mexico, emancipated, and married her. One master was for five years doubtful about selling a man and would not let him marry a woman because he did not like to part husband and wife. Meanwhile the pair had four children. A violent negro wife tried to kill her husband with an axe. The master sold her to a New Orleans trader in order to get her away but he sold her to a nearby planter. She threatened to kill any girl her husband might take; so he had to stay single till her death. One negro man and wife about to be separated committed suicide. A young mulatto girl, favorite of her master and disposed of on his marriage, did likewise when she found that she was not being taken to her mother as promised. At New Orleans a doctor bought an old woman over sixty, mother of twenty-one children, all of whom at different times had been sold in the New Orleans market. In order to induce her to leave home quietly she was told that she would be put with some of her children. "And no," she said, "aldo I suckle my massa at dis breast, yet now he sell me to sugar planter after he sell all my children away from me." At Yorkville, South Carolina, a negress was executed for murdering her child. She did it because she was going to be sold away from her little one. An old man besought a lady with tears to buy his little boys, as his master was about to sell them to Louisiana where he could never see them again. The lady did not want them; so they were carried off. A St. Louis master sold a slave to a driver. Determined not to part from a beloved wife, he said to a prospective purchaser: "If you buy me you must buy my wife too.   [Then] I will willingly go.   But if you don't I shall never be of any use to you."   Repelled, he cut his throat.   In another case the wife became a raving maniac.

Heartrending scenes occurred at slave auctions where families were separated.   A train passenger described pitiful parting of wives and husbands sold apart, at which none of the passengers expressed sympathy.

> Young ladies, daughters of slaveholders, well educated, connected with refined families, were in the cars, but they did not seem to pity the poor despairing slaves.   They laughed at them and ridiculed their expressions of grief.   "Look out here," said one to a schoolmate opposite, "just see those niggers! What a rumpus they are making!   Just as if niggers cared anything about their babies!   See Cuffee kiss Dinah!   What a taking on!   Likely as not he will have another wife next week."

In 1835 the Presbyterian Synod of Kentucky published an address to their churches as follows:

> Brothers and sisters, parents and children, husbands and wives, are torn asunder and permitted to see each other no more. These acts are daily occurring in the midst of us.   The shrieks and agony often witnessed on such occasions proclaim with a trumpet tongue, the iniquity of our system.   There is not a neighborhood where these heartrending scenes are not displayed; there is not a village or road that does not behold the sad procession of manacled outcasts, whose mournful countenances tell that they are *exiled by force*, from all that their hearts hold dear.

A pamphlet on Virginia described slaves driven along fastened by iron chains "attended by a black woman, a reliance on whose conjugal or sisterly affection prevented the application of handcuffs or neck collars."

Professor Andrews, sometime of the University of South Carolina, inquired of a slave-trader near Washington, "Do you often buy the wife without the husband?"   "Yes, very often; and frequently too they sell me the mother while they keep the children. I have often known them to take away the infant from its mother's breast, and keep it whilst they sold her." Farmers near Washington bred slaves like cattle for market and cared no more for mother's agony than for the lowing of a cow. A standing advertisement in Charleston papers read: "Several small boys without their mother." A Georgia female slave had a child by one of the master's visitors. When the child grew up, it was thought desirable for its father's sake to send it away. The mother threatened to sulk and kill the boy. Accordingly she was sold to west Georgia and the boy to South Carolina. "Such separations," says Buckingham, "are quite common, and appear to be no more thought of, by those who enforce them, than the separation of a calf from its . . . parent."

White citizens of North and East often kidnapped negro children and sold them south. Many families of free colored people in free states mourned over relatives who had suddenly disappeared—presumably kidnapped and sold.[127]

Apologists for slavery tried to condone the separation of relatives by comparing it with similar phenomena among free peoples. Thus the laborer places his children to service, many persons left home for the gold regions, and "many in Europe have abandoned their families for Australia, or the United States, or the Canadas." We are told that in practice there was no more separation of children from parents in chatteldom than in New England families whose children as a rule scattered all over the earth. In the writings of a traveller of the early forties we read that "members of the same family of negroes are not so much scattered as are

---

[127] Hood. *United States Constitution and Socialism*, 23; American and foreign Anti-slavery Society. *Tenth Annual Report*, 86.

those of workingmen in Scotland, whose necessities compel them to separate at an age when the American slave is running about gathering health and strength." A northern man thought that "probably in no slave state were there more voluntary separations of husbands and wives among the slaves than in some of the New England states that could be specified for the same period."

The influence of the slave system and the attendant lack of fundamental morality was disastrous to organized religion among both whites and blacks. In general, the clergy were the chattels of the slave power and had to acquiesce in the evil; so that some even came to accept it as right. In Kentucky "in the kitchen of the minister a slave man was living in open adultery with a slave woman" church-member while the slave's wife was on the minister's farm at another place. The minister had had to bring a cook but instead of bringing the man's wife he had brought this other woman. The pastor of an Alabama church had two families of slaves, one pair of whom had been married by a negro preacher. The wife's owner robbed the man of his wife. The other pair lived in concubinage. Both were church-members. Some ministers added a farcical clause to the marriage formula when used on slaves. The reverend Mr. Smith of Sumter County, Alabama, added to "death" "some other cause beyond your control. . ." One Baptist association formally decided that a slave might lawfully have several wives — that if a slave were sold off a plantation ten, twenty, or thirty miles or more, and took another woman, it would not injure his standing in the Baptist church. An Alabama gentleman, questioned regarding the chastity of the so-called pious slaves, admitted that four negro women had borne children in his own house though all were church-members in good standing and none had a husband. The only negro man in the house was also a church-member but the gentleman believed him to be the father of the four children. He said further that he did not know of more than one negro woman whom he could suppose to be chaste, though hosts were members of churches. It was common for a female slave to change husbands and yet retain her church fellowship. In Missouri "most of the churches admitted that the removal of either party sundered the marriage bond."[128]

Not all ministerial consciences rested easy. The Synod of Kentucky (a state where slavery had a precarious hold) confessed in 1834 that

The system produces general licentiousness among the slaves. Marriage, as a civil ordinance, they cannot enjoy. . . Until slavery waxeth old, and tendeth to decay, there cannot be any legal recognition of the marriage rite, or the enforcement of its consequent duties. For, all the regulations on this subject would limit the master's absolute right of property in the slaves. In his disposal of them he could no longer be at liberty to consult merely his own interest. . . Their present quasi marriages are continually . . . voided [at the master's pleasure]. They are, in this way, brought to consider their matrimonial alliances as things not binding, and they act accordingly. We are then assured by the most unquestionable testimony that licentiousness is the necessary result of our system.

In the Lexington *Luminary* of the same period appeared the following:

Chastity is no virtue among them; its violation neither injures female characters in their own estimation, nor in that of their

[128] American Anti-slavery Society. *American Slavery as it is*, 47, 180; Blanchard and Rice. *Debate on Slavery*, 61; Olmsted. *Cotton Kingdom*, vol. ii, 227; American Anti-Slavery Society. *First Annual Report*, 17; Trexler. *Slavery in Missouri*, 87.

master and mistress. No instruction is ever given, no censure pronounced. I speak not of the world. I speak of Christian families generally.

Bishop Polk strove to preserve the sanctity of family life among his servants. He christened their babies and gave them a ceremonial wedding in his own home. If a couple were guilty of misconduct with each other they were compelled to marry but without a wedding feast. A Catholic bishop in 1860 wrote: "Marriage is scarcely known among [the slaves]; the masters attach no importance to it. We can judge of the disorders which must result from such a state of things in a race greatly addicted to the pleasures of the senses." A Unitarian minister of St. Louis wrote indignantly that "the sham service which the law scorned to recognize was rendered by the ministers of the gospel of Christ." He adds that a religious ceremony was "according to slavery usage in well regulated Christian families." The Catholic church in Missouri regularly married slaves and held the tie to be as sacred as any other marriage. One priest stated that Catholics never sold their slaves and thus avoided the severing of church marriages. Record shows, however, that Catholic families bought and sold many slaves.

At an annual Methodist Conference in Georgia about 1850 resolutions were passed in substance as follows:

The preachers are instructed to require the colored members under their charge, who may hereafter take a husband or a wife, to be married in due form by an ordained preacher or authorized officer of law, provided the master do not object. When church-members have heretofore agreed to be man and wife, or may hereafter be married, they are not to be allowed, voluntarily, to separate, except for Scriptural causes.

In North Carolina "the marriage of slaves, whatever the law might say, was held [by the Baptists] to be binding before God, and not to be broken if it could be avoided." Of course it would have been too much to expect the church to attack the system effectively at the potent end.

Apologists for slavery tried to put the best face forward. An article of 1844 said:

> It is in the memory of many persons, that [the negroes] considered clothes as an inconvenient encumbrance, that they were often almost at the age of puberty, seen in·a state of perfect nakedness. . . A feeling of self-respect has been inspired, and this has brought with it pride of character, modesty, chastity. . . The proportion of females of irreproachable virtue is perhaps not greater in the lowest class in any form of society; while those who put away shame and give themselves up to licentious practices are as effectually put out of better society among them as among us. Many are still betrayed into youthful indiscretion, but the connubial tie is now commonly held sacred. There is an increasing disposition to consecrate it by solemnities, and to strengthen it by the obligations of religion. The Episcopal minister of the village in which I live, celebrates the rites of matrimony between as many blacks as whites; the white members of the family, with their most intimate friends, sometimes witness the ceremony. . . Even admitting, that, in the essential quality of female purity, the slave may come short of the class which fills the same place in society where slavery is not known; yet it is . . . with the negro, in his primitive state of wild freedom, that the comparison is to be made. The improvement in this respect is moreover progressive. At intervals of ten or a dozen years a change may be distinctly seen to have taken place, and but little further progress is wanting to place the once degraded and brutish race on a level in this respect with the lower classes of society in the most moral country under the sun.[129]

Negro slaves married early and sometimes often. There were no costly preparations to be considered and no ambition of the bride for a mansion. One reminis-

---

[129] *Effect of the Relation between the Caucasian Master and the African Slave*, 336.

cent gentleman remembered "but two negro bachelors. I believe they only remained [so] for a season." A Mississippi planter said: "They don't very often get married for good . . . without trying each other, as they say, for two or three weeks, to see how they are going to like each other."

Demand for slaves put a premium on fecundity, especially after the African trade was outlawed. Fannie Kemble wrote:

It seems to me that there is not a girl of sixteen on the plantations but has children, nor a woman of thirty but has grandchildren. . . Whereas the increase of this ill-fated race is frequently adduced as a proof of their good treatment and well being, it really and truly is no such thing. . . It is more than recklessness, for there are certain indirect premiums held out to obey the early commandment of replenishing the earth which do not fail to have their full effect. In the first place, none of the cares – those noble cares, that holy thoughtfulness which lifts the human above the brute parent, are ever incurred here by either father or mother. The relation indeed resembles, as far as circumstances can possibly make it . . . the short-lived connection between the animal and its young. . . It becomes mere breeding, bearing, suckling, and there is an end. But . . . they enjoy, by means of numerous children, certain positive advantages. In the first place, every woman who is pregnant, as soon as she chooses to make the fact known to the overseer, is relieved of a certain portion of her work in the field. . . On the birth of a child certain additions of clothing and an additional weekly ration are bestowed on the family; and these matters, small as they may seem, act as powerful inducements to creatures who have none of the restraining influences actuating them which belong to the parental relation among all other people. . . Moreover, they have all of them a most distinct and perfect knowledge of their value to their owners as property; and a woman thinks, and not much amiss, that the more frequently she adds to the number of her master's live stock . . . the more claims she will have upon his consideration and good will. This was perfectly evident to me from the meritorious air with which the women always made haste to inform me of the number of children they had borne, and the frequent occasions on which the older slaves would direct my attention to their children, exclaiming, "Look, missis! little niggers for you and massa; plenty little niggers for you and little missis!"

An overseer said that women constantly shammed themselves pregnant in order to obtain diminution of labor.

J. B. Lamar speaks of negroes increasing like rabbits. Charles Lyell thought that "the rapidity with which they increase beyond the white . . . shows that they are not in a state of discomfort, oppression, and misery." A manager said that slave "women, from their labor in the field, were not subject to the difficulty, danger, and pain which attended women of the better classes in giving birth to their offspring."

One influence retarding fecundity was the promiscuity of girls. Said a manager: "They'd have them younger than they do, if they would marry or live with one man sooner than they do. They often do not have children till they are twenty-five years old." This phenomenon was perhaps accentuated in case of mulatto girls by reason of their superior attractiveness.

Prolific increase of slave population furnishes solace to apologists for exploitation. It is taken as a sign of well being and contentment and

Never did a race increase faster than the slaves of the South. They multiplied rapidly, in many cases the parents living to see more than a hundred descendants. One case in Carolina is well authenticated where the female ancestor lived to be one hundred and four years old, and had, when she died, one thousand descendants. She became a mother at fifteen, had twenty-two children when forty-five, and two hundred grandchildren and great grandchildren when seventy-five.

Hildreth maintained that slave population did not increase so fast as the white (even leaving out immigration). In spite of the absence of prudential checks, he said, and the stimulation of child-bearing, increase was retarded. This fact he attributed to disease and death due to excessive labor and privation. Even in the days of the Confederation, Schoepf had remarked that "the negroes do not multiply in the same proportion as the white inhabitants. Their numbers must be continually kept up by fresh importations." This necessity violated law up to the start of the Civil War.

Henry Clay mistrusted estimates as to increase of slave population in the far Southwest. In the thirties he believed that the births among the slaves in that quarter were not equal to the deaths. The owner of a Louisiana plantation declared that his overseer worked his hands so closely that a woman bore a child while at work in the field; also that he was at a brick-yard at New Orleans where among the hands were twenty to thirty young women in prime of life. He was told by the proprietor that not a child was born to them for two or three years though all had husbands. Catalogs of slave sales on estates would tend to show that fecundity suffered diminution. An agricultural society of Baton Rouge in a report of 1829 estimates the annual net loss of slaves in excess of propagation at two and one-half per cent. An estimate by a congressman from Louisiana made in 1830 agrees. One man tells of a case in Virginia where a woman in travail was neglected by her master, whose custom it was to be thus negligent unless previously notified and asked for aid. A minister who lived in Georgia for some years said that "when women are confined they have no physician, but are committed to the care of slave midwives." Of course any respite from labor or other relief afforded in such cases was a business proposition. In some instances women were whipped till they miscarried at the post. The son of an Alabama pastor says that an overseer beat a pregnant woman so that soon she was delivered of a dead child In Louisiana, when pregnant women were flogged a hole was dug under them in the ground so as not to kill the babe. Women were so maltreated that few children were raised on the sugar-cotton plantations.

Fanny Kemble wrote of a miserable dilapidated infirmary:

> Here lay women expecting every hour the terrors and agonies of childbirth, others who had just brought their doomed offspring into the world, others who were groaning over the anguish and bitter disappointment of miscarriages. [Miserable neglect was in evidence; yet] this is the hospital of an estate where the owners are supposed to be humane, the overseer efficient and kind, and the negroes remarkably well cared for and comfortable.

The reverend Mr. Long says that no respect was paid to sex: women worked in the field, cut wood, drove the ox-cart, made fences. "Indeed, I have often seen them in situations, where, if the pecuniary value of their offspring had been consulted, they would have been removed to the 'quarters' till after a certain time."

A Georgia overseer wrote in 1855:

> Now as regards the wimin loosing children, Treaty lost one it is true. I never heard of her being in that way until she lost it. She was at the house all the time. I never made her do any work at all. She said to me in the last month that she did not know she was in that way herself untill she lost the child. As regards Louisine she was in the field it is true but she was workt as she please. I never said a word to her in any way at all untill she com to me in the field and said she was sick. I told her to go home. She started an on the way she miscarried. She was about five months gone.

On one rice estate rules required that special care

should be taken to prevent indecency in punishing women.

> Lying-in women are to be attended by the midwife as long as is necessary, and by a woman put to nurse them for a fortnight. They will remain at the negro houses for four weeks, and then will work two weeks on the highland. In some cases, however, it is necessary to allow them to lie up longer. The health of many women has been entirely ruined by want of care in this particular. Women are sometimes in such a state as to render it unfit for them to work in water; the overseer should take care of them at these times. The pregnant women are always to do some work up to the time of their confinement, if it is only walking into the field and staying there. If they are sick, they are to go to the hospital, and stay there until it is pretty certain their time is near.

Weston, in the *Progress of Slavery in the United States*, said that free negroes multiplied slowly and cited Tucker of Virginia as saying: "Since the emancipated class are found to increase more slowly than either the slaves or the whites [the legislature] ought to encourage, rather than check, private manumission."[130]

Some light on the characteristics of the slave family may perhaps be gathered from points alleged in extenuation of the current disregard of family ties contracted by chattels. For instance it was said that relatives except husband and wife often preferred being sold to different masters in the same neighborhood, as they found thus excuse for their roving propensity. The reverend Doctor Mallard says: "In our county [Liberty County, Georgia] they were permitted to marry wherever they chose; and their almost universal choice was of husbands and wives at a distance from one to

[130] On slave infecundity, etc. see Hildreth, *Despotism in America*, 60-61; Schoepf, *Travels in the Confederation*, vol. ii, 221; American Anti-slavery Society, *American Slavery as it is*, 37-38, 45-46; Tower, *Slavery unmasked*, 311-312, 331; Weston, *Progress of Slavery in the United States*, 129-130.

fifteen miles. [The negro on his way to his family was a good telegraph]." More than one lady told Olmsted she was sure her nurse loved the mistress's children twice as well as her own. It was maintained also that "cases of violent separation of husband and wife are not so many as the voluntary and criminal separations by the parties themselves." In Virginia the slaves were accused of being "without natural affection toward their offspring." The cruel cynicism that could develop under the chattel system is illustrated in the remark of a lady who said: "You know my theory, that one race must be subservient. . . I do not care which; and if the blacks should ever have the upper hand, I should not mind standing on that table, and being sold with two of my children."

One factor in lessening family love was the separation of relatives living on different plantations. A visit over Sunday or even twice a week was not sufficient guarantee of the marital bond. Another unwholesome element was the bosses' jurisdiction over marriage. An excursionist of 1816 remarks that a dealer "married" all the men and women he bought—ordered them to sleep together; as they sold better thus. Fanny Kemble blamed the negroes' small regard for marriage on the fact that the overseer, if he heard of disagreement, would redistribute the persons concerned to other partners. Negroes sometimes had to flog their own relatives. Parents, moreover, did not possess that claim to their children and their children's obedience and respect that is essential to ideal relations. A North Carolina planter defended the practice of bringing up the children of the estate in common, as it was far more humane not to cherish domestic ties among the chattels. If maternal attachments in slave-mothers were sometimes too short-lived, was not the fault attributable to the fact that from the moment of conception the idea of chatteldom overshadowed maternal solicitude? A slave-mother in one of the "best Christian families" deprecated the possibility of being a mother again: "You feel when your child is born that you can't have the bringing of it up." Fannie Kemble added:

> The father having neither authority, power, responsibility, or charge in his children, is of course, as among brutes, the least attached to his offspring; the mother by the natural law which renders the infant dependent on her for its first year's nourishment, is more so; but as neither of them is bound to educate or support their children, all the unspeakable tenderness and solemnity, all the rational, and all the spiritual grace and glory of the connection, is lost. . .

In a large colored Sabbath school the superintendent exhorted the children to be good—"what a comfort it will be to your masters and mistresses!" An eminent southern divine, Dr. R. I. Breckenbridge, said:

> Slavery, as it exists among us, sets up between parents and their children an authority higher than the impulse of nature and the laws of God; breaks up the authority of the father over his own offspring, and at pleasure separates the mother at a returnless distance from her child, thus outraging all decency and justice.

According to the laws of Maryland a white man could seize a free colored man's children, take them to a magistrate, and have them bound out against their parents' will. A lawyer stated to the court in such a case "that the laws of Maryland did not recognize the parental relation among negroes any more than . . . among brutes."

There was abundant evidence nevertheless that under proper conditions a sound home life was capable of development among the negroes. Family devotion was often touching. A traveller secretly gave a piece of meat to the hungry-looking waiter. He took it to his sick mother who could not eat herring. A negro woman freed by her mistress refused to go to a place of freedom "as she had a husband belonging to Capt. Wm. H. Hoe in King George County, from whom the benefits and privileges to be derived from freedom, dear and flattering as they are, could not induce her to be separated." Many advertisements for runaway slaves indicate the negroes proclivity for seeking to be with their relatives. Thus: "His wife belongs to a Mr. Henry Bridges . . . who started with her . . . to South Carolina, Georgia, or Tennessee. It is supposed he will attempt to follow her." At Baltimore a negro was placed in the penitentiary for stealing his wife. Negroes often made great sacrifices in behalf of the emancipation of their relatives. A free black was trying to buy his wife. Her master kept her till seven children were born. The wife and children were all the while maintained by her husband yet he received no allowance on that account. Another negro worked sixteen years in order to be able to buy himself and family, paying his master one hundred twenty dollars a year and supporting the family himself. He contrived to give his children a good education. Then he gave twelve hundred dollars for himself and family. A quadroon paid fourteen hundred dollars to his own father for his wife and three children born in slavery. Sometimes slaves were allowed to purchase themselves and families at cut prices. Again we find such a case as that of a free negro in Kentucky with a slave wife whose master saddled the man with the cost of maintaining the children and let him pay the poll tax. When the children became valuable the master would take them.

In 1853 Forrest, writing on Norfolk, said:

Often families of slaves "hire their own time," occupy a home, and dwell together in peace; pay a commendable regard to their marriage vows (though sometimes imperfectly solemnized), rear children, perform their family devotions. . . They are generally attentive to one another in sickness, and appear to pay great respect to their dead.

A free woman, in order to save her children, who were in danger of slavery by her being apprehended as a slave, jumped from a housetop and was so mangled as to be unfit for sale. "She knew a whole family of young slaves was too valuable . . . not to turn the scale against her."

Family ties among the negroes were close enough to cause alarm to the master race. A memorial of the citizens of Charleston to the South Carolina legislature of 1822 read thus: "Many of the free negroes have parents, brothers, sisters, and children, who are slaves; should an insurrection occur, they would have every inducement to join it."

The precise tendency of evolution in the treatment of the slave family is not perfectly clear. Exhaustion of border-state soil gave an impetus to the sale of negroes southward. "Oh," said Charles Hammond on his death-bed; "Oh! slavery is not the thing it was when I first knew it in Virginia. Then the slaves were treated like servants – called in to family worship, and considered members of the family. But men have grown sordid now; and God knows where things will end." Helper said: "The diabolical institution subsists on its own flesh. At one time children are sold to procure food for the parents, at another, parents are sold to procure food for the children." Such is the expedient of Virginia planters when crops are short. Moreover the prospect of abolition in northerly slave states led to sales south. A Washington correspondent says: "Scarcely a day passes which does not witness dreadful heartrending cases of the sale of a human being from all his associates and family relations to the far South never to see them again."

On the other end there was a noticeable development toward conservation of the slave family. In 1801 the Virginia Supreme Court of Appeals declared that

> An equal division of slaves in number and value is not always possible and is sometimes improper when it cannot be exactly done without separating infant children from their mothers, which humanity forbids and will not be countenanced in a court of equity, so that compensation for the excess must in such cases be made and received in money.

The right to separate husband and wife and larger children still remained. Judge Bushrod Washington in 1821 told of having bought a number of negroes to prevent separation of families. A South Carolina planter said:

> In my neighborhood, every planter has agreed that, if he has a negro married to a negro woman belonging to another, and he wishes to get rid of the negro or quit the vicinity, he will either offer the slave to the proprietor of the negro woman, or will himself purchase the latter: in this case the price is regulated by other planters.

(This was prior to 1835). A Louisiana law forbade masters to sell parents and children separately before the latter were twelve years of age.

Progress was, however, shamefully slow. A member of the Georgia legislature tried to pass a bill prohibiting the removal of slaves from the estate where they were born. He was a slaveholder but wished to counteract the separation of families. The bill met with no favor from his fellow citizens. About 1855 the governor of Alabama recommended a law by which children under a certain age, say five years, should not be sold from parents. The Richmond *Enquirer* called the proposal unwise and impolitic, a concession to fanaticism. Nothing came of the recommendation. Wives and daughters of free negroes might be insulted by rowdies but their men must hold their tongues.

The growth of finer feelings was not dependent on the slow march of law. A British writer of 1851 noted that feeling was growing up against separation of husband and wife. "The very religious people [said my friend] won't sell the one without the other." Miss Bremer wrote: "The moral feeling, it is said, is becoming more and more opposed to separation of families and of little children from their mothers by sale; and that it now no longer takes place at the public slave auctions." Still, the best slaveholders can not always prevent heart-breaking separations. . . Even though Miss Bremer's statement probably includes some exaggeration it indicates the trend of shame.

A recent historian of Georgia says that:

As a rule families were kept together, and when their master died and division had to be made among the children, they were divided by families. If they were sold by the administrator to pay debts, they were sold by families, and in most cases they had chosen their masters before the sale. Separation of families was the exception and rare occurrence.

Quite to the contrary however is the testimony of Doctor Caruthers of North Carolina:

I have known some instances in which [the slave family] have been permitted to live on in great harmony and affection to an advanced age, but such instances, so far as my observations have gone [were] . . . "few and far between." Generally in a few weeks at most, they have been separated, sold off under the hammer like other stock, and borne away to a returnless distance.

So negroes had too light views of marriage. "A few Christian owners did what they could to prevent the separation of their married slaves, but after their death, if not before, the slaves were sold for debt or to satisfy less scrupulous heirs." In one place the master of an excellent slave couple died in debt. The children were sold and the heartbroken parents succumbed. "I could fill a volume," says Caruthers, "with similar instances." Another North Carolina gentleman offers contrary testimony: "The separations of husband and wife, parent and young child, were not common. My family never did it, nor did any of the families known to me, and I am sure that the great majority of families in North Carolina would not allow it."

Some families arranged for gradual emancipation, a fixed percentage being freed by each generation. By will and otherwise they provided against division of families. Dr. Mallard writing on *Plantation Life before Emancipation* says that marriage was not often voluntarily broken by the master, but was frequently severed by his death or bankruptcy. This divine had known cases of greatest sacrifice by masters in order to keep husband and wife together. His father sacrificed half the value of a slave in order to send him to Liberia to join his family emancipated by their master, and neighboring slaveholders made up the rest. "I have known planters . . . to hire hands they did not need, in order to keep husband and wife together." The appeal to public interest in cases of prospective separation is illustrated by the publication in the New York *Tribune* of a copy of a paper circulated in Washington to the effect that "the wife of Sam. Marshal, a woman of excellent character" is in the slave pen and will be sold from husband and children unless purchased from the trader for eight hundred dollars. An appeal is made for a ransom.   Negroes were glad when the master married and had children; for thus there was prospect that the estate would be kept together.

Negro home and family relations, even when the negroes were free, did not avoid censorship.   According to a North Carolina law of 1787 no free negro was to entertain a slave at his house at night or on Sunday on penalty of fine.   A free negro was forbidden to marry or cohabit with a slave without written consent of the master.   In 1830 the prohibition was extended to cases where the master consented – penalty thirty-nine lashes. In 1826 the courts received authority to bind out children of free negroes under certain conditions.   In 1840 – a free negro charged with the support of a bastard might be bound out for a sum in order to maintain the child.

Under favorable conditions, however, something of normal home life became possible even for ordinary slaves.   In 1800 Sir William Dunbar wrote to David Ross that the slaves "are often allowed to raise hogs for themselves, and every thrifty slave has his pigpen and henhouse.   They have as much bread, and usually as much milk and vegetables as they wish, and each family is allowed a lot of ground, and the use of a horse for raising melons, potatoes, etc."   A writer on "Old Virginia" said:

> They have no anxiety about their families. . . They have ground . . . for . . . gardens and patch of corn. They . . . raise a hog and fowls. The latter they sell to their master or others. . . Provision was made for those . . . too young or too old to labor.

One Georgia budget found makes a specific allowance "for every grown negro however old and good for nothing."

Charles Lyell in his *Second Visit to the United States* wrote of conditions at Tuscaloosa:

> The colored domestic servants are treated with great indulgence. . . One day some of them gave a supper to a large party of their friends in the house of a family which we visited, and they feasted their guests on roast turkeys, ice-cream, jellies, and cakes. . . It is usual not to exact the whole of their time for domestic duties. I found a footman . . . working on his own account as a bootmaker at spare hours, and another getting perquisites by blacking the students' shoes.

The writer of an *Essay on Sea Coast Crops* said that the negroes "are well fed and clothed, well sheltered and cared for in sickness and during the infirmities and helplessness of old age." A Georgia master allowed all to draw shoes save the children and their nurses. "My negroes are not allowed to plant cotton for themselves. Everything else they may plant." Olmsted described a farm on which slave-quarters

> Lined an approach to the mansion, and were well-made and comfortable log cabins, about thirty feet long by twenty wide, and eight foot wall, with a high loft and shingle roof. Each divided in the middle, and having a brick chimney outside the wall at each end, was intended to be occupied by two families. There were square windows, closed by wooden ports, having a single pane of glass in the center. . . [The planter's] manner towards them was paternal, familiar and kind; and they came to him like children who have been given some task, and constantly are wanting to be encouraged and guided, simply and confidently.

One planter had on high ground "a negro house for my negro children to reside in summer" by reason of the "bad summer climate of our rice fields for children."

The reverend John D. Long, whose observations were mainly in Maryland and Delaware where slavery was mildest, said:

> The "quarters" of the large slave-holders are generally mere shells; very few are plastered; and no arrangement is made for

the separation of male and female . . . [Slaves of small farmers] live in the kitchen, mingle with the master's family, eat the same kind of food as the other members of the family, are not generally overworked . . . and are attended to when sick. Their children are raised with their master's children, play with them, and nurse them. . . A strong attachment frequently exists between them and their masters and mistresses.

A North Carolina physician and planter thought that the slave usually fared as well relatively as a child. One not unusual fault was the putting of more than one family in a room.

Booker Washington could not remember a single instance during childhood or early boyhood when his entire family sat down at table together and ate a meal in a civilized way. "My old master had many boys and girls, but not one, so far as I know, ever mastered a single trade or special line of productive industry. The girls were not taught to cook, sew, or to take care of the home." Washington's mother snatched a few moments in early morning and at night for the care of her children. A man that lived in Mississippi for a time reported that

On all the plantations where I was acquainted the slaves were kept in the field till dark; after which, those who had to grind their own corn, had that to attend to, get their supper, attend to other family affairs of their own and of their master . . . and be in the field as soon as it was sufficiently light to commence work in the morning.

The slave home could not, of course, be considered in any sense independent. A Mississippi planter gave the following instructions to overseers:

At least once a week (especially during summer) inspect their houses and see that they have been swept clean, examine their bedding and see that they are occasionally well aired; their

clothes mended and everything attended to that conduces to
their health, comfort and happiness. . . I want all of my
people . . . punished for inhumanity to their children. . . All hands should be required to retire to rest
and sleep at a suitable hour and permitted to remain there
until such time as it will be necessary to get out in time to
reach their work by the time they can see well how to
work. . . Allow such as may desire it a suitable piece of
ground to raise potatoes, tobacco. They may raise chickens
also with privileges of marketing the same at suitable leisure
times.

A South Carolina rice planter directed that

The overseer is every now and then to go round at night
and call at the houses, so as to ascertain whether their inmates
are at home. . . The hands are to be encouraged to finish
their tasks as early as possible, so as to have time for working
for themselves. Every negro, except the sickly ones and those
with suckling children (who are to be allowed half an hour)
are to be on board the flat by sunrise. . . Fighting, particularly among women, and obscene or abusive language, is
to be always rigorously punished.

Under such a system wives and children were protected
to some extent from brutality. This was one advantage
that they enjoyed in comparison with the coarser working population in other regions.

It is almost impossible to generalize about slave-life
on the plantations. On some there was grinding of
children and neglect or sale of the old. On others the
children were well cared for, the sick were nursed and
the old protected. Similar contrasts appear in the
matter of regard for motherhood.

Persons unduly considerate of family welfare among
the servile population were likely to encounter legal
obstacles. A North Carolina case of 1849 is in point.
A man conveyed to certain persons a slave married to a
freeman and gave a house with land, presumably for

her use. The parties to whom the conveyance was made asserted ownership, the family having been conveyed to them in order to avoid a break. They allowed the husband to occupy, for a rental, the house with his wife, and agreed to look after her. The court voided the arrangement as being only qualified slavery and gave her and the children to the heirs of the donor. The donees were held liable "with just deductions" for the profits due from her services and for costs.[131]

Slave children received, as we have seen, very inadequate care. A traveller wrote in 1784 of Virginia that "even when female slaves breed, which is generally every two or three years, they seldom lose more than a week's work thereby, either in the delivery, or suckling the child." Abdy, who was in the United States in 1833-1834, said that on Louisiana cotton plantations "no exemption from toil is granted to the females, many of whom, while suckling their infants are prohibited from seeing them till their return at night." At about the same time the following report was made of facts from North Carolina:

> Women are generally shown some little indulgence for three or four weeks previous to childbirth; they are at such times not often punished if they do not finish the task assigned to them. . . They are generally allowed four weeks after the birth of a child, before they are compelled to go into the field, they then take the child with them, attended sometimes by a little girl or boy, from the age of four to six. . . When . . . no child . . . can be spared . . . the mother after nursing, lays it under a tree, or by the side of a fence, and goes to her task, returning at stated intervals to nurse it. While I was on the plantation, a little negro girl destroyed the life of a child about two months old, which was left in her care. [She tired of carrying it home at night – the mother had to work as long as she could see.]

---

[131] Bassett. *Slavery in the State of North Carolina*, 33-34.

A minister who lived in Georgia from 1817 to 1824 said:

> Women are seen bringing their infants into the field to their work, and leading others who are not old enough to stay at the cabin with safety. . . Others are left at home shut up in their huts. . . Some who have very young ones, fix a little sack, and place the infants on their backs and work. . . Master gives each of his slaves one peck of corn per week (twelve and a half cents). . . It cost me upon an average, when at the South one dollar per day for board. . . Think of the little, almost naked and half starved children, nibbling upon a piece of cold Indian cake, or a potato! Think of the poor female, just ready to be confined, without anything that can be called convenient or comfortable!

A former slave-driver tells likewise of women working in the fields with infants strapt to them—when the child was three weeks old, the mother was put to work.

Some plantations provided nurseries. Emily Burke in *Reminiscences of Georgia* (1850) said:

> Tales are often circulated at the North about the infant children of slaves being left unprotected in the field while the mother is obliged to continue at her task. . . I never saw or heard of any such incident. . . On all plantations of much extent there are always nurseries where all the children from infants a week old, up to ages of four or five are cradled and nursed as well as the aged women to whose care they are entrusted while their mothers are in the field, are capable of doing. . . I doubt not from the cries I have heard from those nurseries, that those helpless little ones often suffer from want of that nourishment nature has provided for infancy.

Miss Bremer noted that on southern plantations everywhere negro children were herded by one or two old women. She saw sixty or seventy or more together under their rods of iron like a herd of cattle.

The amount of care bestowed on negro childhood varied of course with the profit in slave-breeding and with the master's economic insight as well as with hu-

mane considerations. The property sense was fundamental. Thus a negro woman condemned to death for
killing her child (in order to set it free) was reprieved
owing to her pregnancy and the owner's interest in the
prospective child. But when slaves in Virginia were
too cheap, "the damage to service in child-bearing and
the cost of rearing the infant was viewed as involving
a net loss." Harshness of conditions in chatteldom enlarged the mortality rate of infants. Fanny Kemble
speaking of pregnant women who begged for a month's
respite after child-bearing instead of three weeks says
that all had had large families and all had lost half of
their children and some, more. Fanny had had six
children; five were dead. Of Nanny's three two were
dead. Leah had had six; three were dead. Sophy
had had ten, of whom five were dead. Sally had had
two miscarriages and three children born, one of whom
was dead. Charlotte had had two miscarriages. Sarah
had had four miscarriages and borne five dead children and two living ones. She was again with child.
Sukey had had four miscarriages and borne eleven
children; five were dead. Of Molly's nine children
six were alive – the best account received. "There was
hardly one of these women . . . who might not
have been a candidate for . . . hospital, and they
had to come to me after working all day in the fields."
One woman had had fifteen children and two miscarriages. Nine children had died. Die had had sixteen
children and four miscarriages. Fourteen of the children were dead. Venus – eleven children and two
miscarriages; five children had died. Molly – nine children and two miscarriages; six children dead. Another Molly had had eight children and two miscarriages.
Seven of the children had died.

A slave-master writing to a New York paper in order to prove slaves better off than free laborers said of his own plantation: "Our [negro] children are as hearty and as saucy boys and girls as can be shown anywhere." Women with young children come to the cook-house thrice daily besides noon in order to nurse their children. Another planter wrote: "The child's cook cooks for the children at the negro-houses; she ought to be particularly looked after, so that the children should not eat anything unwholesome." One criterion of the usefulness of the overseer was excess of births over deaths and the health of the children. On this estate women with six children alive at any one time were allowed all Saturday to themselves.

It was hard to secure from the negroes proper care of the children. Miss Martineau observes that the mistress is "obliged to stand by and see Diana put clean linen upon her infant, and to compel Bet to get her sick husband some breakfast." Fanny Kemble found that "the negro-women seemed incapable of drying or dressing their own babies." Negro mothers were often so ignorant, so indolent, or so exhausted that they could not be trusted to keep awake and administer medicine to their own children. The mistress often had to sit up all night with a sick negro child. One mistress had to dress daily a negro child's broken arm, because the mother was too indolent. If "it was rare to see a puny, sickly negro child" as a writer on Georgia alleges, the fact may perhaps be due to the high casualty rate.

Slave parents were not model educators: They were too much given to blows and too much encompassed by the conditions of exploitation. Many children went naked in summer. The little ones learned from their parents to regard the white people with fear and to deceive them.   Nor was the master's end of paternal responsibility always duly administered.   Children were cruelly whipped for small offences, and that in the presence of their mothers.   Olmsted reports that

> Until the negro is big enough for his labor to be plainly profitable to his master, he has no training to application or method. . . Before the children arrive at a working age, they hardly come under the notice of their owner.   An inventory is . . . taken on the plantation at Christmas, and a planter told me that sometimes they escaped the attention of the overseer and were not returned at all, till twelve or thirteen years old.   The only whipping of slaves I have seen in Virginia, has been of these wild, lazy children, as they are being broke in to work.

On some well-regulated plantations, however, special effort was made to teach the slave children their duty and "the way of salvation."   The young Africans often shared, also, much of the life of the white children.

XII. RACIAL ASSOCIATION IN THE OLD SOUTH

A considerable proportion of the southern slaves were in effect members of their masters' families; and negro children were playmates of the future masters and mistresses. A Virginian born in 1828 writes that until nine he lived on his father's plantation the life of a Virginia boy "always followed by two or three negro boys of about the same age, my satellites and companions, partners in any mischief and with whom I cheerfully divided any good fortune which came to me in the way of cakes, fruit, or other edibles." Miss Martineau saw "little ones . . . lounging about the court, with their arms around the necks of blacks of their own age."

On the best plantations, especially when the slaves had been inherited, the position of the master was patriarchal. A historian of Mississippi pictures "old massa" as the head of a family of which the blacks considered themselves members; "old missis" as head nurse and stewardess of the plantation "seeing to the sick and the children and distributing clothing and comforts all around. 'Young Missis' spruced up the colored 'gals,' taught them the fashions, and 'Young Marster' stood between the slaves and the overseer, got them out of trouble, and took the boys with him to hunt and fish."

The negroes often manifested great devotion to the white family. Mansion doors often stood open at

night; for while a negro might now and then sequester
a fowl or a pig "the planter knew that, hardly more
than his own children, would his own slaves be tempted
to rob him or otherwise molest his repose."   There
does, indeed, seem to have been a good deal of haunting
fear in the slave states, perhaps without much real
foundation.   Nat Turner refused to murder his own
master and mistress; they "had been too kind to him,"
he said.   One of his lieutenants took a similar stand.
At one place the slaves withstood firmly Turner's gang
and declared that they would "lose every drop of blood
in defence of their master and his family."   Especially
in the regions where slavery was milder was such fondness developed.   In the Valley of Virginia, where
slaves were relatively few and the masters more indul-
.gent, the negroes were much attached to their homes
and to the white children.

In some respects the whites admitted negroes to
great intimacy.   Fanny Kemble observed that the dis-
agreeableness of negroes "does not prevent Southern
women from hanging their infants at the breasts of
negresses, nor almost every planter's wife and daughter from having one or more little pet blacks sleeping
like puppy-dogs in their very bed-chamber, nor almost
every planter from admitting one or several of his
female slaves to the still closer intimacy of his bed."
In many southern houses it was customary to have the
slaves in at family prayers.   Olmsted tells of a master
who at dinner frequently addressed the slave "familiarly, and drew him into our conversation as if he were a
family friend, better informed on some local and domestic points, than himself."   A minister with twenty-
one years' southern experience related that if a son
brought home a bride he introduced her to the servants
in their quarters, particularly to his old nurse.

Many slaves were taught in their owner's family.
In Virginia in the days before the war, "the old gray
headed servants are addressed by almost every member
of the white family as 'uncles' and 'aunts.' The others
are treated with as much respectful familiarity as if
they were white laborers. They never hesitate to apply to their masters or mistresses in every difficulty."
On large farms the doctor for the slaves was paid by
the year. In sickness the white folks acted as nurses
for the negroes. Many Virginia families in the agricultural depression toward the middle of the nineteenth
century were reduced to bankruptcy by their unwillingness or inability to sell their slaves. A distinguished
professor of William and Mary testified, also, that
"there are hundreds of slaves who will desert parents,
wives or husbands, brothers and sisters to follow a kind
master."

The negro race to-day owes much to the fact that
where the slaves were adopted into the household they
soon learned the ways of the master's family. Such
servants largely identified their interests with those of
the white family. It was common to see negroes belonging to different masters refrain from relations with
each other by reason of the difference of rank of the
two families that they considered their own. Social
assimilation of the negro field hands on large plantations was naturally less complete than that of such
slaves as enjoyed more personal contacts with the master race. Especially on the South Carolina islands
where the white folks were likely to be no more than
winter visitors was the transforming process retarded.
The idealization of slavery builded rather on personal
relationships.

The "Mammy" was one of the most important mem-

bers of the master's family.   She often slept in the
room with the white children.   All family secrets were
in her keeping; she was defender of the family honor.
The tie of affection between her and her charges was
never out-grown.   Often she was the confidential adviser of the older members of the household.   To young
mothers she was an authority on first babies.   Both
white and colored esteemed her highly.   "How quietly peach-tree switches dropped from parental hands
when Mammy begged for us.   Mammy's cabin was
the white children's paradise."   Thomas Nelson Page
says that in all that related to the children

> Her authority was recognized . . . second only to that of
> the Mistress and Master.   She tended them, regulated them,
> disciplined them: having authority indeed in cases to administer
> correction. . . Her régime extended frequently through two
> generations, occasionally through three.' . . .   She may have
> been harsh to [her own offspring]; she was never anything but
> tender with [her white children.   When the young masters and
> mistresses grew up, they were still her children].   When they
> parted from her or met with her again after separation, they
> embraced her with the same affection as . . . in child-
> hood. . . Her influence was always for good.

Miss Bremer tells of a wedding at which

> A fat old negro woman sat, like a horrid specter, black and si-
> lent by the altar.   This was the nurse and foster mother of the
> bride, and who could not bear the thought of parting with
> her. . .   These black nurses are cared for with great tender-
> ness as long as they live in white families, and, generally speak-
> ing, they deserve it, from their affection and fidelity.

Next to Mammy ranked the butler and the carriage-
driver.   They had a share in the training of the children.   The butler was awesome.   "Grandma," said
the white child, "are you 'fraid of Unc' Tom?"   The
driver was the boys' ally and the girls' devotee; consequently he "had an ally in their mother, the mistress."

Slaves frequently looked after orphan children of their mistress.

Close attention should be given in the light of modern psychology to the consequences upon white children of constant association with members of the other race. The subject can be merely touched here. The more subtle effects in the realm of the unconscious will suggest themselves. White babes, for instance, commonly had negro wet nurses, and it may be wondered whether in view of the psychic importance of the suckling process there may not have been implanted in the minds of the southern whites certain peculiar attitudes toward negro women and whether this possibility may not be a partial explanation of the sex tastes of the men of the old South.

Jefferson in his *Notes on Virginia* noted the

Unhappy influence on the manners of our people, produced by the existence of slavery among us. The whole commerce between master and slave is a perpetual exercise of the most boisterous passions – the most unremitting despotism on the one part, and degrading submissions on the other. Our children see this, and learn to imitate it. . . The parent storms, the child looks on, catches the lineaments of wrath, puts on the same airs in the circle of smaller slaves, gives a loose rein to the worst passions; and, thus nursed, educated, and daily exercised in tyranny, cannot but be stamped by it with odious peculiarities.

Other writers commented on this tendency of child development. Miss Martineau asked "what is to be expected of little girls who boast of having got a negro flogged for being impertinent to them?" Fanny Kemble exclaimed: "Think of learning to rule despotically your fellow creatures before the first lesson of self-government has been well spelt over!" A Virginia judge, a slaveholder, said in 1832: "A slave population exercises the most pernicious influence upon the manners, habits and character, of those among whom it exists. Lisping infancy learns the vocabulary of abusive epithets and struts the embryo tyrant of its little domain." A minister, who lived in South Carolina at about the same date, tells of a slave woman mercilessly beaten before the family for pouring too much molasses for one of the children. A traveller on an Ohio River steamer saw a five year old white boy go up to a slave child "and deliberately hit him a blow on the face with his fist and then kick him without any provocation. The poor little negro did not resent this." Dickens reported that "the delicate mamma . . . quiets her youngest child . . . by promising the boy 'a whip to beat the little niggers with'." Helper exclaimed vehemently: "The challenger to almost every duel has been an abandoned wretch, who, on many occasions during infancy, sucked in the corrupt milk of slavery from the breasts of his father's sable concubines." Of course some parents tried to save their children from the psychology of arrogance but mere pedagogy can rarely offset the pressure of an economic system.

The Synod of South Carolina and Georgia on one occasion said: "Our children are corrupted from their infancy, nor can we prevent it." Association with the slaves was a prolific source of low ideas and of vitiated manners and morals. Miss Martineau said:

> The generality of slaves are as gross as the total absence of domestic sanctity might be expected to render them. They do not dream of any reserve with children. The consequences are inevitable. The woes of mothers from this cause are such that, if this "peculiar domestic institution" were confided to their charge, I believe they would accomplish its overthrow. . . Among the incalculable forces in nature is the grief of mothers weeping for the corruption of their children.

Slaves often gloried in corrupting the children of their owners.

A gentleman from Kentucky reported the matter thus:

> I shall not speak of the far South, whose sons are fast melting away under the unblushing profligacy which prevails. I allude to the slave-holding West. It is well known that the slave lodgings – I refer now to village slaves – are exposed to the entrance of strangers every hour of the night, and that the sleeping apartments of both sexes are common. . . There is no allowed intercourse between the families and servants after the work of the day is over. . . Should one of the younger members of the family, led by curiosity, steal out into the filthy kitchen, the child is speedily called back, thinking itself happy if it escapes an angry rebuke. . . The slaves . . . roam over the village streets, shocking the ear with their vulgar jestings and voluptuous songs. . . [There is] indiscriminate debauchery . . . in the kitchens of church-members and elders. [In spite of all care the] domestics influence very materially the early education of . . . children. Between the female slaves and the nurses there is an unrestrained communication. As they come in contact through the day, the courtesan feats of the past night are whispered into the ear of the unsuspecting girl to poison her youthful mind. . . The slave states are Sodoms, and almost every village family is a brothel. (In this I refer to the inmates of the kitchen and not to the whites.) . . This pollution . . . springs not from the character of the negro but from the condition of the slave.

Olmsted reports an obscene quarrel of negro nurses occurring on a South Carolina train while the white children listened. *The Southern Cultivator* of June, 1855, contained the following:

> Children are fond of the company of negroes, not only because the deference shown makes them feel perfectly at ease, but the subjects of conversation are on a level with their capacity; while the simple tales, and the witch and ghost stories, so common among negroes, excite the young imagination and enlist the

feelings. If, in the association, the child becomes familiar with
indelicate, vulgar, and lascivious manners and conversation an
impression is made upon the mind and heart, which lasts for
years – perhaps for life. Could we, in all cases, trace effects to
their real causes, I doubt not but many young men and women,
of respectable parentage and bright prospects, who have made
shipwreck of all their earthly hopes, have been led to the fatal
step by the seeds of corruption which, in the days of childhood
and youth, were sown in their hearts by the indelicate and
lascivious manners and conversation of their father's negroes.

Chancellor Harper said: "A greater severity of de-
corum than is required elsewhere, is necessary among
us."

An Alabaman opposed to slavery, among other reasons gave this: "I've got a family of children and I
don't like to have such degraded beings round my home
while they are growing up. I know . . . the
consequences." A southern merchant on his annual
visit to New York said:

When on my brother's plantation just before I came North, I
was informed that each of his family servants were suffering
from [a venereal disease], and I ascertained that each of my
brother's children, girls and boys, had been informed of it, and
knew how and from whom it had been acquired. The negroes
being their familiar companions, I tried to get my brother to
send them North with me to school. I told him he might as
well have them educated in a brothel at once.

Olmsted says:

I never conversed with a cultivated Southerner on the effects of
slavery, that he did not express a wish or intention to have his
own children educated where they should be free from demoralizing association with slaves. That the association is almost
inevitably corrupting and dangerous, is very generally (I may
say, excepting by the extremest fanatics of South Carolina, universally) admitted. The children of a few wealthy men may,
for a limited period, be preserved from this danger, [but] the
children of the million can not be.

A southern college president says that "contaminating and degrading contact" of white children "with negro associates . . . was universal in the best families in ante-bellum times." Yet some attempt was occasionally made to segregate the two races in childhood. On one plantation, white and black children were both punished if found playing together. But until emancipation, white and black children could hardly be kept apart. Nor were the black children lacking in initiative and capacity for leadership.

Personal relations had, too, their saving features. A nurse girl that struck a child that would not go to sleep was told by her mistress that she could never touch the child again – she was free. After pining for weeks, she was allowed to nurse the child again and always resented any reproof or criticism of the child. McDonald's *Life in Old Virginia* draws this picture:

> The slaves are generally affectionate . . . particularly to the children of the family, which lays the foundation of . . . attachments . . . continuing through life. The white children – if they had the desire – are not permitted to tyrannize over the slaves young or old. The children play together on terms of great equality, and if the white child gives a blow, he is apt to have it returned with interest. At the tables you will find the white children rising from them, with their little hands full of the best of everything to carry to their nurses or playmates, and I have often known them to deny themselves for the sake of their favorites. . . When the young master (or mistress) is installed into his full rights of property, he finds around him no alien hirelings, ready to quit his service upon the slightest provocation, but attached and faithful friends, known to him from his infancy, and willing to share his fortunes.

There is some testimony, also, in qualification of the deleterious influence alleged of the association with slaves. A minister who came from Liberty County,

Georgia, says that he played with negroes and that his playmates were never profane and rarely vulgar. A Tennessee lady says: "I do not think, as some do, that white children were contaminated by association with negroes." A minister writing on "Old Kentucky" says: "After long experience and careful thought on the matter, I am satisfied that the influences of old-time Kentucky negroes upon the white children were good."

The most serious risk in the rearing of children among the happenings of chatteldom befell the boys. An ex-mayor of Huntsville, Alabama, once said that "as a general rule, every young man in his state became addicted to fornication at an early age." A distinguished lawyer, elder in a church in a southern city, remarked: "It is impossible to bring up a family of children virtuously in a slaveholding community." A Tennessee slaveholder ventured

> To say, that in the slaveholding settlements of Middle and Southern Mississippi, where I have lived for several years, there is not a virtuous young male of twenty years of age. . . To send a lad to a male academy in Mississippi is moral murder. Now I have four children, three of them boys. I confess I shall never raise them in a slave state willingly.[132]

No system of exploitation ever respects the virtue of

---

[132] On miscegenation see: American Anti-Slavery Society, *First Annual Report*, 27-28, 63; American and Foreign Anti-Slavery Society, *Thirteenth Annual Report*, 150; Schoepf. *Travels in the Confederation*, vol. ii, 92-93; Lambert. *Travels through Canada and the United States*, vol. ii, 173; Janson. *Stranger in America*, 383-384; Candler. *Summary View of America*, 284, 299-300; Abdy. *Journal of a Residence and Tour in the United States*, vol. i, 352-353; Martineau. *Society in America*, vol. ii, 320-329, 335, 339; Martineau. *Retrospect of Western Travel*, vol. i, 268-270; Marryat. *Diary in America*, vol. ii, 107-109; Kemble. *Journal of a Residence on a Georgian Plantation*, 14, 15, 141, 162, 194, 199; Lyell. *Second Visit to the United States*, vol. i, 271-273, vol. ii, 94-95, 215-216; Elliott. *Sinfulness of American Slavery*, vol. i, 151-158, vol. ii, 60-66; Pickett. *History of Alabama*, 213, 299-302; Tower. *Slavery unmasked*, 316-330; Long. *Pictures of Slavery*, 231, 261-263; Olmsted. *Cotton Kingdom*, vol. i, 83, 306, vol. ii, 94, 227, 230; Noel. *Freedom and Slavery in the United States*, 87-90.

women of the subject class. American slavery almost universally debauched slave-women. A minister in the convention held at Danville for the forming of a constitution for Kentucky said that a number of female slaves "have been remarkable for their chastity and modesty. If their master attempts their chastity they dare neither resist nor complain. If another man should make the attempt, though resistance may not be so dangerous, complaints are equally vain." An Englishman who visited the United States prior to 1824 noted that

> At present the seduction of a colored girl is regarded as a venial offence. . . [The colored girls of the South] are not taught to respect themselves and value modesty. [White women seem regardless of their duty to influence them.] A tradesman at Fredericksburg told me, that the seduction of a colored girl was the almost invariable result of her settling in that town.

Early in the nineteenth century, the North Carolina Supreme Court decided that a white man could not be convicted of fornication and adultery with a slave-woman, because she had no standing in court. A speaker in the North Carolina constitutional convention of 1835 said: "A white man may go to the house of a free black, maltreat and abuse him, and commit any outrage upon his family, for all of which the law cannot reach him, unless some white person saw the act."

A traveler of 1832-1834, said of New Orleans:

> The unfortunate quarteroon girls, many of whom have received an education which would be an ornament to any lady, imbibe a belief from infancy, that the Creator has made them subordinate beings, belonging to a race inferior to the whites, and that therefore they are not fit to go through the ceremony of marriage.

At the same period it was reported that if there were any good-looking mulatto girls in a slave gang on its way South the drivers would grant a rebate on their charge. In the business of prostituting mulatto girls, threats and the lash were used where blandishments and gifts failed. In order to secure mulatto young, masters compelled colored women to submit to impregnation by whites and punished barbarously any that resented the duty. Slaves could not bear testimony against whites, hence the way was open for violence and seduction by any white. Women of color were compelled to endure every sort of insult.

Negro men were exasperated by being deprived of their wives – supplanted by their masters. A man in New Orleans was stabbed by a slave under such circumstance. Negroes cherishing revenge were dangerous persons liable to a cruel fate. An overseer took a negro's wife from him and had a child by her. Later she was allowed to return to her husband. A planter had a female slave with whom he desired intercourse. On refusing, she was flogged. Refusing again, she was whipped once more. Finally she yielded. A master tried to seduce a quadroon of irreproachable character and threatened to send her to the rice swamps if she refused. Finally he managed to make her his mistress. Such episodes are but samples of the working of the "peculiar institution."

When the persistence of African mores is coupled with the pressure imposed by slavery, it is not to be wondered at that a large proportion of women of color were of easy virtue. Lambert, who travelled through America in 1806-1808, remarked that "Many of the mulatto girls are handsome and good figures. They are fond of dress, full of vanity, and generally dispense their favors very liberally to the whites." A traveller of a few years later writes:

A mulatto at Petersburg . . . replied to my enquiry why he did not marry, that no white woman would . . . receive his addresses, and that amongst those of his own color, there were only three in the town whose chastity was unimpeached. When making enquiry respecting the state of morals at Norfolk, I receive an account nearly as bad.

A slave-girl detected in infamous practices put on a prudish air and declared that she was greatly pained to be considered immodest—that she had no desire to have any lover save her master. An Alabama lady had carefully brought up a colored girl, who grew up modest and well-behaved but finally bore a mulatto child. The mistress reproached her severely and the girl took the matter much to heart. Later, however, she said that her mother, a native African, had assured her that she had done no wrong and need not be ashamed.

Hildreth wrote in 1854 that

Among the slaves, a woman, apart from mere natural bashfulness, has no inducement to be chaste; she has many inducements the other way. Her person is her only means of purchasing favors, indulgences, presents. To be the favorite of the master or one of his sons, of the overseer, or even of a driver, is an object of desire, and a situation of dignity. It is as much esteemed among the slaves as an advantageous marriage would be among the free. . . Among slaves, every carnal union, tho but for a day, is a marriage. To persons so situated, we cannot justly apply ideas founded upon totally different circumstances.

A light colored Louisiana barber who had lived North said:

I'd never marry in Louisiana . . . there are no virtuous women among the colored people here!

What do you mean?

There are very few, sir.

What, among the free?

Very few, sir. There are some very rich colored people, planters, some of them worth four or five hundred thousand dollars. Among them I suppose there are virtuous women; but they are very few. You see, sir, it's no disgrace to a colored girl to *placer*. It's considered hardly anything different from marrying.

The master's right of rape wiped out female honor. Slave-women were taught that it was their duty to have a child once a year, and it mattered little who was the father. Probably few negresses were like one quadroon girl who maintained her virtue in face of brutal whippings and other urgings. Long wrote: "Many of the female servants are brought up virtuously, sleeping in the same room with their young mistresses. . . The females bring the highest prices in the South. For them there is no virtue after a certain age, unless they die the martyr's death."

It is amusing to find "the white man's burden" shifted to the shoulders of the subject race. Thus in a book on *Dixie* we are informed that "The heaviest part of the white racial burden [in slavery] was the African woman, of strong sex instincts and devoid of a sexual conscience at the white man's door, in the white man's dwelling." A historian of Alabama writes:

> Under the institution of slavery, the attack against the integrity of white civilization was made by the insidious influence of the lascivious hybrid woman at the point of weakest resistance. In the uncompromising opposition of the white mother and wife of the upper classes lay the one assurance of the future purity of the race.

The indecent remarks and jests that attended the sale of female slaves constitute a sidelight on southern manhood quite in keeping with the wholesale profligacy already more than hinted. Small wonder that boys were carried away by the lasciviousness of the times! Respectable young men lived in constant intercourse with colored females. A clergyman who left the South in consequence of slavery "believed there was scarcely a young man in the South but what was more or less contaminated with this sin." A large planter sent his boys North to be educated on the ground that they could not be brought up in decency at home; the evil practice was universal. A traveller said: "Twice it happened to come to my knowledge that the sons of a planter, by whom I was lodged on this journey, lads of fourteen or sixteen, who were supposed to have slept in the same room with me, spent the night in the negro cabins." A southern merchant visiting New York said: "I have personal knowledge that there are but two lads sixteen years old in our town (a small market town of Alabama) who have not already had occasion to resort to remedies for the penalty of licentiousness."

Space fails for the comprehensive citation of the distressing record of the universal debauchery of southern manhood. Such southern men as remained pure must have been paragons of conscience and strength. Often the greater number of the master's children were born of the wives and daughters of his slaves. "In slave states where the colored people are few and the whites numerous, very few slave children can claim persons of color for their fathers." The reverend J. D. Long, a Maryland man, wrote in 1857:

If Joe Smith had been born and brought up in the Slave States, he would never have thought of being the founder of a sect. Among the million of female chattels in the South, the supply would have been equal to the demand. You never hear of free-love associations in the South. From the very structure of slave society there is no necessity for them. . . Amalgamation is increasing at a horrible rate throughout the slave states; and will continue to increase while wealth and luxury prevail in one class of the community, and degradation in the other. There are many pure and virtuous men in the South, who are, and who have been so, even from their childhood; but . . . they labor under a temptation twofold greater than persons who occupy the same social position in the free states. It is admitted, by truthful men in the South, that slavery is a source of unbounded licentiousness. . . It is with pain that I express the conviction that one of the reasons why wicked men in the South uphold slavery is the facility which it affords for a licentious life. Negroes tell no tales in courts of law of the violation by white men of colored females.

Olmsted mentioned a small farmer who had broken up all vices and bad practices among his slaves save that "habits of amalgamation I cannot stop." A Virginia planter using free labor because of dislike for slavery "did not think more than half [the slaves] were full-blooded Africans. . . The owners . . . felt a family attachment to their slaves. . ." A South Carolina planter was asked why he stayed on his plantation during the unhealthy season. He replied that half a dozen girls could no longer be trusted without a husband and that he thought it to his interest and that of the plantation that he should be the first husband. A large planter said: "There is not a likely-looking black girl in the state that is not the concubine of a white man. There is not an old plantation in which the grandchildren of the owner are not whipped in the field by the overseer." A Sabbath school in Jackson after the war had in it many unrecognized children of "first citizens of Mississippi"—children of governors, United States senators, congressmen, members of the High Court of Errors and Appeals, legislators, sheriffs, justices of the peace, doctors, lawyers, ministers, merchants, planters, teachers, blacksmiths, carpenters, and general laborers attending together. A post-bellum legislature legitimized on the father's petition six children by various mothers, some of them negro.

Especially notable was the situation, already mentioned, among the quadroons, particularly in Louisiana. Some of the boys were sent abroad, others were placed on farms, still others sold into slavery. The girls were brought up by their mothers for the career of concubine. Free quadroons "elevated" themselves by such prostitution to whites, especially if the men had wealth or standing, whereas marriage to a colored man would not even protect a woman. The transactions preliminary to the matings were facilitated by formal balls where white men met colored women; when a man was smitten he could bargain with the mother or with the girl. One traveller said of New Orleans: "In some instances I was informed that various families of daughters by the same father appear at the quadroon ball on the very evenings when their legitimate brother is present for the purpose of following the example of his worthy papa." Quadroon concubinage seems to have been normal usage in the crescent city. Numerous men coming to New Orleans on business adopted it as cheaper than boarding.

The quadroon girls entered upon their anomalous function with a high degree of education in externals and with a capacity for the performance of the duties of wifehood, to which they attended "as becomes respectable females;" for success in the role of mistress was the only hold that women of this blood could lay upon the means to the gratification of ambitious interests. Even thus, their tenure was precarious. Every woman believed that her partner would prove an exception to the rule of abandonment (just as every white lady liked to believe that her husband was immune to quadroon allurements) but often the mistress heard of her partner's marriage from the newspapers or from a letter bestowing upon her the house and property. Miss Martineau reported that "the quadroon ladies . . . rarely or ever . . . form a second connexion. Many commit suicide; more die broken-hearted." Of course a man's marriage did not necessarily mean separation from his paramour. Some connections grew into real marital attachment. Often after breaking with his woman in order to marry, the man's attachment to her continued; sometimes on account of their mutual affection he had to have her sold away.

One can with difficulty appraise a civilization in which such an institution was accepted, in which countless "respectable" men lived thus in standardized illicit love to which society was too supercilious to accord legal recognition, and in which all the virtues of womanhood were not sufficient to procure a career of respectability. It was a common boast of the South that there was less vice in their cities than in those of the North; New Orleans could even plume herself on superior morality by reason "of the decent quietness of the streets and theatres." There was room for the ostrich policy. Many children of the shadowy unions were sent to France or the North, were educated, and won social standing where their lineage was unknown. Many assumed the names of their white fathers. Such quadroon men as remained in the South were likely to have to marry darker women.

There was in the South a considerable traffic in women for prostitution. When asked the price of a beautiful quadroon on sale at Alexandria, the dealers said: "We can't afford to sell the girl Emily for less than eighteen hundred dollars. . . We have two or three offers for Emily from gentlemen from the South. She is said to be the finest looking woman in this country." (A woman of thirty who had borne five children was selling for six hundred and fifty dollars.) Large numbers of mulatto girls were carried to the cities and sold at enormous prices into private prostitu-

tion. A New Hampshire gentleman in Louisiana took
a quadroon mistress, amiable and well educated, and
lived happily with her for twenty years. Tho she
warned him that she was not free, he neglected to see
to her manumission. When he died insolvent the creditor reckoned his three daughters (pure white) among
the assets, and in spite of their uncle's willingness to
redeem them at the price of all his property (an excessive valuation from the standpoint of their labor)
they were sold as prostitutes. "A Southern lady of
fair reputation for refinement and cultivation" told
with naïveté that "she had . . . a very pretty mulatto girl, of whom she declared herself fond." A
young man fell in love with the girl. "She came to me
for protection," said the lady, "which I gave her."
The young man left but returned later saying that his
love for the girl was such that he could not live without
her. "I pitied the young man, so I sold the girl to
him for fifteen hundred dollars."

A planter had two beautiful daughters by a slave.
They were educated in England and introduced as his
daughters but he failed to emancipate them; so that on
his death they were snatched away by the creditors and
sold to a purchaser who was to reap his gain from their
prostitution.

The charms of concubinage accounted in large measure for the prevalence of bachelors in the South. A
book of *Letters from the South and West* (1824) noted
that it was very common for rich planters in Virginia to
remain bachelors. A work of 1850 referred to the sale
of mulatto girls "in the far South to the abandoned
white bachelors who abound in this country."

A Virginia slaveholder remarked that "the best blood
in Virginia flows in the veins of slaves. Yes, even the

blood of a Jefferson." It was well known that a considerable proportion of Jefferson's slaves were his own children. If any of them made off he would smile as if to imply that he would not be very urgent in pursuit. He bequeathed freedom to five of his children and the Assembly passed a law allowing them to remain in the state.[133]

So ingrained became the usage of miscegenation that shame dwindled. Men "of worth, politeness and humanity" could listen with composure to their dinner guests facetiously tracing the paternal features in the faces of slave sons waiting at table. Mulatto offspring constituted no barrier to high position in affairs or to the society of "virtuous women of the first rank;" illicit relations with black women were a part of the order of the day and constituted a distinction for the women, who might thereby improve their own position and in negro eyes elevate the social level of their offspring. Yet all over the slave states might be found outcast mistresses working as field hands or domestics having been sold by their fickle paramours. Ministers had not much to say about the régime of adultery; indeed Noel says: "If a pastor has offspring by a woman not his wife, the church dismisses him if she is a white woman, but if she is colored, it does not hinder his continuing to be their shepherd." It was often asserted as an advantage of slavery (for instance, by Chancellor Harper) that its facilities protected the chastity of white women.

Fanny Kemble cited a lady as saying "that, as far as her observation went, the lower class of white men in the South lived with colored women precisely as they

---

[133] Grimké. *Letters to Catherine E. Beecher*, 10; Marryat. *Diary in America*, vol. ii, 108; Abdy. *Journal of a Residence and Tour in the United States*, vol. iii, 232.

would at the North with women of their own race."
Olmsted heard that poor whites associated constantly
in a licentious way with negroes.

Under the reign of degeneracy so far detailed it was
perfectly natural for men to sell their own flesh and
blood, or indeed to beget offspring for profit. A Georgia congressman reared a fine family by a slave woman,
for years acknowledged them as his children, and permitted them to call him "papa." Eventually they
were all sold at auction during his life. Parents placed
their own children under the whip of the overseer; men
were masters of their own brothers and sisters. Some
of the mixed offspring were well treated during the life
time of their fathers, but such leniency might only increase the tragedy, as when girls tenderly reared, well
educated, and in ignorance of their servile status were
claimed by their father's heirs. Many slaveholders
abhorred the practices associated with race mixture.
Legislation had, indeed, to be passed in order to forestall the normal operation of human feeling. In
North Carolina, most of the prosperous free negroes
were mulattoes, often liberated by their fathers. In
that state there also were frequent emancipations of
slave mistresses till the law of 1831 interposed a check.
Miss Martineau wrote:

A gentleman of the highest character, a southern planter, observed . . . that little was known out of bounds, of the
reasons . . . emancipation was made so difficult. . .
The very general connexion of white gentlemen with their female slaves introduced a mulatto race whose numbers would
become dangerous, if the affections of their white parents were
permitted to render them free. . . There are persons who
weakly trust to the force of parental affection for putting an
end to slavery, when the amalgamation of the races shall have
gone so far as to involve a sufficient number! I actually heard
this from the lips of a clergyman in the South.

At Baton Rouge a man that wished to free his children by a mulatto woman complained of the hardship of the law that prevented such emancipation unless the freed persons were sent out of the state. If it had not been for such legislation, many parents would doubtless have provided for their children "from a sense of moral duty" which Grund found operative even in cases where "there was no filial or parental affection visible."

Cases of tragedy occurred in marriages that unwittingly crossed the race line. One man on discovering that a beautiful Cuban girl, his father's ward whom he had treated as an equal, was a slave, managed to marry her to a friend on whom he desired revenge. When the husband learned the truth he sold his wife to a slave-dealer. In another instance, a wife was unable to prove, when claimed by a slave-dealer, that she had not negro blood; so in spite of her pleas her husband abandoned her; she died heartbroken. A young man happily married to his mother's seamstress found presently that she was a slave. "Separation was thought so much a matter of course that [the young man's generosity was commended] because he had purchased her freedom after the discovery and given her the means of setting up as a dressmaker."

When a master left property to his children of color their economic charm sometimes won them white mates; thus the strain of African blood was ultimately diluted and many white families in the South have today traces of negro blood. One Louisiana youth who fell in love with a beautiful (and wealthy) quadroon so light as to be scarcely distinguishable let some of her blood into his veins in order to swear that he had negro blood so that he could marry her legally. How potent property is in spite of sentiment is illustrated in the case of a mulatto woman who died in South Carolina in 1820. She had associated on terms of social equality with her neighbors, though many people refused to associate with her. This was a case of "compromise of feeling for interest," for her moral character was not above suspicion, but she had property to dispose of by will. Her brother was excluded from the white society of his sister. One man hired a young Northerner to marry his beautiful quadroon daughter, well educated and accomplished – gave him a large sum. Money would not always serve, however. A Scotch resident of Virginia married a mulatto and reared a family of children whom strangers would have taken for white. Yet tho he gave them a liberal education and left them large property no white families would associate with them.

Southern sentiment could wink at miscegenation but would not legitimize it. A heavy penalty was imposed on mixed marriages. Great resentment was aroused by the appearance of tracts advocating miscegenation as a solution of the race problem. Croly's *Miscegenation* which appeared during the War was endorsed by prominent Northerners. It predicted that the physically superior black would absorb the physically and morally inferior white and hailed this as a consummation to be desired, and "committed [in southern eyes] the one unforgivable blasphemy, that against the purity of the southern women." A planter who sold all his property and moved to Maine taking a young quadroon woman whom he intended to marry was thought by a crowd discussing the matter to deserve lynching.

Loyal Southerners were prone to compare their system with that of the North to the disadvantage of the latter. One finds a recurrent debate. Candler's *Summary View of America* maintains that "in the northern states . . . the seduction of a colored girl is as rare as that of a white, and prostitution in general is less conspicuous than in some parts of Maryland and Virginia." Chancellor Walworth of New York said he believed there were not north of the Potomac half a dozen virtuous women who would willingly allow their children to marry colored persons. A New York newspaper bitterly attacked a Mr. May of Connecticut for saying that he saw no impropriety in intermarriage. A negro of Boston wrote a pamphlet speaking in scorn and contempt of the negro that would marry a white woman; but an Ohio justice married four white men to colored women one winter; a physician in Cincinnati married a negress. Elliott wrote in 1850: "In the free states there is very little mixture of color. The colored people principally marry among themselves." The reverend J. D. Long speaking of the contention that the white women of the South were more chaste than the same class in the North said:

This I deny. The poor white girl at the South has no more protection against the rich seducer than the poor girl at the North. She has not the same chance, enjoyed by the latter, of getting an honest living. The licentiousness produced by slavery is a clear addition to be set down to a sum-total of wickedness in the slave States which of itself fully equals that existing in the free States.

Olmsted found it asserted by people who had lived both North and South

That although the facilities for licentiousness are much greater at the South, the evil of licentiousness is much greater at the North. Not because the average standard of "respectable position" requires a less expenditure at the South, for the contrary is the case. But it is said licentiousness at the North is far

more captivating, irresistible and ruinous. . . Its very in-
trigues, cloaks, hazards, and expenses, instead of repressing the
passions of young men, exasperate them, and increase its degrading effect upon their character, producing hypocrisy, interfering
with high ambitions, destroying self-respect, causing the worst
possible results to their health, and giving them habits . . .
inimical to future domestic contentment and virtue. Possibly
there is some ground for this assertion with regard to young
men in towns, though in rural life the advantage of the North,
I believe, is incomparable.

On the other hand we find in Dabney's *Defence of Virginia* the amusing assertion that southern society "has
never engendered any of those loathsome issues, which
northern soil breeds, as rankly as the slime of Egypt
its spawn of frogs"—the Mormons, communists, free
lovers, etc.

Southerners maintained heatedly that at all events
the virtue of southern women was unspotted. Doubtless their contention was largely warranted but it could
not be maintained absolutely. Neilson, who spent six
years in the United States prior to 1830, wrote:

Although many white men evince a wonderful inclination for
black women, I never could . . . learn of but one instance,
wherein a white woman was captivated by a Negro, and this
was said to have taken place in Virginia; a planter's daughter
having fallen in love with one of her father's slaves, had actually
seduced him; the result . . . was the sudden mysterious
disappearance of the young lady.

In North Carolina there was a pretty well authenticated story of a white woman who drank some of her
negro's blood in order to swear she had negro blood
in her and marry him. They reared a family. The
reverend Mr. Rankin who was in Kentucky prior to
1835 said: "I could refer you to several instances of
slaves actually seducing the daughters of their masters!
Such seductions sometimes happen even in the most

respectable slave-holding families." Pickett's *History of Alabama* is, however, probably warranted in its generalization that the white women even to the lowest in social position maintained racial purity. Benwell's insinuation that perhaps the ladies are not immaculate "as may be inferred from the occasional quadroon aspect of their progeny" may be a mistaken inference really due to strains of negro blood in white families. A Southerner remarked, however: "It is impossible that we should not always have a class of free colored people, because of the fundamental law, *partus sequitur ventrem*. There must always be women among the lower class of whites, so poor that their favors can be purchased by slaves." The Richmond *Enquirer* of 1855 contains the news of a woman's winning freedom for herself and five children by proving that her mother was a white woman.[134] Lyell said: "There are scarcely any instances of mulattoes born of a black father and a white mother." One of Olmsted's informants said that while white men sometimes marry a rich colored girl he never knew a colored man to marry a white girl. Olmsted subsequently heard of one such case.

It is pretty clear that the crime of rape of white women by negroes was not, as some assert, initiated by the suggestions of Yankee soldiers. As early as 1813 occurs the news that a woman near Richmond has killed a negro that wanted to ravish her while her husband was away in the army. Even earlier a negro in North Carolina was burned for rape of his master's daughter. She had previously received improper lan-

[134] Neilson. *Recollections of a Six Years' Residence in the United States of America*, 297; Bassett. *Slavery in the State of North Carolina*, 43; Abdy. *Journal of a Residence and Tour in the United States*, vol. iii, 29; Olmsted. *Journey in the Seaboard Slave States*, 509.

guage from him but had not reported him for fear of the dreadful punishment her father would give him. One slave made attempts on the chastity of white women and had been heard to boast "that he never would cohabit with those of his own color, if he could, by any means, possess a white woman." The owner had him castrated and informed as to the reason. Three months later the negro said: "Tank ye, massa doctor, you did me much great good; white or blackie woman, I care not for." In 1822 negroes at Charleston had a plot to kill all white men and black women, reserving the choice young white ladies for themselves. They had lists containing names of many of the most accomplished young ladies. A coachman had his master's daughter designed as his wife. The New Orleans *Bee* of 1842 mentions a horrible outrage "by a negro on the person of a young orphan girl, fourteen years old. She was seized by the [negro] while paying a visit to one of her relations, dragged into the woods, beaten most unmercifully, and then treated – in the most infamous manner." In 1854 in Missouri a slave condemned for raping a white girl was pardoned.[135]

Rape was practically unknown in war days when negroes were left as guardians of white women and children. If early laws against it indicate anything more than the white man's fear, the evil tendency must have been largely eliminated. It probably was a source of less distress to white women than was their male relatives' proclivity for miscegenation.[136] Mixed

[135] *Niles' Weekly Register*, vol. v, 279; Janson. *Stranger in America*, 379-380; Neilson. *Recollections of a six years Residence in the United States of America*, 295; *Documentary History of American Industrial Society*, vol. ii, 121; Trexler. *Slavery in Missouri*, 89.

[136] Abdy. *Journal of a Residence and Tour in the United States*, vol. ii, 93-94; American Anti-Slavery Society. *American Slavery as it is*, 16; Elliott. *Sinfulness of American Slavery*, vol. i, 152, 154, vol. ii, 69; Lyell. *Second*

offspring of white lust became a "source of jealousy to the lawful wife, and of shame and vexation to legitimate children." Southern women felt intensely on the subject. A sister of President Madison said: "We southern ladies are complimented with the name of wives; but we are only the mistresses of seraglios." A Virginia woman wrote deploring amalgamation as the one great evil in the South:

> The white mothers and daughters of the South have suffered under it for years – have seen their dearest affections trampled upon – their hopes of domestic happiness destroyed, and their future lives embittered, even to agony, by those who should be all in all to them, as husband, sons, and brothers. I cannot use too strong language in reference to this subject.

One planter's wife declared in the bitterness of her heart that a planter's wife was only "the chief slave of the harem."

Lyell's *Travels in the United States* records that "the anxiety of parents for their sons, and a constant fear of their licentious intercourse with slaves is painfully great. . . Here it is accompanied with a publicity which is keenly felt as a disgrace by the more refined of the white women." A Methodist clergyman long a pastor in Kentucky and Tennessee talked with a lady in Iowa formerly of Kentucky. She lamented the lack of domestics in Iowa.

> The preacher remarked to her that times had very much changed in Kentucky since they left there – now over twenty years ago – that in consequence of "illicit" connections of white husbands with the slaves, the lives of the slaveholders' wives were embittered; and confusion reigned in the families. . .

Visit to the United States, vol. i, 271; Tower. *Slavery unmasked*, 322-323; Benwell. *Englishman's Travels in America*, 95, 204-205; Olmsted. *Cotton Kingdom*, vol. i, 307-308; American Anti-Slavery Society. *Twenty-seventh Annual Report*, 31, 34-35; *Subdued Southern Nobility*, 16; Noel. *Freedom and Slavery in the United States*, 88; Morgan. *Yazoo*, 320; Dubois. *Negro American Family*, 25.

The lady could hardly credit the narrative. [On a visit to Kentucky she made inquiry and found it true.] She joyously thanked God for her deliverance from the domestic evils of slavery, and very contentedly bore the inconveniences of her situation in a new free state.

The jealousy of white women was sometimes visited on their dusky rivals. One mistress, out of ungrounded jealousy, had slaves hold a negro girl down while she cut off the forepart of the victim's feet. The girl was then thrown into the woods to perish. A man saved her and her master freed her in order to get her away from the resentment of his wife who did her best to get the poor creature into her power again. An English traveller reported that it was by no means uncommon for men

To inflict chastisement on negresses with whom they are in habitual illicit intercourse, and I was credibly informed that this cruelty was often resorted to, to disabuse the mind of a deceived and injured wife who suspects [her husband]. I apprehend . . . that they are [influenced to cruelty by their wives] who are notoriously jealous of their sable rivals.

A negress condemned to death in Alabama for the murder of her child said that her owner was the father and that her mistress, aware of the fact, treated the little one so cruelly that she had killed it in order to save it from further suffering and also in order to remove a provocation to ill treatment of herself. A congressman who had a child by a mulatto woman not belonging to him would have bought the child, he said, were it not for his wife. The little girl "is the innocent proof of his own faithlessness to solemn vows, and must be removed to a safe distance." In one instance a planter came home and patted a beautiful mulatto woman under the chin. His wife rushed down, caught the woman by the hair, and pummeled her face. Then

the slave-holder was summoned and the husband had
to sell the woman.

A New Orleans lawyer, a native of New York, had
as mistress for seven years a beautiful mulatto girl
while courting an accomplished young lady. When
he married, his new mistress required him to discard
her black colleague and the girl became a maniac. A
man who by many years' slave-trading from Virginia
to Mississippi and Louisiana had made enough money
for good social standing decided to marry. He had
for years kept a beautiful mulatto woman in a richly
furnished house with servants to wait on her and her
babies rocked in a mahogany cradle; she believing that
they were all free and would inherit their father's
wealth. One dark night they were surprised in their
slumbers, gagged, put aboard a steamboat, carried to
New Orleans and sold. The bride knew all this.

The fact that Southern women endured the personal
affront thrust upon them by the slave system and did
not rise in mass opposition is perhaps the best condemnation of the institution. Thus an English gentleman at Charleston said: "Few girls would refuse a
man who possessed a goodly number of slaves, though
they were sure his affections would be shared by the
best-looking of the females . . . and his conduct
towards the remainder that of a very demon." A traveller remarked:

> These sentiments I very soon ascertained to be in no way libel-
> lous. A Southern wife, if she is prodigally furnished with dol-
> lars to "go shopping," apparently considers it no drawback to
> her happiness if some brilliant mulatto or quadroon woman en-
> snares her husband. Of course there are exceptions, but the
> patriarchal usage is so engrafted in society there, that it elicits
> little or no comment.

But how could women raise effective opposition in view
of their utter economic dependence?

XIII. THE WHITE FAMILY IN THE OLD SOUTH

Courtship among the southern aristocrats was reminiscent of the age of chivalric gallantry. Schoepf said of the Virginia youth:

> At fifteen, his father gives him a horse and a negro, with which he riots about the country, attending every fox hunt, horserace, and cock-fight, and does nothing else whatever; a wife is his next and only care.

Thomas Nelson Page says that white "men were lovers almost from their boyhood."

The maidens in whom their interest centered were exquisite products of the class-system—"languid, delicate, saucy; now imperious, now willing; always bewitching," says Page of the girls of ante-bellum Virginia. The girl of his idealizations grew up apart from the great world yet was not provincial. As a child she was self-possessed and able to entertain her mother's callers in proper fashion. She began to have beaux in girlhood and exacted a protracted devotion of her lovers. Her chief attraction was not her beauty, though that was often dazzling, but an indefinable composite of many attractions. Living in an atmosphere created for her, "she was indeed a strange creature, that delicate, dainty, mischievous, tender, God-fearing, inexplicable southern girl" with her deep foundation of "innate virtue, piety and womanliness." Hodgson wrote from Charleston, 1820, of the patrician damsels as "delicate, refined, and intelligent, rather distant and reserved to strangers, but frank and affable to those

who are familiarly introduced to them by their fathers
and brothers."

Girls were kept and cherished in right romantic fashion.   Extreme modesty was assiduously cultivated; self-
help was not expected.   John F. Watson, who arrived
in New Orleans in 1804, said of that region:

> Gentlemen cannot visit young ladies often unless they declare
> themselves as intended suitors. . .   Young ladies do not dare
> to ride out or appear abroad with young gentlemen. . .
> Girls are never forward or garrulous in conversation; they are
> all retired and modest in their deportment, and very mild and
> amiable.   I have never seen a presumptuous, talkative rattle-
> cap or hoyden here.   The ladies seldom appear abroad before
> the evening; then they sit at their doors or walk on the levee.

A woman recalling her girlhood of 1840 in New Orleans says:

> It was not *comme il faut* for a young lady to be seen too fre-
> quently on the street or to make calls alone. . .   The miscel-
> laneous education we girls of seventy years ago in New Orleans
> had access to culminated by fitting us for housewives and
> mothers, instead of writers and platform speakers, doctors and
> lawyers – suffragettes.

Another writer says:

> No set of girls in Christendom were watched with more vigilant
> eyes . . .   in all ways more surely girdled about, as with
> a wall of fire, from the sensual temptations of society, at home
> and elsewhere, than the Southern young women of the more fa-
> vored sort in these early days.

We of to-day should consider that surveillance and
custody went to extremes.   In ante-bellum Washington the chaperon was omnipresent.   Gifts from young
men were restricted.

> As for a buggy alone, perish the thought!   Nor was it consid-
> ered at all the thing for the escort to furnish the conveyance to
> a ball.   If the family coach was non-existent, the harmless,
> necessary hack was provided by the mother of his belle, while
> he sought her shrine on foot, or in the horse-car.

A northern governess remarked on the fact that

In the North the young lady is left alone with her beaux and pa and ma retire. In the South it is deemed indecorous for them to be left alone . . . and the mother or some member of the family is always in the room; and if none of these, a female slave is seated on the rug at the door. . . Young girls are kept in very strict bounds by mammas in this respect; and I was told by a married gentleman, a few days since, that his wife never took his arm till she took it to be led to church on her wedding day; and that he never had an opportunity of kissing her but twice while he was addressing her (they were six months engaged!) and in both cases by means of a stratagem he resorted to of drugging a peach with laudanum which he gave to the attending servant, and thereby put her into a sound sleep.[137]

Flirtation was in order. The *Letters from Virginia* refer to a Virginia coquette who drove poor wights crazy. Page says that the Virginia girl was generally a coquette, often an outrageous flirt, not from heartlessness but as a normal expression of her life. "She played upon every chord of the heart. Perhaps it was because, when she grew up, the surrender was to be absolute." It was said that the worst flirts made the most devoted wives. We find, moreover, an early complaint from the *Alabaman* that woman is often doomed by man's inconstancy to a desolate life.

There were runaway matches. Greensboro, North Carolina, served as a Gretna Green for Virginians. Excessive restriction upon sex acquaintance furthered such clandestine matches. "The lover is piqued and begins to regard the whole matter as a fair field for strategy." The girl's mother is an enemy to be circumvented. Thinking the same, the daughter flees with her sweetheart.

[137] Mayo. *Southern Women in the recent Educational Movement in the South*, 46; De Leon. *Belles, Beaux, and Brains of the Sixties*, 136-137; Ingraham. *Sunny South*, 224-225.

In other cases, circumstances resulted in diffidence or relative coolness in the ways of love. Buckingham in his *Slave States of America* said:

> We never knew or even heard, thus far at least of any romantic attachment, accompanied by acts of such self-devotion as is often seen in England: and neither in the social intercourse which we have enjoyed among the young, nor in the domestic conversations of the middle-aged, have we ever witnessed that ardent attachment, and reciprocal sacrifice of all selfish considerations, which characterize the communion of passionate lovers everywhere else. All is decorous, orderly, and irreproachable: but everything is also formal, indifferent, and cold. . . Both physical and mental causes may contribute. . . The youth of America have not that vigorous and robust health, and that full flow of blood, which characterize the youth of England, and which forms a large element in the capacity to feel intense and passionate love. [They have less leisure for courtship.] When they meet the other sex it is either at a public dinner table, with fifty or a hundred other guests, where none remain more than a quarter of an hour, and where there is no time for conversation; or at balls and crowded parties, where the opportunities of indulging an interchange of sentiment and feeling are too broken and interrupted, to feed the passions of fervent feeling, or to suit the gravity of sentimental love. Social evening visits, without invitation or preparation, are rare indeed in any part of America; and to morning visits to ladies, gentlemen are rarely admitted. [They rarely sing together.]

In South Carolina about 1815 a young lawyer proposed at a wedding a marriage scheme. He asked each young man and woman to write his or her name on a slip of paper with the name of the person preferred as spouse, reciprocal choices to be made known to the pair, other preferences to be kept secret. There were twelve reciprocal choices and eleven weddings followed soon. Eight of the eleven men said they were so diffident that "they certainly would not have addressed their respective wives if the above scheme had not been introduced."

The reverend J. D. Long wrote that courtship and marriage were especially important and exciting questions in the slave states.

> Among a sparse population, where there are comparatively few social topics to enlist attention, many long winter evenings and summer days are spent in discussing the minutest incidents of a courtship. If a marriage is to come off, the bride's lace or her nightcap is a subject of criticism. Colored people take a deep interest in the marriage of their owners. Courtships are frequently conducted through them. They carry the mail and the letters are not always sealed. Many a young man has borne off a beautiful and wealthy bride, in spite of opposition from relatives, through the good offices of Uncle Toby and Aunt Dinah. Many a man has lost a fair lady by incurring the displeasure of servants. Reader, did you ever hear the servants in the kitchen criticizing Miss Julia's beau? One mimics his voice; another his language. Bill shows how he walks. Aunt Sucky, in tracing his genealogy, relates how his grandfather killed a negro, and how his father sold one to Georgia. If Miss Julia gets him, Tom expects to be sold to the Georgia trader. . . Uncle Lester says that Mr. Willard's slave girl, Nell, is his half-sister and that he is too intimate with Mr. Sturgeon's yellow girl, and hopes Miss Julia won't have him.

Especially was the old mammy often a great aid to the young folks during courtship.[138]

It might have been supposed that southern girls educated in the North would have a great influence over their young men but, said an observer at Charleston in the thirties,

> They are brought out before either their judgment or knowledge of the world are sufficiently matured to make them aware of the existence of certain abuses or of their own power of reforming them. Then again, marrying very young, they commonly quit society, in a great measure, at the moment the influence of their example might be of the greatest service to it.

Marriage occurred at a sufficiently early age. When the daughter of the old southern household came home

[138] Long. *Pictures of Slavery*, 269; McDonald. *Life in Old Virginia*, 93.

from school, after a short run in society she almost always "succumbed to the common fate of an early marriage and joined the procession of hard-working, heavy-laden wives and mothers who were the heart and soul of her dear Southland." Old maids were rare. Every girl, so to speak, married. Strange combinations occurred. The Savannah *Ladies' Magazine* of 1819, for instance, reported the marriage of a man of seventy-five to a girl of twelve, the daughter of his former wife. At the same time the girl's brother married the old man's daughter. Also a man of seventy-four had married a girl of eighteen. In a land where marriage was woman's one career, no wonder that women sometimes sought to make the most of it.

In New Orleans in the fifties "only Catholics went to the sanctuary for a wedding ceremony. Protestant weddings were . . . confined to family and nearest friends." Vulgar notoriety was not sought nor were wedding presents made. Page says of Old Virginia: "There were no long journeys for the young married folks in those times; the travelling was usually done before marriage. When a wedding took place, however, the entire neighborhood entertained the young people."

Southerners have always been proud of the status of women under the old system. She figures as the soul and grace of old southern life. The reverend Dr. Ross of Alabama spoke before the Presbyterian General Assembly at Buffalo in 1853 congratulating the South on its freedom from bloomer girls, women's rights conventions, and the like. "Oh, sir," he declaimed, "if slavery tends in any way to give the honor of chivalry to southern young gentlemen toward ladies, and the exquisite delicacy and heavenly integrity and love to southern maid and matron, it has then a glorious blessing with its curse." Chancellor Harper said: "It is related as a matter of tradition, not unmingled with wonder, that a Carolinian woman of education and family proved false to her conjugal faith."

But it is particularly in the romanticism of the new southern literature that the woman of the old South shines as queen and saint, a being of rare social gifts and sensibility to exalted sentiments and embodying in her person the quintessence of all that was lovely in the civilization of an effulgent people. Modesty, refinement, and sweet gentility grace the memories of her that linger in the thoughts of her children. Her "highest ambition was to be president of home."

To some extent the status and functions of the middle and upper class women of the old South merited the encomiums that are bestowed. The southern women of the middle class were modest, virtuous, industrious housekeepers, devoted wives and mothers. They were frequently gullible, knowing little of the world, and aloof from public diversions. Having to look after the wants of the few slaves – the making of their garments and the like – the labors of these ladies were onerous. They lived "only to make home happy."

In general there could be no complaint of lack of domesticity in southern wives. Marriages prefaced a life-time of self-devotion; sprightly girls became sober, retired wives, bent on making home a man's delight, and devoted to family welfare; their husbands' relatives and connections became their own. The married woman was not a figure in society; romance is built about the young girl; the social functions of the little cities consisted chiefly of balls and dances that brought the young of the two sexes together. After marriage women lived in plantation isolation; only the few that maintained town houses and spent part of the year in

Richmond, Charleston, or New Orleans retained their social connections "and for them a staid and modified social life was deemed fitting. For them the dance was over." De Leon says that in Richmond

> The male element at all functions ranged from the passé beau to the boy with the down still on his cheek; ancient husbands and young bachelors alike had the open sesame! But if a married woman, however young in years of wifehood, passed the forbidden limits by intent or chance . . . she was promptly and severely made to feel that the sphere of the mated was pantry or nursery, not the ballroom.

The matron of old Virginia became timid and dependent as her daughters came on and found new ways; yet when need was she could assert her deeper wisdom and overtower them all.

Dr. George Bagby who visited in Virginia families before the War said of the Virginia mother:

> Her delicacy, tenderness, freshness, gentleness; the absolute purity of her life and thought, typefied in the spotless neatness of her apparel and her every surrounding, it is quite impossible to convey. Withal, there was about her a naïveté mingled with sadness, that gave her a surpassing charm.

It is easy to fancy the women of the southern aristocracy as pampered idlers; but this conception is in need of grave qualification. A northern governess of ante-bellum days wrote: "The southern girls . . . never do anything themselves, being always attended by a shadow of a little negress or an ancient mammy;" and it is true that girls "were, generally in the towns and invariably in the slave crowded plantations, scarcely permitted to lace their own slippers or stays." But Mrs. Ravenel in her work on Charleston says of the old South:

> Girls were carefully brought up. Mothers studied Mrs. Montague's and Mrs. More's books on female training. So

the girls became good housekeepers and good managers – mistresses of many servants; generally mothers of many children.

In Ramsay's *History of South Carolina* occurs the statement

> The women are generally well educated. . . The name of the family always depends on the sons; but its respectability, comfort, and domestic happiness, often on the daughters. . . [Their youthful] vivacity is in general so well tempered by sweetness of disposition, and discretion, as leaves little room for anxiety to parents. . . No pursuit of pleasure interferes with duty to a father, or affectionate attention to a brother; so that the happiness as well as cheerfulness of a family is increased in proportion to the number of daughters. . . Nor are there wanting examples of those who, remaining single, perform admirably well the duties of daughters, sisters and friends, and have been eminently useful in assisting to train up and educate their younger connexions.

The *Letters from the South and West* reported that "the matrons, in the upper classes, are industrious, affable, and accomplished in a high degree." Perhaps the southern lady contributed less in labor (at least in manual labor) to the maintenance of the household than women of like rank elsewhere; but the mistress of many slaves needed to be competent in strenuous supervision and the crudities of servile labor left many a burden for the lady.

Mrs. Ripley's recollections of New Orleans in the forties record:

> Though we had ever so many servants, our family being a large one, my semi-invalid mother, who rarely left her home and never made visits, did a thousand little household duties that are now, even in families where only one or two servants are kept, entirely ignored by the ladies of the house. . . Every woman had to sew.

The duties of a plantation mistress were often truly formidable. Many a plantation was a crude industrial plant comparable as to household comfort with a mining camp. On such estates many a lady lived. If slavery released the lady from manual drudgery, it overworked her in other ways; she was typically deficient in vitality, often nervous and sensitive, yet she often had to contend with an aggravated form of the servant problem, for slaveholders did not always manage to get rid of trying and unprofitable servants. Except perhaps a butler and a head housemaid the help was often idle, incompetent, and in need of constant supervision. Olmsted wrote of Virginia:

> Really well-trained, accomplished, and docile house servants are seldom to be purchased or hired at the South, though they are found in old wealthy families rather oftener than first rate English or French servants are at the North. [One must pay] to get a certain amount of work done, three or four times as much, to the owner of the best sort of hired slaves, as they do to the commonest, stupidest Irish domestic drudges at the North, though the nominal wages . . . are but little more than in New York. . . The number of servants . . . in a Southern family of any pretension, always amazes a Northern lady. In one that I have visited, there are exactly three [house] negroes to each white.

A southern lady of an old and wealthy family visiting in New York said: "Your two servants accomplish a great deal more, and do their work a great deal better than our twelve."

Every household operation had to be under scrutiny. Every consumable thing had to be kept locked up, hence the mistress carried a huge bunch of keys and doled out "on incessant requests" whatever was wanted for the household. Continually she was being called upon to attend to some want of one of her many dependents. The plantation nurse brought a list of the sick and the serious cases had to be visited. The wagons came with the carcass of a beef or sheep and the mistress saw to the cutting up. The makers of garments had to receive attention and "it often fell to her lot to go down on her knees on the floor and cut out garments for hours at a time." A scared mother would ask her to "just run up to de quarter to see little Nancy who is fall into a fit;" or perhaps a man and wife had decided to part and a lesson in ethics had to be instilled.

The sovereignty allotted to the matron by the division of jurisdiction between her and the master was real enough, but it was a realm of contrasts. Waited on at every turn, "unhabituated often even to putting on her dainty slippers or combing her soft hair – she possessed a reserve force which was astounding." Miss Martineau declared:

> Some few of these ladies are among the strongest-minded and most remarkable women I have ever known. [The barbarous society over which they rule demands strength. At the other extreme are] perhaps the weakest women I have anywhere seen – selfishly timid, humbly dependent, languid in body and with minds of no reach at all.

Underwood says in his *Women of the Confederacy* that

> The busiest women the world has ever seen were the wives and daughters of the Southern planters during the days of slavery. . : It is no wonder that a Georgia woman, when she heard the negroes were really free, gave a sigh of relief and exclaimed: "Thank heaven! I shall have to work for them no more!"

She was but one of the southern ladies that exulted in their own emancipation.

The sterling quality of the women of the South was manifested in times of emergency and stress (as will be evidenced further in a study of war days). Revolutionary women had borne like privation. Ramsay said in his *History of South Carolina* (1809):

> When the war was ended and their husbands and fathers were by its ravages reduced in their circumstances, they aided by

their economy and retirement from the world to repair the losses. . . In Carolina, where sickness and health, poverty and riches, frequently alternate in rapid succession, wives and daughters bear incredible fatigues and privations with exemplary fortitude.

He testified to the efficiency of widows left with insolvent estates:

In such extremities the female character in Carolina has shone with peculiar luster. Two obvious and common resources are open . . . to keep a lodging-house or open a school. In these or some other modes of making a "living" widows engage, and often with surprising success. . . By their judicious management, estates have been retrieved – families reared – sons and daughters, knowing that their prospects of paternal fortune are cut off, are educated strictly and early taught to depend on their own exertions. . . Speculating, intemperate, mismanaging husbands advance their families by dying and leaving to their widows the sole management of their embarrassed fortunes. In the lower grades of life, where there are no fortunes to repair, the industry and economy of the wife produces similar results eminently conducive to the advancement of the common interest.

A chief indictment against the system of the South is that it afforded no proper sphere for the largest usefulness of the potentialities of woman; in fact it is probable that her opportunities progressively died away as the chattel system plunged toward its fall. There was no saving grace in serving as a pinnacle to the precarious structure of slavery. Mrs. Houstoun in *Hesperos* remarks of New Orleans:

The French Creole ladies are remarkably indolent and are apt to grow extremely corpulent, when early youth is past: they are very slightly educated, and beyond the subject of dress, I doubt their ideas extending with anything like distinctness. Love-making sometimes occupies them violently for a time, but it requires too much thought and exertion to be a very popular amusement with them – "Il parle si bien toilette," seems to be the highest praise they can bestow on a male acquaintance.

Benwell noted that the Charleston ladies were inert. Active women, he said, were seldom to be met with, the wives of affluent men being in general like pampered children and suffering dreadfully from ennui. Especially astonishing is the news item from Fairfax County, Virginia, in 1834, where a young lady was lawfully qualified as a selectman; a situation held by her mother for many years before her.[139]

The necessity of self-support rarely if ever befell the woman of "good family." Brothers and other male relatives never allowed such women to toil. A young woman writes:

Before the war, self-support was the last resort with respectable women in the South, and such a thought was never entertained so long as there was any male relative to look to for support, and men felt responsible for the support of even remote female relatives. . . I have heard of instances where refined and able-bodied women would allow themselves to be supported by the charity of their friends rather than resort to work for self-support – and this not because they had any reluctance to work, but because charity seemed to them the more respectable.

The other course would compromise self and family.[140]

Gallantry to woman was the gallantry of the harem. Nowhere in the world were women shown more surface respect than in the South, yet degradation of the sex was obvious. Women of the oligarchy were exempt from menial cares but licentious secrets (or disclosures) smothered wholesome comradeship and woman became the chief ornament of the house or merely its keeper. Miss Martineau wrote:

I have seen, with heart sorrow, the kind politeness, the gallantry, so insufficient to the loving heart, with which the wives of the South are treated by their husbands. I have seen the horror of a woman's having to work . . . the eagerness to

---

[139] *Man*, March 8, 1834.
[140] Tillett. *Southern Womanhood as affected by the War*, 12.

ensure her unearned ease and rest; the deepest insult which can
be offered to an intelligent and conscientious woman. . .
One gentleman who declares himself interested in the whole
subject, expresses his horror of the employment of women in
the northern states, for useful purposes. He told me that the
same force of circumstances which, in the region he inhabits,
makes men independent, increases the dependence of women,
and will go on to increase it. Society is there, he declared "always advancing towards orientalism."

Softness, gentleness, and grace disguised a chattel.
Ladies of the old South might stitch and make music,
but even to teach school was to risk social standing.

An English farmer who visited America a little before Miss Martineau's coming comments pointedly on
the appearance of divinity that sat upon woman in the
South. As always under Parasitism, woman was cruel
to woman and ignorance abounded. Extreme propriety in the presence of ladies was sufficient compensation
for infidelities. Here, if ever, the sable sisterhood of
shame were the vicarious guardians of the formal purity of their more favored rivals.

It is scarcely necessary to say that southern chivalry
did not include within its purview the wretched women
of the "poor whites." Men that would almost jump
out of their boots to wait on a wealthy dame would
treat with contempt a poor woman. "These are the
men generally," says Long, "who contend that there
are no virtuous women in the world."[141]

It must not be supposed that the southern theory on
woman's sphere was essentially different from the phil-
osophy of the North. The following citation from the
North Carolina University *Magazine* of 1859-1860
might well have appeared in the North:

[Woman's sphere is the household.] Wherever she is found
to have placed the boundaries of her position at defiance, and to

---
[141] Long. *Pictures of Slavery*, 272.

have made innovations upon the grounds of lordly man's estate, she is divested of that halo of female beauty and confiding love that is the natural accompaniment to her proper sphere, and presents a spectacle of horrid deformity and misshapen beauty. . . She seems to have been created as a repository of man's troubles, in whom he is sure to find a sympathizing and noble friend, who soothes his harassed and weary mind, and in turn leans upon his strong arm for protection, to be guarded from the rude breath of adversity, and shielded from the demoralizing influence that a contact with the world is apt to generate. . . She should always be found occupying a position of equality. . . Wherever she is found occupying a menial position, and regarded as an inferior, barbarism and ignorance, superstition and irreligion, is an invariable concomitant.

Unfortunately, fine words were of small advantage to the essentially degraded womanhood that so universally characterized the South.[142]

Angelina Grimké nobly assailed the perverted conception of womanhood regnant in her day. She denied the need of romantic chivalry and contended that human rights are not founded on sex; what is right for man to do is right for woman.

This regulation of duty by the mere circumstance of sex . . . has led to [a] multifarious train of evils. . . Man has been converted into the warrior, and clothed with sternness, and those other kindred qualities, which in common estimation belong to his character as a man; whilst woman has been taught to lean upon an arm of flesh, to sit as a doll arrayed in "gold and pearls and costly array," to be admired for her personal charms, caressed and humored like a spoiled child, or converted into a mere drudge to suit the convenience of her lord and master. Thus have all the diversified relations of life been filled with "confusions and every evil work." [Man is free to be despotic, selfish, proud, arrogant, lustful, brutal. Woman is reduced to the status of tool.][143]

---

[142] An excellent treatment of "The Lady of the Slave States" is found in Putnam, *The Lady*, 282-323.

[143] Grimké. *Letters to Catherine E. Beecher*, 107, 115-116.

Unfortunately there was not much chance for a progressive movement among southern women. A very interesting *Ladies' Magazine* begun at Savannah in 1819 was forced to suspend at the end of six months for lack of patronage. The lady of the archaic South left little written record. As in the North, woman received no worthy education. An actor remarked in 1842 upon the rarity of daughters of the far South among the vast number of women magazine writers. Gentlemen of the old régime in the South would say, "A woman's name should appear in print but twice — when she marries and when she dies."[144] There was no economic opportunity for women outside the home. If there had been, social status would have debarred woman from acceptance of it. Miss Martineau found that mantua-making was "almost the only employment in which a white southern woman can earn a subsistence." Abdy remarked upon the dishonor shown to industry in Washington and the consequent danger to female virtue in that center of gay idleness and profligacy.

In a blind way, southern ladies were intense in their political sentiments. Politicians could count on unstudied backing. A northern woman who spent five years in the South wrote: "The Tennessee ladies are all politicians, I believe the most zealous to be found anywhere, and I have caught their spirit." The atmosphere that surrounded southern ladies adapted them admirably to the blind loyalty so much in demand among the followers of the standard-bearers of exploitation.

The snuff-dipping propensities of ante-bellum ladies seem incongruous with the famed gentility. The practice was supposed to brighten the eyes and im-

---

[144] Avary. *Dixie after the War*, 23 *footnote*.

prove the complexion of the young, hence rose (in theory) above the level of mere self-indulgence. But it was detrimental to health and character. Long said: "It is blasting the health of many a young mother, while a broken hearted husband stands by and can render no relief. No wonder that Southern men are irritable, passionate, and headstrong, if born of such mothers." Other causes contributed to ill health. Long further remarked:

I have no doubt that the white ladies of the South have worse health than any class of females in any enlightened nation. . . It is the result of slavery, which exempts them from all labor of a domestic character. . . It is considered a mark of gentility to be feeble, effeminate, dyspeptic, and nervous. . . Some resort to acids to reduce their bulk, and thus ruin their teeth, their breath, and their health. . . We . . . fear that many bosoms that appear natural, are but cotton after all. . . Southern ladies die early, and bequeath multitudes of motherless children to step-mothers. It is no uncommon thing to find men who have been married two, three, and four times.

Even the chastity of the southern women (a monopolized excellence) was scarcely a virtue, but rather a matter of course. Men sedulously shielded their female perquisites of white blood. A young lady of South Carolina got a verdict of one thousand dollars against a man (of moderate means) for imputation of unchastity. Education and public opinion were strained to the preservation of the purity of free women, or rather of such as belonged to the master race. Somewhat of the spirit of the regnant male may be glimpsed in the remark of a Natchez gentleman about 1808: "The ladies in general are extremely delicate, which never fails to please, and excite the warmest sensations in the beholder. . . Tho chaste as the virgin queen before the Gordian knot is tied, yet indulgent as the Cyprian goddess for ever after."

We need not be surprised at unworthy traits in some of the women of the South. They were the product of six or seven generations of an execrable economic system and could not altogether escape its taint. If women attended negro sales and were not always entirely refined in their manipulations; if, as Miss Grimké reported, a woman that conducted daily family worship showed extreme brutality to slaves; if a Baltimore lady "richly and fashionably dressed, and apparently moving in the best society" derived her income from the sale of children of negro women whose husbands belonged to other masters—there is no occasion for wonderment. Miss Martineau mentioned the case of a young man full of the southern pride who married a young lady who

> Soon after her marriage showed an imperious and cruel temper towards her slaves. Her husband gently remonstrated. She did not mend. He warned her . . . that, if she compelled him to it, he would deprive her of the power she misused. Still she did not mend. He one day came and told her that he had sold all his domestic slaves for their own sakes. . . It rarely happens that free service can be hired; and this proud gentleman assists his wife's labors with his own hands.

A Virginian was quoted in 1853 as saying:

> I must remark . . . that Southern ladies are not always "amiable and domestic." Some . . . are real viragos, and make no more of giving a negro man nine-and-thirty with a cowhide than they do of taking a chew of tobacco. Some of them are indolent, fashionable, and fond of pleasure, and careless alike of husbands, children, or slaves.[145]

Almira Lincoln Phelps, a southern woman, after

---

[145] Neilson. *Recollections of a six Years Residence in the United States,* 285; American Anti-Slavery Society. *American Slavery as it is,* 22; Martineau. *Society in America,* vol. ii, 315; American and foreign Anti-Slavery Society. *Thirteenth Annual Report,* 152.

telling of good housekeeping by New England ladies, said:

> Most of you young ladies from the Southern States are not under the necessity of performing household labors. It would be a mistaken kindness in you to do the labor and let the menials live in idleness. But yet it is well for you to know what labor is. . . No family can be well ordered or even comfortable, where the care, as well as the labor, is thrown upon servants.

Housekeeping is more important, she said, than merely ornamental living; accomplishments should be valued chiefly as an aid to refinement and cheer of the domestic circle, whereas most young ladies thought they were means to gain admiration in society, that it is a waste of time to practise them on their families.

In a young man's letter from Richmond a few years before the middle of the century was the assertion that an alarming deterioration was affecting woman's ways.

> I look upon these changes that are now occurring among the young women of our cities in their language, habits, and manners, as more important than questions in government; for they exist among those who rule and direct the men who carry out the government. . . Woman can alter the dialect, change the manners, dictate the dress and habits of life, and control the morals of every community. . . Young ladies who have received education in northern schools, or who have gone to northern cities for the purpose of obtaining "an air" (airs, not graces, are thus received) [have adopted plebeian prouncation.]

A mid-century writer on Richmond lamented that such works as the *Lady's Book* are more popular than the *Southern Literary Messenger* though they are full of garbage, sickly sentimentality, and "romantic tales adapted to the capacity and the unripe minds of boarding-school young ladies."[146]

Death and widowhood in the old South complicated the problem of keeping intact the family name and

---

[146] Little. *Richmond*, 73-74, 84.

dignity. Schoepf reported of Confederation days in South Carolina that

> Under this zone, the male sex is exposed to more and more dangerous diseases than the female, or rather the men expose themselves to disease, because they permit themselves vastly more extravagances of all sorts and give a freer rein to their passions. Men therefore die frequently in the bloom of their years and leave behind for others young and rich widows.

In the first half of the nineteenth century Tennessee experienced, like Virginia in colonial days, a belleship of widows. In old eastern Virginia it was not expected that a widow would remarry and usually she did not. It was almost a matter of course for a husband to make enjoyment of the estate conditional on non-marriage; the chief gospel was the preservation of family name and these restrictions were not considered cruel.[147]

Conservatism retarded the introduction of divorce. In New Orleans of the forties divorces were practically unknown in polite circles. In some cases men sent erring wives abroad and made them stay there. There was no need of divorce in such a case, or of open scandal.[148] South Carolina was already wedded to her present conservatism. Hecke heard, indeed, in Maryland and Virginia that various men had deserted as many as four wives, many with four or five children.

Family affection was a strong asset in the prosperous circles of the South. The isolation of families constituted each into a community bound together by closest ties of affection, dependence, and interest. Every economic and social force contributed to family solidarity. Joel C. Harris says:

> The home life of the plantation . . . was larger, ampler, and more perfect than that which exists in the republic today,

---

[147] Warner. *Studies in the South and West*, 23.
[148] Ripley. *Social Life in old New Orleans*, 91.

not because it was more leisurely and freer from care, but because the aims and purposes of the various members of the family were more concentrated.

Home was the center of all life. In the sparsely peopled rural districts public diversions of a commercial sort did not exist to lure young folks away from parental supervision. Relations between parents and children were ordinarily spontaneous and affectionate. Dyer asserts that

It was this rural home off to itself, fixing its own policies, and directing its own activities, more than any other institution, more than all other institutions, that gave to the South its distinctive type of civilization. . . . Such life and influence can never come from a city home.

Cook remarks that "the Kentucky children were taught that character was everything . . . that home was a sacred retreat, and that he who invaded its sacred purity might expect death." Hale and Merritt in their *History of Tennessee* recall that "the home was a home in the best sense – a domestic center of absolute family order and discipline, rather free from distracting cares, and refined. The women were ladies in the old high sense of the word." Aged Southerners still

Remember the genteelness, the industry, the kindness of rule and deportment, that were general in planters' families before the War; how they often breakfasted with the sun-rise, and how they and their sons, in the day, laid out and superintended work in the fields, and their wives and daughters did the like in the house and the cabinyard, how the early evening was given to reading and family discussion.

Religion had a profound influence on southern family life. The Scotch-Irish reared the family altar. The house of worship, whether high church or low, was a family institution in the South. Among the early settlers of Kentucky, "whatever other books were wanting,

each family had its Bible, and this being almost the
only book in the household, it was highly prized, and
its lessons instilled into the minds of the little ones."
Michaux, however, who travelled in the West in 1802,
said of Kentucky:

> Whenever there is an alliance between families, the difference
> of religion is never considered as an obstacle; the husband and
> wife pursue whatever kind of worship they like best, and their
> children, when they grow up, do just the same, without the
> interference of their parents.

In so far as city life developed, the simplicity of the
family life tended to disappear.   At Richmond in 1800
"the higher circle consisted of the families of the neighboring planters, who left their estates to the management of overseers, and spent the larger part of the year
in Richmond because of its social advantages."   At
New Orleans the perpetual shifting on account of fever
was a serious evil to sober families and very injurious
to the minds and habits of children.   King says however of French New Orleans in ante-bellum days:
"There were no summer trips then beyond the atmosphere of Louisiana, none of the periodical separations,
which, year after year . . . break through the
union of families and friends."   But in New Orleans
even as early as 1835 there were bachelor apartments.

The first tendency of the spirit of Revolutionary
days was to do away with artificial social distinctions.
Primogeniture was abolished in Virginia and Maryland; so that only by will could estates be maintained
intact (as was in fact done in some notable cases for the
sake of prestige).   In Maryland, following the Revolution there was an open contempt for anything savor-
ing of caste and nobility.   "Coats of arms were destroyed and even erased from family silver in some
cases, and all evidences of pride of lineage frowned

down by the American patriots and their descendants, so that not to know one's grandmother was not rare." [149]

After the Revolution, soil exhaustion in the older states and competition in tobacco reduced old families to poverty and oblivion. Jefferson made a pathetic attempt to keep up the old hospitality; Mrs. Madison received charity. As early as 1820 "the absence of the privilege of primogeniture, and the consequent repeated subdivision of property are gradually effecting a change in the structure of society in South Carolina, and will shortly efface its most interesting and characteristic features." By the early thirties at Charleston abolition of primogeniture had undermined old families. "Comparatively few of the old families now remain who are wealthy. . . Therefore, the sons of the best men of the South are wisely placed in counting-houses in the great trading cities, or . . . bred to some useful calling." (But there were many showy idlers.) The South Carolina planter no longer inherited enough to send his sons to English universities. Division of property was killing patrician notions. At the same period Abdy

> Asked a very shrewd man, who looked like a farmer, how long estates remained in the same family in Virginia. "The longest period," he replied, "may be three or four generations. I do not think I could point out one in possession of an estate that belonged to it at the revolution. The poor and industrious soon succeed to the rich and extravagant; and a perpetual interchange is going on between them."

By 1845, the once numerous large estates had in many instances gradually dwindled, the descendants retaining the pride without the means. Many preferred to subsist on the bounty of friends rather than work. Olmsted remarked in 1861 that a large percentage of

[149] Richardson. *Sidelights on Maryland History*, vol. i, 178-179.

families composing the Virginia and South Carolina gentry before the Revolution had passed through dismantling poverty very dissipating to hereditary breeding. Very few were the real "old families" that remained at all "well-bred."

The Revolution itself had divided families and the political divisions that followed had somewhat of a similar effect. Federalist fathers had Republican sons. A young man objectionable on account of his party eloped with a young lady and had to fight a duel with an irate brother-in-law before he could get into the family affections. In another case months of intercession were required.

The democratic disposition to deal with individuals, not families, bore fruit in a Maryland statute of 1818 to the effect that

> No children shall be answerable for the passage money of their parents, dead or alive, nor parents for their deceased children, nor a husband for his deceased wife, nor a wife for her deceased husband, any pretence of custom in contract, promise or agreement made beyond sea, to the contrary notwithstanding.

In spite, however, of all contrary tendencies, the family in the South was a much more potent institution than elsewhere in the republic. Old families held the day. In Kentucky, family feuds cost sundry lives. The eldest son of the old Virginia families was regarded as representative of the kin. In old east Virginia, family was a fetich. Estates were entailed to the limit of the law – one generation, and the heir commonly renewed religiously the entail. The tidewater owner of large estates would have been insulted by the idea of selling his home. The ancestral abode was the one spot on earth. A writer of 1837 protesting against soil wastage and abandonment too common (in Florida) said: "It is something to preserve the fruits that we have planted, and the improvements that we have made in early life, or those which we have received from our ancestors."

Relationship was traced by Southerners to a remote degree. The bond of fellowship stretched to include all that were worthy, even tho they had removed to distant places. A post-bellum writer on North Carolina said: "In the many political canvasses which I have made, from East to West, I have never, to my best recollection, visited a county however distant, without being asked by some one about his kinsmen living in my county." It would be hard to overestimate the power of a great and strongly entrenched southern family connected with a dozen like families all holding a common point of view and action. Marriage and intermarriage and the tangle of consanguinity welded the slave power. Intercourse consequent to intermarriage made Virginians clannish. A traveller prior to 1825 found an old couple in Mississippi "who had settled nine children in their neighborhood . . . giving each . . . about one thousand acres . . . and a stock of negroes, and retaining for themselves only just sufficient for their wants and to supply a little occupation." By 1845 the rich lands bordering the Altamaha (in Georgia), with adjacent islands had been acquired by a few families.

Christmas was the time for reunions. "It was not uncommon to see from twenty-five to sixty relatives seated at the bounteous board." In Old Virginia some relations were always present on a visit. There was a great deal of visiting between Kentucky families. A historian of Mississippi recalls the early custom of going "with one's family to the home of a 'neighbor' a few miles distant to remain from Saturday until Monday or even longer." A writer on Georgia says:

> An aunt of mine has said to me that, when a young lady in her father's house, she scarcely remembered sitting down to the dinner table with less than twenty-four. And I have often been told of the gentleman and his wife, who, being asked to dine at a residence on St. Simon, found that during the meal a boat had been sent to Darien, fifteen miles distant for their luggage, and that so much pleased were host, hostess, and guests with one another, that the stay was prolonged until two children had been born to the visiting couple.

Hospitality in the old South prevented the establishment of good hotels, yet one finds many instances showing lack of hospitality. Hence we are inclined to doubt the universal receptivity of the southern home. It seems probable that kindred or other social ties or interests drew rather narrow lines.

Outbreeding in so far as it occurred had significant social results. Mixture with the French tended to a lessening of austerity. Marriage of creoles with lawyers and merchants from the North helped to cement the sections. The children of many southern families even prior to 1825 were

> Educated, the young men at colleges in the northern and eastern States, and the young ladies at boarding-schools in Philadelphia; and some of them have formed matrimonial connections with northern families. . . One happy consequence is a degree of repugnance to the slave-system on the part of some of the younger members of the community.

A northern governess remarked that ninety-nine per cent of the governesses, tutors, professional men, and others who flock to the South (ten thousand yearly) in order to improve their fortunes remain (the young ladies, if they can find southern husbands).

On the whole, the South was probably more conservative than the North in its treatment of the young.

In New Orleans of 1840 "children were neither seen nor heard. . . They led the simple life, going and coming in their own unobstrusive way." In Old Kentucky, "children were taught to love and venerate their parents, and were always ready to help them and vindicate them, and a boy would fight quicker for his father's or his mother's honor than for his own." A southern man that had lived north wrote in 1860:

> The parental discipline is more rigid [in the South] and Young America is rarely met with, save in the large towns and villages. . . The better portion of southern boys are taught to consider themselves boys so long as they remain in their teens, and the valuable advice of Hebrew Solomon is followed to the letter, in case they seek to imitate the vices or to ape the manners of their elders before the down has ripened on their boyish cheeks.

Page says of old Virginia:

> There was something in seeing the master and mistress obeyed by the plantation and looked up to by the neighborhood which inspired the children with a reverence akin to awe which is not known at this present time. It was not till the young people were grown that the reverence lost the awe and became based only upon affection and admiration.

The customary subduction of girlhood was not sufficient to quench normal exuberance. *Letters from the South and West* noted that "when out on the green terraces, or in the parterres, and orchards, the young girls run wild as the boys." Page says of Virginia:

> There were the little girls in their great sun-bonnets, often sewed on to preserve the wonderful peach-blossom complexions, with their small female companions playing about the yard or garden, running with and wishing they were boys, and getting half scoldings from mammy for being tomboys and tearing their aprons and dresses.

The South had certain pathologies of child behavior and child control. In 1853 a manual school was urged for Norfolk orphan boys. "A number of subjects are daily running wild through our streets, exempt from all control or protection, engaging in every kind of mischief and vice, and treading that path which must inevitably lead them to crime and infamy." There was also in the ante-bellum South a type of man with "Yankee" characteristics—cold and repellant to wife and children, anxious to keep them from fee simple inheritance. While he buried himself in sordid acquisition his children were free to give themselves to dissipation and senseless love of pleasure or else, unreasonably stinted and curbed during his life and on his death coming into possession of wealth which they did not know how to use wisely, they fell into unwise expenditure. From these southern mammonists, it was alleged, sprang "in the main our cotton snobs and rich southern bullies." The cotton snob went off to college and bought harlots. When he married, the family vaunted its wealth in gaudy display.

Child care was far from scientific. For instance, the New Orleans creole beauties were said to be excessively indulgent mothers. Fanny Kemble noted, too, that their overseer's wife was suckling a baby two and a half years old and remarked that American women injure themselves thus.

As in colonial days, education in the rural South was a serious problem. Schoepf remarked of Charleston in Confederation days: "It has long been nothing extraordinary for the richer inhabitants to send their children of both sexes to Europe for their education." People of other states did likewise, at least for the boys. Northern colleges received many southern boys before the War in spite of the danger of heretical infection as to sacred institutions. In the early days free thought touched the South. It is learned that prior to 1816 "Liberty" and "Infidelity" crept into William and Mary. "Dissipation followed. . . Reflecting parents at last took the alarm, and silently withdrew their children from an institution where they could no longer trust them with safety to their morals, and hardly to their lives." [150]

The system of tutors and governesses was also employed. Many of these pedagogs came from the North. One recorded that usually the governess holds a place midway between the lady and the overseer's wife. She can't get a husband inasmuch as a gentleman will not court a teacher.

> This line of distinction between the governess and the mother of the young children she teaches is more strongly defined in the older and more aristocratic families. [The higher the fashion of the family, the lower the station of the governess.] In general the planters keep their daughters under governesses till they are fourteen, and then send them to some celebrated school, North or South, to remain a year or two to graduate. . . Since the recent agitation of the slavery question, the Mississippians are disposed to be shy of northern teachers.

Preparatory training at home was likely to be deficient and to subject the lads to sharp transition when they went to college.

The public school system of the South was crude. It grew under difficulties, in the face of the individualistic or aristocratic propensities of the people.

In the latter part of the eighteenth century at Ellicott's Mills, Maryland, the company built a schoolhouse for the children of the village and of the adjacent neighborhood. All of suitable age were admitted irrespective of their parents' means. In Rockingham County, Virginia, the Methodists started a school in

[150] *Letters from Virginia*, 130.

1794. "The scholars shall attend at eight oclock in the summer and half past eight in the winter, and the teacher shall regulate the time of attendance in spring and autumn according to the length of the day." An hour was allowed for recreation in winter and two in summer. Dismissal was at six in summer, four in winter. "No gaming of any kind, nor instruments of play shall be tolerated. The scholars shall be examined in the 'Instructions for Children' once a week except the children of such parents as disapprove the same."

In 1811 the South Carolina legislature "on petition of several counties, established what was meant to be a working system of free common schools open to all the white children of school age," preference to be given to destitute orphans and children of the poor in case of shortage of funds. One hundred thirty-three schools were established at once. This was the first free school system founded in America, and continued with various degrees of success down to the Civil War. On the proposed repeal of the act in 1813 one legislator spoke effectively in its defense, showing that the country people have no means to educate their children, that genius may be found buried in lowly cottages, and that the free schools had been a godsend. "It is contended that the children should be boarded, as well as educated, at public expense because" the schools are remote from their homes! "One gentleman has said that his constituents disdain to be enlightened at public expense." [151]

In 1820 Virginia inaugurated a state system of free schools for the poor. Maryland established a state school system in 1825. In 1839 North Carolina put a state system in operation. The modern system of free schools began in New Orleans in 1841. Louisiana es-

---

[151] Dyer. *Democracy in the South before the Civil War*, 71-72; Courtenay. *Education in Charleston*, 5.

tablished her public school system in 1845. Dyer
maintains that "the idea of a State Fund for the education of those who were not able to pay their tuition
originated in the South. The idea of the education of
the poor children by the state came from the South."
The school system of the South, however, scarcely could
be called a success. Abdy observed of Virginia in the
early thirties that there were no public schools as in the
North. Commissioners of the poor sent children to
private schools along with those able to pay. "Rather
than expose them to humiliation, many parents keep
their children at home, where they receive little or no
education." He added that there was little provision
for popular education in the South. Page in the "Old
Dominion" mentioned a small free school in his neighborhood established by a bequest of 1844 – a farmer left
his estate for the education of children of his poor
neighbors. A physician writing in 1851 on Richmond
said:

> The mass of children are taught in private or in denominational
> schools. . . It is better to place education under church in-
> fluence than under that of the state. . . The government
> cannot, itself, educate the community, it can only act by a cloud
> of irresponsible and ignorant school masters; nor would it be
> right for it to exercise the power if it possessed the ability of im-
> parting a good education. It is no more a part of government
> to provide education to the people, than it is to provide labor
> and wages; nor is it right to tax one section of a community to
> educate the other.

In Georgia fear of paternalism retarded adoption of a
common school system. There was also lack of interest in education.[152]

---

[152] On this paragraph see: Dyer, *Democracy in the South before the Civil
War*, 71-77; Abdy, *Journal of a Residence and Tour in the United States*,
vol. ii, 238, 254-257; Page, *Old Dominion*, 342-344; Little, *Richmond*, 81;
Smith, *Story of Georgia and the Georgia People*, 488-489.

In 1851 William Gregg speaking on manufactures before the South Carolina Institute said:

> While we are aware that the northern and eastern states find no difficulty in educating their poor, we are ready to despair of success in the matter, for even penal laws against the neglect of education would fail to bring many of our country people to send their children to school. . . We have collected at [Graniteville] about eight hundred people, and as likely looking a set of country girls as may be found – industrious and orderly people, but deplorably ignorant, three-fourths of the adults not being able to read or write their names. . . With the aid of ministers of the Gospel on the spot, to preach to them and lecture them on the subject, we have obtained but about sixty children for our school, of about a hundred which are in the place. . . The only means of educating and Christianizing our poor whites, will be to bring them into such villages, where they will not only become intelligent, but a thrifty and useful class. . . Notwithstanding our rule, that no one can be permitted to occupy our houses who does not send all his children to school that are between the ages of six and twelve, it was with some difficulty, at first, that we could make up even a small school.

"The Child That Toileth Not" was not a twentieth century discovery. Charles T. James in De Bow's *Industrial Resources of the Southwest* said that "Boys and girls, by thousands, destitute both of employment and the means of education, grow up to ignorance and poverty, and, too many of them to vice and crime. [Manufacturing is the cure.]"[153]

A writer on Tazewell County, Virginia in 1852 said that schools were poor and that there was need of conveying children to school. In 1855 we find at Norfolk a free school for the benefit of indigent children. "It is hoped that this school will become a useful institution to the community in rescuing many friendless children from ignorance and vice."

---

[153] Tower. *Slavery unmasked*, 351-356.

In the country schools and academies of the old
South coeducation was the rule and much benefit came
from this companionship.[154]   The South was conservative in respect to education of women.   Some of them
gained intellectual charm from contact with cultured
men or by effective general reading.   Fiction did not
have right of way everywhere.   It is rather amusing
to think of ladies secretly reading the *Vicar of Wakefield* or *Paul and Virginia*.[155]   From Georgia came a
plea for more attention to the education of women that
they might be better fitted to train their children.   The
Ladies' Magazine of Boston quoted, in 1833, a Georgia
educator as saying that "too much show and too little
solidity has marked the course of girls' education, and
woman has been looked upon rather as a creature to
please, than as a being designed for the exercise of
thought."   One could wish that more men had shared
the view of the University of Virginia student who
wrote home in 1849 urging the education of his sister
and alleging that "if an educated woman does not make
a good wife, it is because the man who received her
hand was unworthy of it, and because it was the hand
of a slave, and not of a wife and an equal that was the
object of his desire."[156]   Yet Georgia had the first college in the world to bestow diplomas on women – Wesleyan at Macon.[157]

   Hundley indicated in his *Social Relations in our
Southern States* that

In most instances the daughters of [a middle-class, modest]
southern matron resemble their mother, save that they possess
a little more modern polish and culture, and hanker more eagerly after the vanities of the world; but even the daughters are

---

[154] Curry. *The South in the olden Time*, 41.
[155] Hale and Merritt. *History of Tennessee and Tennesseeans*, vol. ii, 409.
[156] Smedes. *Southern Planter*, 136.
[157] Rutherford. *Georgia Day Programme*, 1910, 19, 32.

often quite uneducated in the current literature of the times, and in all things else evince a simplicity of mind and character altogether refreshing. Sometimes, 'tis true, they are sent to boarding schools (which are becoming more common in the South of late years), are there exposed to a false and shallow system of hot-bed culture for a few sessions; and emerging therefrom in due time make their debût in life, possessed of full as much pride and affectation, as well as conceit and vanity, as of artificial graces of person and manner; and boasting a superficial knowledge of twenty different branches of learning, but in reality having a perfect mastery and comprehension of none. Southern young ladies of this character, however, are usually the daughters of tradesmen, village store-keepers, and the like, who constitute a pretty fair proportion of the southern middle classes. . . [These men frequently educate their children so senselessly] that they almost invariably grow up to be nothing better than doddling fops and parvenues.[158]

The lot of the girl of the humbler classes of southern whites just before the war did not include even the minimum of schooling allotted to the boy. The only exception was in the new public schools in a few cities, in some of which excellent high schools for girls were established. From these sources was developing a large class of enthusiastic girls, precursors of woman's free education in the South. Ante-bellum southern girls were largely dependent on female colleges established chiefly by churches. Isolation and lack of good local facilities   hindered   women's   enlightenment.   "Nowhere was the opportunity for educational and social development more persistently withholden from the majority of women of the lower orders than in the older Southern States previous to 1860."[159]

Various arrangements were made in the old South for the care of dependent children. A Maryland act

[158] Hundley. *Social Relations in our Southern States*, 100, 111.
[159] Mayo. *Southern Women in the recent Educational Movement in the South*, 38-43.

of 1818 empowering orphans' courts to bind out free
black children neglected or not usefully employed by
parents provided that courts might require the child to
be taught to read or write, or in lieu thereof that thirty
dollars be given in addition to the ordinary dues at
freedom. (As with whites, the wishes of parents were
to be consulted in the choice of master.) The code of
1860 stated that it was not necessary, in binding out colored children, to require education.

In Virginia

Prior to 1805 [it was] customary . . . to provide instruction for slaves . . . servants . . . free negroes.
Church wardens and overseers of the poor upon binding out a
bastard or a pauper child, black or white, specifically required
that he should be taught to "read" and "write" and "calculate," as well as to follow some profitable form of labor.[160]

Various orphan asylums were in operation. In 1797
Dr. De La Howe of South Carolina left his estate to
be used in the education and training in manual and
domestic labor of twelve boys and twelve girls—a permanent blessing to homeless, needy orphans. The
South Carolina Huguenot Society looked after many
children. A movement started in Savannah in 1801
for the foundation of a female asylum shows good sense
views on the treatment of orphans:

It is a matter of certainty, that notwithstanding the attentions
paid to the poor in this city, many female orphans suffer for
want of early patronage. . . We are most deeply penetrated
with the sufferings of our own sex. . . Our design is to
raise funds for the benefit of female orphans and other poor
children, from three to ten years of age, and to board them with
some capable discreet woman, who shall teach them to read,
write, sew, and do all kinds of domestic business, until they are
old enough to be placed in virtuous families. . . At a suitable time they shall be placed in good families, until the age of

---

[160] Ballagh. *History of Slavery in Virginia*, 109.

eighteen years, except such . . . as may be taught mil-
linery, mantua-making, or some business of a similar kind. . .
They have since had the happiness of placing [six persons] all
lately under the chilling influence of adversity; but now, neatly
attired, well fed, and assiduously instructed, [they] inspire
in every benevolent beholder, the most pleasing reflections.

Captain Hall of the British navy, who travelled in
America in the later twenties, considered the orphanage
at Charleston

A most interesting sight, however questionable the policy may
be, which, by holding out artificial means of subsistence to families, gives a hurtful degree of stimulus to the increase of population, already but too apt to run into excess. [His own remarks seem to emphasize, however, the need of such an institution. After speaking of the way in which American families
scatter and members lose sight of one another he said:] It
often happens, that the heads of a household die off, or wander
away, no one knows where, and leave children, if not quite destitute, at least dependent on persons whose connexion and interest in them are so small, that the public eventually is obliged
to take care of them. . . At Charleston, Savannah, and
other parts of the country where . . . yellow fever occurs,
and where that still more dreadful curse of America – spirit-
drinking – prevails, to at least as great an excess as in the other
states, it very often happens that children are left, at the end
of the sickly season, without any relations or natural protectors
at all. Of course, I speak now of the poorer inhabitants, part
of whom are made up of emigrants, either from foreign countries or from other parts of America.

Abdy pointed out in 1835 that in New Orleans "a gam-
bler can provide for his family, while he is pursuing
his amusements; the Orphan Asylum in that city being
supported out of the licenses [of gambling dens]."

Poverty abounded in the ante-bellum South and
class cleavage was clear-cut. The slave-holding oligarchy was a meager fraction of the population. Many
of the whites were in a position to envy the slave. Miserable housing, scanty subsistence, absence of educa-

tion, lack of opportunity on account of the degradation of labor resulting from the slave system, conspired to depress the moral tone and to lower the quality of family institutions. Sometimes a very poor family owned a slave or two and these miserable chattels shared in the extremities of fortune that fell upon their masters. At the beginning of the century an observer expresses the conviction

That in nine cases in ten, the hardships and sufferings of the colored population of lower Virginia is attributable to the poverty and distress of its owners. In many instances, an estate scarcely yields enough to feed and clothe the slaves in a comfortable manner, without allowing anything for the support of the master and the family; but it is obvious that the family must first be supported, and the slaves must be content with the surplus; and this on a poor, old, worn out tobacco plantation, is often very small and wholly inadequate to the comfortable sustenance of the hands.[161]

A dealer gave the information that in some instances masters were obliged to sell slaves in order to save their families from ruin.[162]

The Augusta *Chronicle* in 1819 gave a glimpse of the depths of poverty that were possible even for whites. "Passed through . . . from Greenville District bound for Chatahouchee, a man and his wife, his son and his wife, with a cart but no horse. [The men were harnessed to the vehicle], the son's wife rode . . . and the old woman was walking, carrying a rifle and driving a cow."[163]

Candler observed of Virginia (in his work published in 1824) that

The log houses of the poor whites and free coloured people were little adapted to exclude cold and wet. All seemed dor-

[161] *Documentary History of American Industrial Society*, vol. ii, 63-64.
[162] — *Idem*, 67.
[163] — *Idem*, 196.

mant. . . The small occupier of land in the free states is
an independent, industrious man with children industrious as
himself. In the slave states, he is poor and lazy, and his children are brought up without having their powers either mental
or corporeal properly developed. The house of the former is
comfortable, that of the latter miserable.

A writer in *Niles' Register* prior to 1835 said of Maryland:

The character of the white laboring population in Maryland,
as well as their numbers, and efficiency, is declining in all the
chief slave holding counties. . . Hundreds of landholders
whose fathers lived in affluence are reduced almost to poverty,
without any personal act of indiscretion to cause it.[164]

Buckingham's book of 1842 calls attention to the fact
that in Georgia back country clearings all, young and
old, must work.

We saw many boys and girls, of not more than six or seven
years of age, some using small axes, others carrying wood, and
others assisting in domestic duties. In general they were very
dirty . . . the mother being too weary to wash them.
[Parents and children looked pale, haggard, overworked.]

Smith says that in ante-bellum Georgia "the toilers did
not often mate with the aristocrats nor intrude upon
them socially." In the mountains and pines common
folks had settled in advance of the schoolmaster; so the
children's only chance for learning was from mothers'
love. The women would teach all that they remembered. The father was too busy or tired. "Before
the war there were in north Georgia at least two generations that had grown up with but a limited education—in fact, with none to speak of, for it was rare to
find a man among them who could read or write."[165]

Buckingham said of North Carolina that at every

---

[164] Candler. *Summary View of America*, 251, 254; Abdy. *Journal of a
Residence and Tour in the United States*, vol. i, 383.

[165] Buckingham. *Slave States of America*, vol. i, 231-232; Smith. *School
History of Georgia*, 136.

farmhouse they saw eight or ten lazy men and boys hanging around. The women seemed equally lazy; niggers did the work. A southern-born gentleman, long a resident of South Carolina, said of poor whites on the banks of the Congaree in that state that they

> Are the descendants of the former proprietors of nearly all the land of the region; but for generations, their fathers have been gradually selling off to the richer planters moving in among them, and living on the purchase money of their lands, and their children have been brought up in listless, aimless, and idle independence.

This remark is but one evidence of the deterioration that befell the poor whites. Mr. Tarver of Missouri in 1847 published a paper containing the following observation:

> I lament to say that I have observed of late years that an evident deterioration is taking place in this part of the population, the younger portion of it being less educated, less industrious, and in every point of view less respectable than their ancestors.

Soil exhaustion was in part to blame but doubtless the hookworm played his usual rôle. Stirling's *Letters from the Slave States* mention "handsome dwellings here and there" and also "poor, mean-looking homesteads" but note the lack of "the neat farm-houses that dot the landscape of New England, and speak of comfort, equality, and intelligence." [166]

Slavery was in part responsible for racial decay among the whites. The slavery of whites with all its atrocities had gradually come to an end but negro slavery reacted on the white race. Olmsted was told in Virginia that

> Poor white girls never hired out to do servant's work, but they

---

[166] On this paragraph see: Buckingham, *Slave States of America*, vol. ii, 198-199; Olmsted, *Journey in the Seaboard Slave States*, 505-506; Tower, *Slavery unmasked*, 346; Stirling, *Letters from the Slave States*, 45.

would come and help another white woman about her sewing
and quilting and take wages for it.   But these girls were not
very respectable generally, and it was not agreeable to have
them in your house, though there were some very respectable
ladies that would go out to sew.

He found that the poor whites of North Carolina lived
wretchedly.   A gentleman said that he had several
times appraised on oath the whole household property
of such people at less than twenty dollars.   The travelling agent of a religious tract society read in a church
in Charleston from his diary:

Visited families, numbering two hundred twenty-one souls over
ten years of age; only twenty-three could read, and seventeen
write.   Forty-one families destitute of the Bible. . . All of
one family rushed away when I knelt to pray, to a neighbor's,
begging them to tell what I meant by it.   Other families fell
on their faces instead of kneeling.

Hundreds of southern families lived in log cabins
ten or twelve feet square "where the children run
around . . . naked . . . and a bedstead or
chair was not in the house, and never will be" said a
farmer living in Illinois.[167]

Hundley (a southern man who had lived North)
said that the sand-hillers were quite prolific, every
house having half-a-dozen children.   In the main, the
entire family occupied one room; "but it is a rare circumstance to find several families huddled into one
poor shanty, as is more often the case than otherwise
with those unfortunates in cities, who are constrained
to herd together promiscuously in tenant houses and in
underground cellars."[168]

Poor white folks were unwilling to have their children taught manual trades inasmuch as negroes gave to

[167] On this paragraph see: Olmsted, *Cotton Kingdom*, vol. i, 82, 188, vol.
ii, 285, 293, 308-309.
[168] Hundley. *Social Relations in our Southern States*, 265.

such occupation the servile taint. Charles T. James, in De Bow's *Industrial Resources of the South and West*, said that the southern "poor white man will endure . . . pinching poverty, rather than engage in servile labor under the existing state of things, even were employment offered him, which is not general." The white girl was not wanted at service and if she were she could not condescend to such degradation; hence she was subjected to want and misery.

So long as the newness of pioneer country lasted, the class lines were indistinct. In Mississippi prior to 1830 there was little contrast between rich and poor; the wealthy often preferred to live on a level with their less fortunate neighbors. "A failure to ask a neighbor to a house-raising, a clearing, or chopping frolic, or his family to a quilting was considered a great insult— such a one too as had to be answered for at the next muster or county court." But presently the chattel system developed a class of wealthy planters who became sharply distinguished from the lower class of poor white laborers. Exhaustion of the fertility of the southern soil by "mining methods" of plantation agriculture made it hard for the small farmer to compete save by the same methods that ended in ruin.

In 1850 De Bow said that poor whites

Are fast learning that there is almost an infinite world of industry opening before them, by which they can elevate themselves and their families from wretchedness and ignorance to competence and intelligence. It is this great upbearing of our masses that we are to fear so far as our institutions are concerned.

The *Southern Banner* of Athens, Georgia, voiced in 1859 the aspirations of the working class: "We want to see labor high. . . In every country the honest faithful laborer ought to be able to supply himself and family by his labor, not only with the necessaries, but the comforts of life." Olmsted reported[169] that at Columbus, Georgia, a great manufacturing town, "The operatives in the cotton-mills are said to be mainly 'cracker girls' (poor whites from the country), who earn, in good times, by piece work, from eight to twelve dollars a month." Great numbers of the laborers in industries there were on the borders of destitution.

Some persons objected to the industrial movement of the South on the ground that manufacturing establishments would be hotbeds of crime; the retort was to point to existing conditions and the beauties of the system that was to supplant the old order. Even before the Civil War the class struggle among the whites was gathering bitterness. After 1850 opposition to slavery in North Carolina was augmenting, in main due to the small farmer and workingman who saw in slavery a bar to progress for self and children.[170] It was possible to combine this resentment with the propaganda for capitalism, as is done in Helper's book of bitterness, *The Impending Crisis.* He points out that slavery exhausts the soil; small planters move away; large planters who can live on smaller profits spread. He quotes the honorable C. C. Clay as writing of Madison County, Alabama: "One will discover numerous farmhouses, once the abode of industrious and intelligent freeman, now occupied by slaves, or tenantless, deserted and dilapidated. . . 'one only master grasps the whole domain' that once furnished happy homes for a dozen white families." Speaking to the slaveholders Helper said: "You have absorbed the wealth of our

[169] Olmsted. *Cotton Kingdom*, vol. i, 273-274.

[170] North Carolina University, James Sprunt Historical Publications, vol. x, no. 1. *Benjamin Sherwood Hedrick*, 5.

communities in sending your own children to northern seminaries and colleges, or in employing Yankee teachers to officiate exclusively in your own families, and have refused to us the limited privilege of common schools." He added that the proportion of free white children from five to twenty who are in school is over three times as great in the free states as in the slave states.

To the argument that the South is too hot for white men, Helper rejoined:

It is not too hot for white women. Time and again, in different counties in North Carolina, we have seen the poor white wife of the poor white husband, following him in the harvest field from morning till night, binding up the grain as it fell from his cradle. In the immediate neighborhood from which we hail, there are not less than thirty young women, non-slaveholding whites, between the ages of fifteen and twenty-five . . . who labor in the fields every summer; two of them in particular, near neighbors to our mother, are in the habit of hiring themselves out during harvest time, the very hottest season of the year, to bind wheat and oats – each of them keeping up with the reaper; and this for the paltry consideration of twenty-five cents per day. [Slavery, he says, has entailed on them poverty, ignorance, and degradation.] We want to see no more plowing, or hoeing, or raking, or grain-binding, by white women in the Southern States; employment in cotton-mills and other factories would be far more profitable and congenial to them, and this they shall have within a short period after slavery shall have been abolished. . . [He appeals to non-slaveholders to wipe out slavery.] Your children, now deprived of even the meager advantage of common schools, will then reap the benefits of a collegiate education.

In answer to a gentleman solicitous for the widows and orphans that would suffer by abolition, Helper says that slavery has "reduced thousands and tens of thousands of non-slaveholding widows and orphans to the lowest depths of poverty and ignorance." He quotes William Gregg as saying before the South Carolina Institute: "Many a mother . . . will tell you that her children are but scantily provided with bread, and much more scantily with meat; and, if they be clad with comfortable raiment, it is at the expense of these scanty allowances of food."

A citizen of New Orleans, writing in *De Bow's Review*, deplores the scantiness of opportunity for employment of women and affirms the danger of demoralization; in a slave state menial female labor is "in the lowest depths, a lower deep" owing to the fact that "by association it is a reduction of the white servants to the level of their colored fellow-menials." Helper asserts that in North Carolina

> Industrious, tidy white girls, from sixteen to twenty years of age, had [last spring] much difficulty in hiring themselves out as domestics in private families for forty dollars per annum — board only included; negro wenches, slaves, of corresponding ages, so ungraceful, stupid and filthy that no decent man would ever permit one of them to cross the threshold of his dwelling, were in brisk demand at from sixty-five to seventy dollars per annum, including victuals, clothes, and medical attendance.

Exploitation was a severe strain on morals of the poor whites. Olmsted said that the Sand-Hillers of South Carolina put very slight value on female virtue.

> A Southern physician expressed the opinion to me that if an accurate record could be had of the births of illegitimate children . . . it would be found to be as great, among the poor people in the part of the country in which he practised, as of those born in wedlock. A planter told me that any white girl who could be hired to work for wages would certainly be a girl of easy virtue. [A northern gentleman who had been spending a year in South Carolina expressed his conviction that] real chastity among the young women of the non-slave-holding class in South Carolina was as rare as the want of it

among farmers' daughters at the north. [Olmsted goes on to say:] It is often asserted as an advantage of slavery . . . that the ease with which the passions of men of the superior caste are gratified . . . is a security of the chastity of white women. I can only explain this, consistently with my impression of the actual state of things, by supposing that these writers ignore entirely, as it is a constant custom for Southern writers to do, the condition of the poorer class of the white population.[171]

[171] Olmsted. *Journey in the Seaboard Slave States*, 508-509.

XIV. EFFECTS OF THE CIVIL WAR

The Civil War had a great disturbing influence on the traditional functions of the sexes. The men were called to the front leaving even the farm work in some regions to be done by new machinery and women. A missionary writing from Iowa said:

I will mention that I met more women driving teams on the road and saw more at work in the fields than men. They seem to have said to their husbands in the language of a favorite song,

> Just take your gun and go;
> For Ruth can drive the oxen, John,
> And I can use the hoe!

. . . In one township beyond, where I formerly preached, there are but seven men left, and at Quincy, the county seat of Adams Co., but five.

From Kansas one wrote: "In many cases the women must harvest the corn and take care of the stock, in addition to their ordinary work." Another wrote:

Yesterday I saw the wife of one of our parishioners driving the team in a reaper; her husband is at Vicksburg. With what help she can secure and the assistance of her little children, she is carrying on the farm. In another field was a little boy of ten years, similarly employed; and in another a girl of about twelve, doing the same. Men cannot be found in sufficient numbers to secure the harvest; the wives and children, therefore, are compelled to go into the fields.

The same conditions were observed in Ohio, New York, and other states.[172] Home life was transformed.

---

[172] Fite. *Social and industrial Conditions in the North during the Civil War*, 8-9.

Women were keyed above ordinary domestic cares to the national emergency.

They had to be; inasmuch as the ordinary spirit of profit-seeking and accumulation did not yield to the call of patriotism.   The promises of wealthy men in many communities that wives and families of absent soldiers should be cared for were not always fulfilled. The following appeal is extremely significant:

> Friends, please do not stand idle with your unsoiled hands folded and witness these ladies cut and haul their own wood, day after day and week after week, as you have already done, after urging their husbands to leave them in a state of utter helplessness, promising, and that surely, to care for their wants: and also that you would furnish them with comfortable homes and wearing apparel.   Please do your duty at home, if you are not on the bloody battlefield.

The Milwaukee Chamber of Commerce had to be browbeaten by a woman into liberality toward war relief.[173]

A writer on *Woman's Work in the Civil War* said:

> The Aid Societies and the direct oversight the women sought to give the men in the field very much increased the reason for correspondence between the homes and the tents.   The women were proud to write what those at the hearthstones were doing for those who tended the campfires, and the men were happy and cheery to acknowledge the support they received for this home sympathy.   The immense correspondence between the army and the homes, prodigious beyond belief as it was, some regiments sending home a thousand letters a week, and receiving as many more back; the constant transmission to the men of newspapers, full of the records of home work and army news, produced a homogeneousness of feeling between the soldiers and the citizens, which kept the men in the field civilians, and made the people at home, of both sexes, half soldiers.

Frederick Law Olmsted expressed the opinion

Formed through his long and effective service with the Sanitary Commission during the Civil War, that the two things that did

---

[173] Wallach. *Patriots of Property.*

most to keep the soldiers well were music and letters from home.[174]

The significance of such phenomena as the above is marked. The conditions in the agricultural section indicate that in spite of their individualism the Americans were ready to subordinate the family to what they conceived to be the social need. The readiness with which woman did the man's work and kept the family together would place her in a new light, or at least entitle her to greater esteem and prominence in family circles. In many cases, the prolonged absence of the father followed by his return, must have softened and endeared domestic relations to a notable degree; while in cases where he did not return the family had acquired a new center of union – a family hero – whose memory would hallow the family bond. No doubt many a family received permanent uplift from the idealization of a lost member who would have been only a liability had he remained at home.

Females of the sixties could scarcely have been otherwise than delicate by reason of high heels, long heavy skirts, crinoline, and diabolical corsets. The shock of war seems to have awakened American women from ladylike futility.

> Listless young girls and fancied invalids rose from their sofas, at first to wind bandages and pack supplies . . . later to do the household work, which there were no servants to perform, or to earn their living in unaccustomed occupations that there were no men to undertake.[175]

Having yielded their men to the ranks, women proceeded to organize coöperation with them, not in a spasmodic and sentimental way

But with a self-controlled and rational consideration of the

---

[174] Brockett and Vaughan. *Woman's Work in the Civil War*, 64; *Survey*, vol. 39, Oct. 6, 1917, p. 3.

[175] Reed. *Female Delicacy in the Sixties*, 857-858, 863.

wisest and best means of accomplishing their purpose, which showed them to be in some degree the products and representatives of a new social era, and a new political development.

The distinctive features in woman's work in the war, were magnitude, system, thorough coöperativeness with the other sex, distinctness of purpose, business-like thoroughness in detail, sturdy persistency to the close.

Man, caught in the press of urgency, could not afford to manifest his customary jealousy of expanding womanhood. Thousands of women learned contempt for frivolity, gossip, fashion, and idleness; learned to consider seriously and fairly the capacities of their sex; and thus laid a strong and practical basis for the advancement of the rights of woman. Women went as nurses; many "scandalized their friends at home . . . or they left their families under circumstances which involved a romantic oblivion of the recognized and usual duties of domestic life; they forsook their own children, to make children of a whole army corps; they risked their lives."[176] It is said, indeed, that the plan of the strategic campaign of the Tennessee was made by a woman–Anna Ella Carroll.[177]

The opening of remunerative occupations to women was another positive advance occasioned partly by the exigencies of the War. It is estimated that at the opening of the war women performed one-fourth of the manufacturing of the country. War times naturally advanced wages; and in order to resist increase, more employment was given to women. Men were superseded by women; "thus to many men, whose positions they usurped, the low wages of women were far from being a matter of commiseration." Women were doing more work in industrial lines, in teaching, and in

[176] Brockett and Vaughan. *Woman's Work in the Civil War*, 56-61.
[177] Harper. *Life and Work of Susan B. Anthony*, vol. i, 239.

clerical work; in the sphere of charity and religion "their opportunities and achievements seemed boundless;" they were forging ahead in the professions, particularly in medicine; and their education advanced. Ultra-radicals were agitating for woman's rights and some had adopted short skirts. In 1864 it was estimated that there were in the North between two hundred fifty and three hundred women physicians, regularly graduated from medical schools. At least five medical institutions admitted women, tho there was great prejudice against such schools and their graduates. Women supplanted men as teachers to the extent almost of a revolution. In Illinois the number of women teachers increased by four thousand and in one year one thousand men quit their positions.[178] By 1864 women had come to be employed in the government departments at Washington; the chief reason assigned was that they worked better and more cheaply. This circumstance was assailed as shameful on the score that they could not live more cheaply. Consideration was in order for "delicate women and girls . . . going out into the world to do their labor there, and for that very reason losing often social caste."[179]

It must not be supposed that the war was the sole cause of the invasion by woman of the industries and professions. The movement was not a new one; and other causes contributed, as for example the ordinary desire of the capitalists for cheap labor. Moreover the higher education of woman was bearing fruit. The whole movement signifies an extension of woman's economic independence of man, and the breaking down of that barrier of inequality that had so long served to

[178] Fite. *Social and industrial Conditions in the North during the Civil War*, 188, 244-246.

[179] *Arthur's Home Magazine*, vol. xxiii, 214.

keep woman in a subordinate place in the household.
While the Civil War did not start the movement, it did
greatly stimulate it, and thus, together with the other
influences mentioned, helped to unsettle the foundations of the "mediaeval" family which was now passing out and through a transition of storm and stress
yielding to the new family of equality and comradeship.

It may be observed, also, that woman's experience on
the Sanitary Commission, etc., during the war, seemed
to give an impetus to woman's organizations, clubs, etc.,
in which woman since then so largely functions.[180] It
would seem that these are in cases, tho not necessarily
so, rivals of the home, and indicative, if not causes, of
weakened family devotion.

The turbulent times of war gave rise to immoralities
that shocked the people of that day. Thus the Springfield *Republican* commented:

> It is a sad, a shocking picture of life in Washington which our
> correspondents are giving us. A bureau of the Treasury De-
> partment made a house of seduction and prostitution. The
> necessities of poor and pretty women made the means of their
> debauchery by high government officials. Members of Con-
> gress putting their mistresses into clerkships in the departments.
> An honorable senator knocked down in the streets by a woman
> whom he has outraged. . . . "Washington was never quite so
> villainously corrupt" [writes our most careful correspondent, a
> long resident at the capital].[181]

Burn knew of many women that "unwived themselves"
in their husbands' absence, "and profligacy and prodigality were the order of the day." How could women
of the industrial classes continue to obtain expensive

---

[180] Hillis. *Serious Note in the Education of Women*, 853; Wells. *Women
in Organizations*, 360; Warfield. *Moral Influence of Women in American
Society*, 112.

[181] Rhodes. *History of the United States*, vol. v, 212.

dresses "when every article of wearing apparel had increased to at least four times the old price?" How could a young working girl give eighteen shillings (nine shillings English) for bonnet strings?

The bonnets themselves, such as worn by the working classes, vary from six to twenty dollars, and mantles or cloaks can not be had for less than twenty dollars. It is seemingly . . . of no consequence what people do for a living; they will have dress, and that too in the first style of fashion.[182]

We must make allowance, also, for the profligacy, sex vice, and venereal disease to which the soldiers in the field were introduced. Dabney in his *Defence of Virginia*, published shortly after the War, said:

The mass of letters found upon [the Yankee] slain, and about their captured camps, disclosed a shocking prevalence of prurient and licentious thought, both in their armies and at home. And our unfortunate servants seduced away by their armies, usually found . . . that lust for the African women was a far more prevalent motive, than their pretended humanity, for their liberating zeal. Such was the monstrous abuse to which these poor creatures were subjected, that decent slave fathers often hid their daughters in the woods, from their pretended liberators, as from beasts of prey.[183]

An immediate effect of the Civil War was to check the natural increase of population. There was a temporary reduction of the birthrate in consequence of the withdrawal of hundreds of thousands of men from domestic life. The indirect effect, in increase of town life in tall houses without yards, followed by imitation of foreign fashions, was also followed by decline in natural increase. Moreover the death of hundreds of thousands of men tended to leave many women unmarried. This

[182] Burn. *Three Years among the Working-Classes in the United States during the War*, 85.

[183] Dabney. *Defence of Virginia and the South*, 286-287.

tendency is less significant as to mere number than would seem at first sight, for in 1860 there was a larger excess of seven hundred fifty thousand males. Moreover between eighteen hundred and sixty and eighteen hundred and seventy, four hundred and fifty thousand more males than females entered the ports of Boston and New York; so that in 1870 the excess of males was still some four hundred and fifty thousand. Eugenics would not overlook qualitative distinctions, however. It may be that the loss of the boys of the nation (for the war was fought largely by boys) meant a loss of germ plasm that can not be replaced. It would be worth while, however, to be able to extend Crum's *Study of the Birth-rate in Massachusetts, 1850-1890*, in which he points out that the excess of males born in that state was greater during the Civil War than in any other of several quinquennial periods.[184]

Besides the children that were not born owing to the premature death of possible fathers, thought must be given to those that were not fathered as they should have been or when they needed attention. The Civil War lasted long enough to yield a sufficiency of instances. E. S. Martin says:

Of half a dozen boys that I remember in one Civil War family when the father was for three or four years in the field and for years before and after in intense political life, only two came to satisfactory maturity, and they were the older ones whose boyhood was passed under their father's eye. . . Disaster, moral or mental, befell the others, first or last, though not until several of them had demonstrated the exceptional quality of their natural abilities. It has always seemed to observers who knew that family, and the father's extremely valuable public services, and how they tore him out of his family life and monopolized him for fifteen years, that his younger

184 Walker. *Our Population in 1900*, 493; Dixon. *White Conquest*, vol. ii, 311; Crum, *Birth-rate in Massachusetts, 1850-1890*, 252.

boys were as much sacrificed to their country as though they had been killed in war.[185]

The reader may speculate at will as to the extent of feminization and demoralization due to this factor.

The negro family suffered in a peculiar way from the circumstances of war. In the Senate, Wilson said:

The enlistment of colored men causes a vast deal of suffering; for a great wrong is done to their families, and especially is that so in the state of Missouri. Those wives and children who are left behind, may be sold, may be abused; and how can a soldier fight the battles of our country when he receives the intelligence that the wife he left at home, and the little ones he left around his hearth, were sold into perpetual slavery – sold where he would never see them more? Sir, if there be a crime on earth that should be promptly punished, it is the crime of selling into slavery, in a distant section of the country, the wives and children of the soldiers who are fighting the battles of our bleeding country. Now wife and children plead to the husband and father not to enlist – to remain at home for their protection. Pass this bill [to free wives and children of soldiers], and the wife and children will beseech that husband and father to fight for the country, for his liberty, and for their freedom.

Brown said:

You have the fact before you, that these colored soldiers are going into the army. . . You have the further fact before you, that slave-owners are hounding on a persecution in the Border States, and selling the wives and children of these soldiers, making merchandise of their flesh and blood, and doing it as a punishment for their entry into our army as volunteers for our defense. Shall we tolerate that scene? Shall we legislate here, sending men day after day to sacrifice their lives for our protection, and yet sit quietly by, with no legislation to prevent, and see others sending the wives and children of those men day after day into further and harsher bondage because they have done so?

Clark spoke likewise:

Everywhere in these loyal States . . . are men . . .

185 Martin. "Use of Fathers," in Harper's *Magazine*, vol. cxvii, 763-764.

in sympathy with the rebellion. We know that men in the loyal states are opposed to the negroes going into the service. Many of these men – I will not say all – would be willing to punish the negro if he went in, if they are in sympathy with the rebellion, by the abuse of his wife and children. They wish to deter him from going into the service if they can; and they say to him, "Not only shall your wife and children have no care, no food, no protection, but they shall be sold into slavery; and when you return from fighting the battles of the Union you shall find your home desolate, your wife gone no one knows where in slavery, and your children all sent away."

One man said that the sales in Missouri were more in view of impending emancipation. The bill in question did not come to vote in the Senate at that session.[186]

The Civil War helped to usher in the new era of city industrialism so pregnant with menace to the integrity of the family. By practically cutting off foreign intercourse it accelerated immensely the growth of American industries and thus proved a turning point in economic development and social life. The trend was magnified by the increased demand for standardized manufactured products as army supplies. The rise of prices occasioned by excessive issues of legal tender paper joined with the war tariff to stimulate business. While the purchasing power of the West was increased by its development and improved transportation, the long-run outcome favored the cities and manufacturing at the expense of rural life.[187]

The southern family had its peculiar trials by reason of the war. In the border states the struggle sometimes set father against son, brother against brother, wife against husband. In any case, the demands of the

---

[186] Wilson. *History of the Anti-slavery Measures of the Thirty-seventh and Thirty-eighth United States Congresses*, chapter xvi.

[187] Walker. *Great Count of 1890*, 416; Bookwalter. *Rural vs. Urban*, 245-246, 267-268.

Confederacy broke up, at least temporarily, well-nigh every southern family. In the Union there were many families that had no near relative under arms; in the Confederacy it was a rare family that had neither husband, father, son, nor brother in service: hardly a household escaped bereavement. Many an expectant bride sadly postponed marriage and sent her lover to join the colors.

The common notion, however, that the aristocracy waived its prerogatives is untenable. The sons and brothers of influential families were to some extent kept out of danger by an ingenious system of details. The favored aristocrat would get "detailed" to some "bomb-proof" position, as the saying went. Men were slipped into every comfortable berth that the government could reach; and as the government assumed various kinds of business, it soon became hard for an old or infirm person to get light employment. Young men were detailed from the army to oil car-wheels; others to carry lanterns for them. After the fall of Fort Donelson the Confederate Congress, made up of slave-owners and their lawyers, passed a series of acts exempting all owners of over twenty slaves from military service. The number was later reduced to ten. It was not uncommon for big slave owners to divide their chattels among their sons in order to exempt them from the war.

Nearly every landed proprietor has given bonds to furnish meal to obtain exemption. Over one hundred thousand landed proprietors, and most of the slave-owners, are now out of the ranks, and soon, I fear, we shall have an army that will not fight, having nothing to fight for. The higher class is staying at home making money, the lower is thrust into the trenches. Lee complains that the rich young men are elected magistrates to avoid service in the field.

Old Confederate soldiers who were prisoners at Camp

Chase in Ohio have said that "they never saw one single commissioned confederate officer call the roll in the morning to ascertain the names of the boys that had died during the night." It is not to be wondered that the soldiers did not appreciate mere cheers. "Many a time," said one woman, "I have heard them yell back at the ladies who cheered them, 'Go to hell! If you care for us, come out of your fine clothes and help us!'"[188]

Women bore a large part of the burden of the War. They brought into use old spinning-wheels and looms and thus supplied the scarcity of clothing for family, slaves, and soldiers; they labored gallantly to cheer, comfort, and sustain the men at the front. Girls became women in a day. The intensity and heroism of female loyalty inspired and prolonged the struggle; they outdid the men, if anything, in the blindness of patriotism. It was rare to find a disloyal woman. Many reared in ease and luxury had to engage in all the drudgery of farm and shop. Many toiled in the fields in order to raise food for their households. Female clerks were employed in the government departments and proved efficient and useful. "By this means many young men could be sent into the ranks, and . . . the work . . . was better done."[189] School-teaching now fell to women. At Richmond industries employed women and girls as well as men and boys. An English merchant who spent two months in the Confederacy said:

> Southern women have taken to work. At the dinner-hour many
> of the streets of Richmond and other cities are thronged with
> thousands of young women hastening to or from the large
> clothes, cartridge, or cotton factories.[190]

---

[188] Trowbridge. *The South*, 190; Ameringer. *Life and Deeds of Uncle Sam*, 46, 48; *Diary of a Rebel War Clerk*, 290.

[189] Underwood. *Women of the Confederacy*, 117.

[190] English Merchant. *Two months in the Confederate States*, 176, 278.

The war demonstrated that the women of the South were capable of better things than the delicacy in which so many had been reared.

> They proved able to do man's work. [They] descended, as one woman, from the pedestals upon which the Quixotic chivalry had elevated them, and wrought to the bitter ending, and after it, in wholly unused methods and places, as though born to effort and to success. They sewed rough fabrics for rough men with their delicate hands, cooked wonderful messes for camp and hospital out of slenderly stocked pantries; they dressed wounds with never a tremor or a flush of false modesty.[191]

Women at home starved in order to send everything to the front. Their activity as substitutes for husbands and fathers opened new channels, taught them new lessons, and won them new consideration. Confederate writings are full of gratitude to the women. A company of girls in Tennessee even formed a cavalry company and scoured around taking help to friends in the army. They were captured by Unionists.[192]

Men in the field denied themselves for the sake of dear ones at home. The strain on the soldiers at the front was augmented by their fears for the safety of the women. Mistrust of the negroes turned out to be unfounded; but there were ruffians prowling about the country shirking duty, and the men of the aristocracy who shirked service were in a position to put pressure on the unprotected wives and daughters of the soldiers. Some soldiers early in the war sent home their revolvers to be used by the women and children. It was hard for men to remain faithful to discipline under the terrible pressure of letters and messages disclosing suffering, starvation, and despair at home. The strain

[191] De Leon. *Belles, Beaux, and Brains of the Sixties*, 136-137.
[192] Hale and Merritt. *History of Tennessee and Tennesseeans*, vol. iii, 663-665.

was most felt by the husbands of young wives and the fathers of young children, whom they had supported by labor. Most of the desertions from the Confederate army occurred during the latter part of the war, many of them by reason of the most pitiful letters from home. For instance, a gallant soldier from the lower South had enlisted on the assurance of a rich planter that he would guarantee the support of the young wife and child. One day a letter came saying that the wealthy neighbor now refused to give or sell her food unless she would submit to his lust and that unless he came home she saw only starvation ahead. Unable to obtain a furlough, he told the general he would go home even if the result should be death. The officer said he did not blame him. On reaching home, the man moved his wife and child to a place of safety and made provision for their support; then he caught his treacherous neighbor, tied him to a tree, and administered a memorable flogging. Returning to the army on the eve of action he behaved so gallantly as to consign his offense to oblivion. In another case the wife of a soldier who had deserted on account of his family's dire need sent him back when she found he had no furlough. On trial he said: "I was no longer the Confederate soldier, but . . . the father of Lucy and the husband of Mary, and I would have passed these lines if every gun in the battery had fired upon me."[193]

Major Robert Stiles tells of a young woman who in presence of his men sent word to her husband to desert. On being challenged she said:

This thing is over, and has been for some time. The government has now actually run off, bag and baggage – the Lord knows where – and there is no longer any government or any

---

[193] Underwood. *Women of the Confederacy*, 168, 170, 171.

country for my husband to owe allegiance to. He does owe allegiance to me and his starving children, and if he doesn't observe this allegiance now, when I need him, he need not attempt it hereafter when he wants me.

She was won, however, by an appeal to her husband's record, her pride in which led her to acquiesce, and she said, "Tell him not to come." [194]

In the last days of the struggle things became desperate. The Federals sent in circulars offering indefinite paroles and free transportation home – a terrible test of loyalty.

The conflict of the classes was more in evidence in the confines of the Confederacy than is commonly supposed. The diary of a "rebel" war clerk spoke of a

Frightful list of deserters – sixty thousand Virginians. . . The poor men in the army can get nothing for their families, and there is prospect of their starving. . . Gen. Early's cavalry, being mostly men of property, were two-thirds of them on furlough or detail, when the enemy advanced on Charlottesville, and the infantry, being poor, with no means either to bribe the authorities, to fee members of congress, or to aid their suffering families, declined to fight in defence of the property of the rich and absent neighbors. . . I saw a captain, a commissary, give his dog a piece of beef for which I would have paid a dollar. Many little children of soldiers were standing by with empty baskets. A poor woman yesterday applied to a merchant in Carey St. to purchase a barrel of flour. The price he demanded was seventy dollars. "My God!" exclaimed she, "how can I pay such prices? I have seven children. What shall I do?" "I don't know madam," said he, coolly, "unless you eat your children!" [195]

Many of the poorer white women of the South worked for others and were paid, frequently in provisions. Doubtless charity was bestowed in certain cases. Thus a poor North Carolina woman told after the war

[194] Underwood. *Women of the Confederacy*, 198-201.
[195] *Diary of a Rebel War Clerk*, 291-292.

how a South Carolina planter had refused to take pay
for corn that she got.

The women of the South were to some extent subject
to indignities at the hands of the invaders.   Officers in
Sherman's army turned robbers stealing even daguerre-
otypes of dear ones.   One lady of delicacy and refinement was compelled to strip before them that they
might find concealed valuables under her dress.   In
North Carolina Sherman ordered a venerable citizen
with a family of nearly twenty children and grandchildren, mostly females, to vacate his house on a few
hours' notice.   At New Orleans Butler ordered that
when a woman insulted or showed contempt for a soldier she should be liable to the treatment of a prosti-
tute; but none of the soldiers took advantage of this
order.   In Kentucky in 1864 provost marshals began
to arrest and confine women on charge of sympathy
with the rebellion, etc.   Women with children were
banished from the state to Canada, under a guard of
negro soldiers, or sent to prison.   "Women whose children, brothers, and husbands were in the Confederate
army, or dead on its battle-fields, were naturally given
to uttering much treason.   .   ." [196]

Many were the homes desolated by the march of the
invader.   Of Sherman's march through South Carolina a private wrote:

> The great evil of all is the destitution in which we leave the
> poorer classes of these people. I have often seen them sitting
> with rueful faces as we passed, sometimes weeping. Not a
> thing has been left to eat in many cases; not a horse, or an ox,
> or a mule to work with. . . A woman told me, with her
> cheeks wet with tears, that she drew the plough herself, while
> her husband, old and quite decrepit, held it, to prepare the soil
> for the corn they raised last year.

[196] Underwood. *Women of the Confederacy*, 140-141, 172, 175-176; Shailer.
Kentucky, 348.

A private wrote thus of a Virginia incident:

> Most of the elegant furniture was left in the house. The rich carpets remained upon the floor. In three hours time they were completely covered with mud. . . It made my heart ache to see [the soldiers] break mahogany chairs for the fire, and split up a rosewood piano for kindling.

Thus the rich could not escape the costs of their war. A sand-hiller said of one of his rich neighbors:

> He swore he could drink all the blood as would be spilled in the war; but long befo' Sharman come his oldest gal was a ploughin' corn with the bull, and his wife a bobbin' fur cat-fish in a cypress swamp.

The war made the soldier an object of worship. Families of soldiers came in troops to see their relatives in hospital. Their devotion complicated administration and made trouble; one wife even gave birth to a baby in the army hospital. Of two Randolph weddings in war times we are told that at the first the feminine interest was largely overshadowed by the men; the war and its heroes were fresh and the uniforms were new. At the time of the second suitable men were lacking; attendants at the church were girls; and priest, groom, and the aged father of the bride were the only males present. Small wonder if in both cases the masculine element possessed unwonted importance.

It should not seem strange that in the midst of battle men thought of love. When the blood of the race is seeping away, procreation is in order. It seems strange that there were not more war brides – that "for four years the daughters of the South waited for their lovers, and alas! many waited in a life widowhood of unutterable sorrow." At one time there seemed to be "a perfect mania for marriage." "Some of the churches may be seen open and lighted almost every night for bridals, and wherever I turn I hear of marriages in prospect. . . My only wonder is that they find time for love-making amid the storms of warfare." [197]

The attitude of the victors toward the marriage of "rebels" was unbelievable. In April of 1865 General Halleck wrote to General Stanton: "I forward General Orders No. 4. . . You will perceive from paragraph V. that measures have been taken to prevent, as far as possible, the propagation of legitimate rebels." The paragraph read:

> No marriage license will be issued until the parties . . . take the oath of allegiance to the United States; and no clergyman, magistrate, or other party authorized by state laws to perform the marriage ceremony will officiate . . . until himself and the parties . . . shall have taken the prescribed oath. . .

On a personal appeal of a would-be bridegroom the order was suspended a few days; the news was disseminated as widely as possible and three weddings took place in Richmond on Sunday. The Tennessee Senate passed a bill forbidding women to marry till they took the test oath but the House had sufficient sense to reject it.[198]

Emancipation, coming by catastrophe and prematurely, effected in the South a revolution in family life that would ultimately have come about by the gradual weakening of the slave system. The slaves did not always leave immediately the white family; but the days of the old association were numbered. The great estates could not be held together; for the collapse of the old system gave to the younger generation an impetus toward the city or in some cases toward North or West and in any case provision had to be made for cultivation on a new plan. Ancestral estates continued

[197] Underwood. *Women of the Confederacy*, 116.
[198] Avary. *Dixie after the War*, 125-126, 128.

to vanish. The housekeepers of the New South were destined to a new and trying servant problem. Women were to find a new place in the economic and social world, a less protected place; for even chaperonage was weakened by the war, and the old pseudo-chivalry would ultimately give way and open personal opportunity to womanhood. The negro family, also, was thrown on its own resources and subjected to the strains of transition to a new era.

BIBLIOGRAPHY

ABBOT, EDITH. Study of the early history of child labor in America.
In *American Journal of Sociology* (Chicago, 1908-1909), vol. xiv, 15-37.
—— Employment of women in cotton mills.
In *Journal of Political Economy* (Chicago, 1908-1909), vol. xvi, 602-621, 680-692; vol. xvii, 19-35.
—— Industrial employment of women in the United States.
In *Journal of Political Economy* (Chicago, 1906), vol. xiv, 461-501.
—— Harriet Martineau and the employment of women in 1836.
In *Journal of Political Economy*, vol. xiv, 614-626.

ABDY, EDWARD S. Journal of a residence and tour in the United States (London, 1835), 3 vols.

ADAMS, ALICE D. Neglected period of anti-slavery in America (Boston, 1908).
Radcliffe College Monographs, no. 14.

ADAMS, CHARLES FRANCIS. Familiar letters of John Adams and his wife Abigail Adams during the Revolution (Boston, [1875]).
—— Letters of Mrs. Adams, the wife of John Adams (Boston, 1848).

ADAMS, ELIASHIB. Autobiography (Bangor, 1871).

ADAMS, JOHN QUINCY. Diary: life in a New England Town (Boston, 1903).

ADAMS, N. Southside view of slavery (Boston, 1855).

ADAMS, ROMANZO. Public range lands.
In *American Journal of Sociology* (Chicago, 1916), vol. xxii, 324-351.

ALBACH, JAMES R. Annals of the West (Pittsburg, 1857).

AMERICAN ANNALS of Education and Instruction (Boston, 1831, etc.).

AMERICAN AND FOREIGN ANTI-SLAVERY SOCIETY. Annual reports (New York, 1834-1861).

AMERICAN ANTI-SLAVERY SOCIETY. Annual reports (New York, 1834-1861).
—— American slavery as it is (New York, 1839).

AMERINGER, OSCAR. War.
In *Milwaukee Leader*, May 23, 1914.

AMERINGER, OSCAR. Life and deeds of Uncle Sam (Milwaukee, 1912).

ANDREWS, ETHAN A. Slavery and the domestic slave trade in the United States (Boston, 1836).

ANTHONY, SUSAN B. Status of woman, past, present, and future.
   In *Arena* (Boston, 1896-1897), vol. xvii, 901-908.

ARFWEDSON, KARL D. United States and Canada (London, 1834), 2 vols.

ARTHUR, T. S. Children – a family scene.
   In *Ladies' Wreath* (New York, 1848-1849), vol. iii.

ARTHUR'S Home Magazine (Philadelphia), *passim*.

AVARY, MRS. MYRTA. Dixie after the war (New York, 1906).

BALLAGH, JAMES C. History of slavery in Virginia (Baltimore, 1902).
   In Johns Hopkins University *Studies in Historical and Political Science*, extra vol. xxiv.

BARNES, EARL. Woman in modern society (New York, 1912).

BARNES, MARY S. Studies in American history (Boston, 1897).

BASSETT, JOHN S. Slavery in the state of North Carolina.
   In Johns Hopkins University *Studies in Historical and Political Science* (Baltimore, 1899), vol. xvii, no. 7-8.

—— Slavery and servitude in the colony of North Carolina.
   In Johns Hopkins University *Studies in Historical and Political Science* (Baltimore, 1896), vol. xiv, nos. 4-5.

BEARD, CHARLES A. Economic interpretation of the constitution of the United States (New York, 1913).

BEAUJOUR, FELIX DE. Sketch of the United States, translated by Walton (London, 1814).

BEECHER, CATHERINE E. Essay on slavery and abolitionism (Boston, 1837).

—— True remedy for the wrongs of women (Boston, 1851).

—— Woman's profession (Philadelphia, 1872).

BEECHER, LYMAN. Autobiography, correspondence, etc., edited by Charles Beecher (New York, 1864-1865), 2 vols.

BENWELL, J. Englishman's travels in America (London [1857?]).

BESTE, J. RICHARD. The Wabash (London, 1855), 2 vols.

BICKLEY, GEORGE W. L. History of the settlement and Indian wars of Tazewell County, Virginia (Cincinnati, 1852).

BJÖRKMAN, F. M. and PORRITT. Woman suffrage – history, arguments, results (New York, 1915).

BLACKWELL, ELIZABETH. Laws of life (Philadelphia, 1852).

BLANCHARD, J. and RICE. Debate on slavery (Cincinnati, 1846).

BODICHON, BARBARA L. S. Women and work (New York, 1859).

BONNET, J. ESPRIT. États Unis de l'Amérique a la fin du dixhui-tième siècle (Paris [1802]).

BOOKWALTER, JOHN W. Rural versus urban (New York, 1911).

BOWNE, ELIZA S. Girl's life eighty years ago. Selections from the letters of Eliza Southgate Bowne (New York, 1887).

BREMER, FREDERIKA. Homes of the New World (New York, 1853), 2 vols.

BRISTED, JOHN. Resources of the United States (New York, 1818).

BROCKETT, LINUS P. and VAUGHAN. Woman's work in the Civil War (Philadelphia, 1867).

BROWN, WILLIAM. America (Leeds, Eng., 1849).

BROWN, WILLIAM W. My southern home (Boston, 1880).

BUCKINGHAM, J. S. Slave states of America (London, [1842]), 2 vols.

BUNN, ALFRED. Old England and New England (Philadelphia, 1853), 2 vols. in one.

BURN, JAMES D. Three years among the working classes in the United States during the war (London, 1865).

BURNAP, GEORGE W. The health of American women.
In *Ladies' Wreath* (New York, 1848-1849), vol. iii, 185-188.

CAMPBELL, HELEN. Women wage-earners (Boston, 1893).

CANDLER, ISAAC A. Summary view of America (London, 1824).

CARLIER, AUGUSTE. Marriage in the United States, translated by Jeffries (Boston, 1867).

CARLTON, FRANK T. History and problems of organized labor (Boston, [1911]).

CHENEY, MRS. EDNAH D., editor. Louisa May Alcott: her life, letters, and journal (Boston, 1889).

CHEVALIER, MICHAEL. Society, manners, and politics of the United States (Boston, 1839).

CLAIBORNE, JOHN H. Seventy-five years in old Virginia (Washington, 1904).

COBBETT, WILLIAM [Peter Porcupine]. Year's residence in the United States (London, 1828).

COLLINS, S. H. The emigrant's guide (Hull, 1830).

COMMONS, JOHN R. Amalgamation and assimilation.
In *Chautauquan* (Chautauqua, 1904), vol. xxxix, 217-225.

COOK, JOSHUA F. Old Kentucky (New York, 1908).

COOLEY, THOMAS M. Michigan (Boston, 1905).

COOPER, JAMES F.   Notions of the Americans picked up by a travelling bachelor (Philadelphia, 1839), 2 vols.

COURTENAY, WILLIAM A.   Education in Charleston (Charleston, S. C., 1881).

COXE, MISS.   Claims of the country on American females (Columbus, 1842), 2 vols.

CRÈVECOEUR, MICHEL G. J. DE.   Letters from an American farmer (London, 1782).

CRUM, F. S.   Birth-rate in Massachusetts, 1850-1890.
   In *Quarterly Journal of Economics* (Boston, 1896-1897), vol. xi, 248-265.

CURRY, JABEZ L. M.   The South in the olden time.
   In *Publications of Southern History Association* (Washington, 1901), vol. v.

DABNEY, ROBERT L.   Defence of Virginia and the South (New York. 1867).

DECAY of the family affections.
   In *Nation* (New York, 1869), vol. viii, 291-292.

DE LEON, THOMAS C.   Belles, beaux, and brains of the sixties New York [1909]).

DE SAUSSURE, MRS. N. B.   Old plantation days (New York, 1909)

DE TOCQUEVILLE, ALEXIS.   Democracy in America, translated by H. Reeve (London, 1835-1840), 4 vols.

DIARY of a Rebel War Clerk.
   Extract in W. H. MACE's *Working manual of American History* (Syracuse, 1895), 290-293.

DIXON, WILLIAM H.   White conquest (London, 1876).

DOCUMENTARY HISTORY of American Industrial Society (Cleveland, 1910-1911), 11 vols.

DODDRIDGE, D. J.   Notes on the settlement and Indian Wars of the western parts of Virginia and Pennsylvania (Wellsburgh, Va., 1824).

DUBOIS, W. E. B., editor.   Negro American family (Atlanta, 1908).
   Atlanta University *Publications*, no. 13.

DUGARD, M.   La Société Américaine (Paris, 1896).

DUNCAN, MRS. MARY G. L.   America as I found it (London, 1852).

DWIGHT, THEODORE.   Travels in America (Glasgow, 1848).

DWIGHT, TIMOTHY.   Travels in New England and New York (New Haven, 1821-1822), 4 vols.

DWIGHT's American Magazine (New York, 1845), vol. i.

DYER, GUS W. Democracy in the South before the Civil War (Nashville, 1905).

EARLE, ALICE M. Customs and fashions in old New England (New York, 1893).

EARLY, RUTH H. By-ways of Virginia history (Richmond, 1907).

EFFECT of relations between the Caucasian master and the African slave.
> In *Southern Literary Messenger* (Richmond, 1844), vol. x, 329-339, 470-480.

ELLIOTT, CHARLES. Sinfulness of American slavery (Cincinnati, 1850), 2 vols.

ELY, RICHARD T. Outlines of economics (New York, 1909).

ENGELMANN, GEORGE J. Education not the cause of race decline.
> In *Popular Science Monthly* (New York, 1903), 172-184.

ENGLISH MERCHANT. Two months in the Confederate States (London, 1863).

EVEREST, ROBERT. Journal through the United States and part of Canada (London, 1855).

FAMILY CIRCLE – how shall it be preserved?
> In *Democratic Review* (New York, 1859), vol. xliii, 243.

FARRAR, MISS C. C. S. The war, its cause and consequence (Memphis, 1864).

FEARON, HENRY B. Sketches of America (London, 1819).

FEATHERSTONHAUGH, GEORGE W. Excursion through the Slave States (London, 1844), 2 vols.

FERRALL, S. A. Ramble of six thousand miles through the United States of America (London, 1832).

FITE, EMERSON D. Social and industrial conditions in the North during the Civil War (New York, 1910).

FORREST, MARY. Women of the South (New York, 1865).

FORREST, WILLIAM S. Historical and descriptive sketches of Norfolk, Va. (Philadelphia, 1853).

FRANKLIN, BENJAMIN. Works, Sparks edition (Chicago, 1882), 10 vols.
> Especially vols. ii and iv are valuable for this study.

FRANKLIN, JAMES. Philosophical and political history of the thirteen United States of America (London, 1784).

GAGE, MRS. FRANCES D. Husbands and wives.
> In *Presbyterian Magazine* (Philadelphia, 1852), vol. ii, 67-68.

GAGE, MATILDA J. Woman, church, and state (Chicago, 1893).

GEORGIA Analytical Repository (Savannah, 1802), vol. i.

GOLOVIN, IVAN. Stars and stripes (London, 1856).

GÖRLING, ADOLPH. Die neue welt (Leipzig, 1840).

GÖRTZ, CARL VON. Reise in Nordamerika.
  Erster Brief von einer Reise um die Welt in 1844-1847. In E. Widenmann und Hauff's *Reisen und Länderbeschreibungen*, etc. (Stuttgart, 1835).

GRAHAM'S MAGAZINE (Philadelphia, 1842-), vol. xx-.

GRATTAN, THOMAS C. Civilized America (London, 1859), 2 vols.

GRAVES, MRS. A. J. Woman in America (New York, 1855).

GREELEY, HORACE. Hints toward reforms, second edition (New York, 1853).

—— Recollections of a busy life (New York, 1868).

GRIMKÉ, ANGELINA E. Letters to Catherine E. Beecher (Boston, 1838).

GRUND, FRANCIS J. Aristocracy in America (London, 1839), 2 vols.

—— The Americans. . . (London, 1836-1837), 2 vols.

GUIZOT [F. P.]. Histoire de la civilisation dans l'Europe, 10me édition (Paris, 1868).

GUROWSKI, ADAM G. America and Europe (New York, 1857).

HALE, WILL T. and MERRITT. History of Tennessee and Tennesseeans (Chicago, 1913), 8 vols.

HALL, BASIL. Travels in North America (Edinburgh, 1829), 3 vols.

HALSEY, FRANCIS W., editor. Great epochs in American history (New York [1912]), 10 vols.

HAMILTON, THOMAS. Men and manners in America, second edition (Philadelphia, 1833).

HAMMOND, J. H. Speech in the Senate, March 4, 1858.
  In *Congressional Globe*, Appendix, p. 71.

HARPER, IDA H. Life and work of Susan B. Anthony (Indianapolis, 1899), vol. i.

HECKE, J. VAL. Reise durch die Vereinigten Staaten von Amerika (Berlin, 1820), 2 vols.

HECKER, EUGENE A. Short history of women's rights (New York, 1910).

HELPER, HINTON R. Impending crisis (New York, 1857).

HENNIGHAUSEN, LOUIS P. History of the German Society (Baltimore, 1909).

HILDRETH, RICHARD. Despotism in America (Boston, 1854).

HILLIS, ANNIE P.   The serious note in the education of women.
In *Outlook* (New York, 1910), vol. xciv, 851-855.

HODGE, H. L.   On criminal abortion (Philadelphia, 1854).

HODGSON, ADAM.   Letters from North America (London, 1824), 2 vols.

HOLMES, ISAAC.   Account of the United States (London, [1823]).

HOOD, SILAS [Henry T. Jones].   United States constitution and socialism (Milwaukee, 1911).

HOUSTOUN, MRS. M. C.   Hesperos (London, 1850), 2 vols.

HOWARD, GEORGE E.   History of matrimonial institutions (Chicago [1904]), 3 vols.

HOWE, M. A. D.   Life and letters of George Bancroft (New York, 1908), 2 vols.

HUGUENOT SOCIETY OF SOUTH CAROLINA.   Transactions (Charleston, 1889-), nos. 2, 5, 6, 7, 13, 15.

HUMPHREY, H.   Domestic education (Amherst, 1840).

HUNDLEY, DANIEL R.   Social relations in our Southern States (New York, 1860).

HUNT, G.   Life in America one hundred years ago (New York, 1914).

HUSBAND HUNTING.
In North Carolina University *Magazine* (1857-1858), vol. vii, 41-49.

IMLAY, GILBERT.   Topographical description of the western territory of North America, third edition (London, 1797).

[INGERSOLL, C. I.].   Inchequin, the Jesuit's, letters (New York, 1810).

INGRAHAM, J. H.   Southwest (New York, 1835).

—— Editor.   Sunny South, or the southerner at home (Philadelphia, 1860).

JANSON, CHARLES W.   Stranger in America (London, 1807).

JOHNSTON, R. M.   The planter of the old South.
In *Publications of Southern History Association* (Washington, 1897), vol. i.

KEMBLE, FRANCES A. [Mrs. Butler].   Journal of a residence on a Georgian plantation (New York, 1863).

KENNGOTT (GEORGE F.).   Record of a city (N. Y., 1912).

KINGDOM, WILLIAM, JR.   America and the British colonies (London, 1820).

KINGSBURY, SUSAN M., editor.   Labor laws and their enforcement (New York, 1911).

KIRKLAND, W.   The West, the paradise of the poor.
    In United States *Democratic Review* (New York, 1844), vol. xv, 182-190.

KITCHIN, S. B.   History of divorce (London, 1912).

LADIES' MAGAZINE (Boston, 1828-).

LADIES' MAGAZINE (Savannah, 1819), vol. i.

LADIES' REPOSITORY (Boston, 1846), vol. xiv.

LADIES' REPOSITORY (Cincinnati, 1841-).

LADIES' WREATH (New York, 1848-1850), vol. iii, v.

LADY'S BOOK (Philadelphia, 1836), vol. xii.

LAMBERT, JOHN.   Travels through Canada and·the United States
    (London, 1813-1814), 2 vols.

LETTERS FROM VIRGINIA, translated from the French (Baltimore,
    1816).

LIEBER, FRANCIS.   Stranger in America (Philadelphia, 1834).

LITERARY AND SCIENTIFIC REPOSITORY (New York, 1820-1822),
    vols. i and iv.

LITERARY FOCUS (Oxford, O., 1827-1828), vol. i.

LITERARY MAGAZINE (Philadelphia, 1804), vol. ii.

LITERARY MAGAZINE and American Register (Philadelphia, 1803-
    1804), vol. i.

LITTLE, JOHN P.   Richmond (Richmond, 1851).

LONG, J. D.   Pictures of slavery (Philadelphia, 1857).

LOWER NORFOLK COUNTY, Virginia, Antiquary (Baltimore, 1897-),
    vol. iv.

LYELL, CHARLES.   Second visit to the United States (New York,
    1849-1855), 2 vols.

—— Travels in North America (New York, 1856), 2 vols. in one.

LYMAN, WILLIAM D.   The Columbia River (New York, 1909).

McCONNELL, J. L.   Western characters (New York, 1853).

McCRACKEN, ELIZABETH.   Women of America (New York, 1904).

McDONALD, J. J.   Life in Old Virginia (Norfolk, 1907).

McINTOSH, MARIA J.   Woman in America (New York, 1850).

MACKAY, ALEXANDER.   The western world (London, 1849), 3
    vols.

MACKAY, CHARLES.   Life and liberty in America (New York,
    1859).

MACKENZIE, ENEAS.   Historical, topographical, and descriptive
    view of the United States of America and of upper and lower
    Canada, first edition (Newcastle-upon-Tyne [1819]).

McMaster, John B. Acquisition of political, social, and industrial rights of man in America (Cleveland, 1903).

—— History of the people of the United States (New York, 1902-1913), 8 vols.

McVey, Frank L. Modern industrialism (New York, 1904).

Mallard, R. I. Plantation life before emancipation (Richmond, 1892).

Man, The (New York, 1834).

Mansfield, Edward D. Legal rights, liabilities, and duties of women (Salem, 1845).

Marryat, Fred. Diary in America (Philadelphia, 1839), 2 vols. in one.

—— Diary in America, part 2 (London, 1839), 3 vols.

Martin, Edward S. Use of fathers.
    In *Harper's Magazine* (New York, 1908), vol. cxvii, 763-766.

Martineau, Harriet. Retrospect of western travel (London, 1838), 3 vols.

—— Society in America (London, 1837), 3 vols.

Massachusetts Historical Society. Proceedings (Boston).

Maury, Sarah M. Englishwoman in America (London, 1848).

Mayo, A[mory] D. Southern women in the recent educational movement in the South (Washington, 1892).
    Bureau of Education, Circular of Information, no. 1, 1892.

[Mazzei, Alfonso]. Recherches historiques et politiques sur les États Unis, par un Citoyen de Virginie (Paris, 1788), 4 vols.

Melish, John. Travels in the United States of America (Philadelphia, 1812), 2 vols.

Methodist Episcopal Church. General Conference Journals, 1796-.

Michaux, François A. Travels to the westward of the Allegheny Mountains (London, 1805).

Milburn, J. Pioneer preacher (New York, 1858).

Morgan, A. T. Yazoo (Washington, 1884).

Mormon Family.
    In *The Mormon point of view* (Provo City, 1904), vol. i, 335-412.

Münsterberg, Hugo. The Americans (New York, 1904).

Murat, Achille. America and the Americans (New York, 1849).

Murray, Charles A. Travels in North America (New York, 1839), 2 vols.

Myers, Gustavus. History of the Supreme Court of the United States (Chicago, 1912).

NAUMANN, JACOB. Nordamerika (Leipzig, 1848).

NEILSON, PETER. Recollections of a six years' residence in the United States of America (Glasgow, 1830).

NEW ENGLAND QUARTERLY MAGAZINE (Boston, 1802).

NEWMAN, F. W. Character of the Southern States of America (Manchester, 1863).

NEW YORK CABINET (1829), vols. i and ii.

NILES' WEEKLY REGISTER, 1811-1822 (Baltimore).

NOEL, BAPTIST W. Freedom and slavery in the United States of America (London, 1863).

NORTH AND SOUTH, or slavery and its contrast (Philadelphia, 1852).

NORTH CAROLINA Baptist Historical Papers, April, 1898 (Henderson).

NORTH CAROLINA UNIVERSITY. Jas. Sprunt Historical Publications (Chapel Hill, 1911), vol. x, no. 1: Benjamin Sherwood Hedrick.

NORTH CAROLINA UNIVERSITY Magazine (Chapel Hill, 1857-1859), vols. vii and viii.

OLDMIXON, JOHN W. Transatlantic wanderings (London, 1855).

OLMSTED, FREDERICK L. Cotton kingdom (New York, 1861), 2 vols.

—— Journey in the seaboard slave states (New York, 1859).

ONEAL, JAMES. Workers in American history (St. Louis, 1912).

OSSOLI, MARGARET F. Woman in the nineteenth century, and kindred papers (Boston, 1855).

OZANNE, T. D. South as it is (London, 1863).

PAGE, THOMAS N. Old Dominion (New York, 1908).

—— Social life in old Virginia before the war (New York, 1898).

PARK, R. E. Race assimilation in secondary groups.
    In *American Journal of Sociology* (Chicago, 1913-1914), vol. xix, 606-623.

PARSONS, ELSIE C. Old fashioned woman (New York, 1913).

PAULDING, J. K. Letters from the South (New York, 1817).

PAXTON, ALEXANDER S. Memory days (New York, 1908).

PHILLIPS, WENDELL. Speeches, lectures, and letters [first series] (Boston, 1884)

PICKETT, A. J. History of Alabama, new edition (Atlanta, 1896).

PLANTER, THE, or thirteen years in the South by a northern man (Philadelphia, 1853).

Powell, Lyman P. History of education in Delaware (Washington, 1893).
> Bureau of Education, Circular of Information, no. 3, 1893.

Power, Tyrone. Impressions of America (Philadelphia, 1836), 2 vols.

Powers, Stephen. Afoot and alone (Hartford, 1872).

Presbyterian General Assembly. Minutes, 1789-1860.

Presbyterian Magazine (1851-1854), vols. i-iv.

Putnam, Emily J. The lady (New York, 1910).

Quentin, Carl. Reisebilder und Studien aus dem Norden der Vereinigten Staaten von Amerika (Arnsberg, 1851), 2 Teile.

Ramsay, David. History of South Carolina (New York, 1809), 2 vols.

—— Sketch of the soil, climate, weather, and diseases of South Carolina (Charlestown, 1796).

Ravenel, Harriott H. Charleston, the place and the people (New York, 1912).

Redpath, James. The roving editor (New York, 1859).

Reed, Amy L. Female Delicacy in the Sixties.
> In *Century* (New York, 1915), vol. lxviii, 855-864.

Reitzel, Charles E. Trend of colleges for women.
> In *Harper's Weekly* (New York, 1914), vol. lix, 310-311.

Rhodes, James F. History of the United States (New York, 1900-1906), 7 vols.

Richardson, Mrs. Hester [D.]. Sidelights on Maryland history (Baltimore, 1913), 2 vols.

Riley, Franklin L. School history of Mississippi (Richmond, 1900).

Ripley, Eliza M. McH. Social life in old New Orleans (New York, 1912).

Robbins, Chandler. Memoirs of Hon. William Appleton (Boston, 1863).

Robinson, Harriet H. Loom and Spindle (New York, [1898]).

Roosevelt, Theodore. Winning of the West, Standard Library Edition (New York, 1903), 4 vols.

Ross, F. A. Slavery ordained of God (Philadelphia, 1857).

Royall, Mrs. Anne. Letters from Alabama (Washington, 1830).

—— Sketches of history, life, and manners in the United States (New Haven, 1826).

RUTHERFORD, MILDRED L. Georgia day, 1910, programme (Atlanta, 1910).

SAINT JOHN, J. H. Same as Crèvecoeur.

SAINT VICTOR, JACQUES B. M. B., COMTE DE. Lettres sur des États Unis en 1832 et 1833 (Paris, 1835), 2 vols. in one.

SCHAFF, PHILIP. America (New York, 1855).

SCHOEPF, JOHANN D. Travels in the Confederation (Philadelphia, 1911), 2 vols.

SCHOULER, JAMES. Americans of 1776 (New York, 1906).

SCOTCH-IRISH, Society of America. Congresses, 5, 8, 10 (Nashville, 1893-1901).

SCUDDER, HORACE E., editor. Men and manners in America one hundred years ago (New York, 1876).

SEALSFIELD, CHARLES [Karl Postel]. The United States (London, 1828).

SEWALL, MAY WRIGHT. Domestic and social effects of the higher education of women (Indianapolis, 1887).

SHALER, N[ATHANIEL] S. Kentucky (Boston, 1885).

SHERRILL, C. H. French memories of eighteenth century America (New York, 1915).

SIDONS, C. Die Vereinigten Staaten von Nordamerika (Stuttgart, 1827), 2 vols.

SIMONS, A. M. Social forces in American history (New York, 1911).

"SINGLETON" [H. C. KNIGHT]. Letters from the South and West (Boston, 1824).

SKETCHES of incidents and adventures in the West (Cincinnati, 1848).

SMEDES, SUSAN D. Southern planter (New York, 1900).

SMITH, ADAM. Wealth of nations (Edinburgh, 1817).

SMITH, CHARLES H. School history of Georgia (Boston, 1893).

SMITH, GEORGE G. Story of Georgia and the Georgia people, 1732-1860 (Macon, 1900).

SMYTH, JOHN F. D. Tour in the United States of America (London, 1784), 2 vols.

SOUTH CAROLINA historical and genealogical magazine (Charleston, 1900-), *passim.*

SOUTH in the building of the nation (Richmond, 1909), 12 vols.

SQUIRE, [V.] BELLE. The woman movement in America (Chicago, 1911).

STANTON, ELIZABETH CADY *et al.* History of woman suffrage (Rochester, 1889 [etc.]), 4 vols.

STIRLING, JAMES. Letters from the slave states (London, 1857).

STORER, HORATIO R. On the decrease of the rate of increase of population now obtaining in Europe and America.
  In *American Journal of Science and Arts* (New Haven, 1867), second ser., vol. xliii, 141-155.

SUBDUED southern nobility (New York, 1882).

SUPPRESSED BOOK about Slavery (prepared for publication, 1857), (New York, 1864).

TASISTRO, LOUIS F. Random shots and Southern breezes (New York, 1842), 2 vols.

THORNDYKE, EDWARD L. Professor Pearson on the distribution of fertility.
  In *Popular Science Monthly* (New York, 1903), vol. lxiii, 84.

THORNTON, JOHN. Diary of a tour through the Northern States of the Union and Canada (London, 1850).

TILLETT, WILBUR F. Southern womanhood as affected by the war.
  In *Century* (New York, 1891), n. s., vol. xxi, 9-16.

TOWER, PHILO. Slavery unmasked (Rochester, 1856).

TREXLER, HARRISON A. Slavery in Missouri.
  In Johns Hopkins University *Studies in Historical and Political Science* (Baltimore, 1914), vol. xxxii, no. 2.

TROLLOPE, MRS. FRANCES. Domestic manners of the Americans (New York, 1832).

TROWBRIDGE, J. T. The South (Hartford, 1866).

UNDERWOOD, JOHN L. The women of the confederacy (New York, 1906).

VAN BUREN, A. DEPUY. The women of our pioneer epoch.
  In Michigan *Pioneer and Historical Collections* (Lansing, 1908), vol. xiv, 517-528.

VANCE, ZEBULON B. Sketches of North Carolina (Norfolk, Va., 1875).

VIGNE, GODFREY T. Six months in America (London, 1832), 2 vols.

VON RAUMER, FREDERICK G. America and the American people (New York, 1846).

WAKEFIELD, E. G. Social and political status of England and America (New York, 1834).

WALKER, FRANCIS A. The great count of 1890.
  In *Forum* (New York, 1891), vol. xi, 406-418.

WALKER, FRANCIS A. Our population in 1900.

In *Atlantic Monthly* (Boston, 1873), vol. xxxii, 487-495.

WALLACH, MARVIN W. Patriots of property.

In Milwaukee *Leader*, Dec. 11, 1913.

WARDEN, DAVID B. Statistical, political, and historical account of the United States of North America (Edinburgh, 1819), 3 vols.

WARFIELD, E. D. Moral influence of women in American society.

In *Annals of the American Academy of Political and Social Science* (Philadelphia 1909), vol. xxxiv, 106-114.

WARNER, C. D. Studies in the South and West (New York, 1889).

WASHINGTON, BOOKER T. Up from slavery (New York, 1901).

WAYLAND, JOHN W. History of Rockingham County, Virginia (Dayton, Va., 1912).

WELLS, KATE G. Women in organizations.

In *Atlantic* (Boston, 1880), vol. xlvi, 360-367.

WESTERN frontier life.

In *Overland Monthly* (San Francisco, 1870), vol. iv, 520-525.

WESTERN people and politicians forty years ago.

Sub-title of "Recallings from a Public Life" in *Scribner's Monthly* (New York, 1877-1878), vol. xv, 255-263.

WESTON, GEORGE M. Progress of slavery in the United States (Washington, 1857).

WETHERELL, ELLEN. Among the cotton mills.

In *International Socialist Review* (Chicago, 1913-1914), vol. xiv, 416-419.

WILKESON, SAMUEL. Early recollections of the West.

In *American Pioneer* (Cincinnati, 1843), vol. ii, nine installments.

WILSON, HENRY. History of the anti-slavery measures of the thirty-seventh and thirty-eighth United States Congresses (Boston, 1864).

WOODRUFF, CHARLES S. Legalized prostitution (Boston, 1862).

WRIGHT, FRANCES. View of society and manners in America (London, 1821).

WYLLY, CHARLES S. The seed that was sown in the colony of Georgia, 1740-1870 (New York, 1910).

WYSE, FRANCIS. America, its realities and resources (London, 1846), 3 vols.

INDEX

Note: The Index on the following pages covers all three volumes of *A Social History of the American Family.* The volume is indicated by Roman numerals, and the page references within that volume are indicated by Arabic numerals.

of various, I, 244, 245, 256, 294, 304, 319; offices, I, 233; slave register, I, 211

Courts: acquittal, I, 139; appeal to, I, 138; on alimony, I, 302-303, III, 256; and assault, I, 93; bias, I, 180-181; and castration, I, 328; and children, I, 120, 172, 295, 309; circuit, I, 92; clerk, I, 266; county, see *County* above; decree reversed, I, 303; and divorce, I, 147, 148, 181, 301, II, 44, III, 263, 264, 273, 278; of Domestic Relations, III, 175, 268; indictment, I, 275; and family, I, 71, 74, 77, 141, 142, 167, 178-179, 181, 186-187, 301, 302; General, see *General Court*; courthouse, I, 263; on intestacy, I, 122; juvenile, III, 174; life, I, 39; and marriage, I, 61, 62, 67, 71, 146, 156, 165, 262, 264, 304, 313, 324, III, 223; and miscegenation, I, 210; and property, I, 234, III, 108, 274; prosecutions, I, 319, 321; provincial, I, 302-303; records, I, 136, 169, 210, 264; and seduction, I, 196, 210; ruling, I, 261; of Sessions, I, 154; settlement, avoidance of, I, 180; and sex offences, I, 136, 139, 147, 149, 182, 304, 318, 319; and slander, I, 170; and slavery, I, 81-82, 212, 326, II, 268; see *Supreme Court*; testimony, I, 314; and wives, I, 93, 142, 180, 299, 302-303, III, 317; and women, I, 55, 101, 138, 319

Courtships: I, 29, 35, chap. III, 78-79, 83, 129, 130, 131, 138, 206, 218, chap. XIV, 264, II, 13, 30, 71, 72, 75, 122, 311-315, 334, III, 193, 214, 322; see also *Suitors*

Cowley, C: cited, III, 167, 230, 231, 232, 242, 256, 265

Credit: I, 95, 120, 234, 239, 300

Crime: I, 67, 111, 113, 135, 148, 154, 162, 182, 197, 210-211, 220, 251, 275, 322, 328, III, 172, 173, 202, 256, 273, 278, 312, 315; Robbery, I, 309-310; see also under various heads

Criminal: abortion, I, 135; code, I, 328; prosecution, III, 278; violence, I, 148

Crouch-Hazlett, Ida: cited, III, 24 *note*

Cruelty: I, 95, 121, 143-144, 146, 178, 179, 195, 208, 302, II, 46, 127, III, 273, 292, 294, 298

Culpepper Co. (Va.): I, 256

Custis, Frances: I, 304-305

Custom: of bundling, I, 129-131; of burial, I, 241; of charity, I, 173; and city life, III, 266; continental, I, 153; of country, I, 309; Dutch, I, 158; as to education, I, 193, 194; of England, I, 262; fusion of, I, 190; of Gavelkind, I, 122; Indian, I, 325; as to marriage, I, 138, 154-162, 166, 207, 245, 262, 266, III, 266; renounced, I, 335; of rest, I, 115; rural, III, 266; as to servants, I, 240; of Saturday holiday, I, 126; under slavery, I, 326-327; for son to work, I, 288; of Spain, I, 335; of unreasonable hours, I, 114; as to woman's place, I, 188

DAKOTA: III, 222, 229

Daughter, Daughters: beaten, I, 142; behavior of, I, 36-37; clothing of, I, 281; courtship of, I, 54, 253, 254; of Col. Dangerfield, I, 292; divorce for, I, 147; dower of, I, 235, 244, 253, 254; of Gov. Dudley, I, 85; education of, I, 42, 203, 290-291, 304; of Thos. Evens, I, 292; and father, I, 178-179, 182, 253, 254, II, 245, III, 155, 158, 212; of freeholders, I, 238; gifts to, I, 244, 245, III, 212; harboring of, I, 75, 180; of Harvard president, I, 110; as heirs, I, 95, 97, 121, 123, 176, 225-226, 235, 237, 239-240; incest with, I, 182; of Indians, I, 166; of landlord, I, 246; -in-law, I, 123, 269; marriage of, I, 34, 41, 54, 79, 123, 124, 155, 156, 160, 187, 250, 251, 266, 270, 285, 298, 324, 331, III, 148, 164, 183, 214; of Milton, I, 42; of minister, I, 78-79,

The American Family

liminaries, I, 35-36, 55, 131, 132, 156, 165, 188, 335, II, 30, 31, III, 275; problems, III, 193, 260; promise, I, 20, 56, 138, 140, 164-165, 196, 210, 256, 270, 313, II, 216, III, 220; promotion of, I, 14, 68, 216, 218, 333, III, 222, 321, 322; proposal, I, 78, 163, 205, 268; as prostitution, II, 215, III, 269, 305-306; purpose of, III, 247, 312; rate, I, 249, III, 242; registration, I, 45, 59, 185, 261-268, 335, III, 295; regulation, etc., I, 14-15, 25, 142, 154, 160, 186, 189, 195, 199, 205, 206, 212, chap. xv, 317, II, 30, 37, 39-42, 374, III, 175, 275-276, 278, 280-281, 283, 287-288, 290, 291, 293, 303, 306, 312, 329; religion and, I, 22-25, 44-47, 61, 79, 100, 141, 155, 158-160, 185, 186, 189, 190, 191, 199, 200, 205, 206, 268-271, 323, 324, 335, II, 35, 39-42, 46, 153, 332, III, 29, 270, 277, chap. xiii; repeated, I, 158, 169, 170, 320, 321; see also *Remarriage*, etc.; romantic, III, 123, 257; runaway, II, 313; sacred, I, 46-47, 136, 148, 205, 207, 315, II, 223, III, 284-287, 297, 304-307, 312, 318, 321; servants', I, 187, 210, 212, 271-272, 285, 286; as slavery, III, 129; and society, I, 100, II, 37, 203, 335, III, 192, 278, 287, 291, 301, 312, 321, 326, 327, 329; Socialism and, III, 325, 326, 330; in South, I, chaps. xiv, xv, II, 34, 77, 218, 311-317, III, 12, 17, 18, 81; of strangers, III, 276, 308, 310; successful, I, 41, III, 169, 275; tie, 182, III, 269-270, 274; trouble with, I, 269, II, 33, 34, III, 185; usages, I, 51; values, III, 128; and venereal disease, III, 271; war and, II, 367, 373-374, III, 106-107; Wisconsin, II, 36; woman and, I, 15, 34, 37, 40, 44, 54, 56, 65-69, 83, 138, 141, 165, 189, 211, 218, 237, 247-251, 256, 258, 260, 261, 264, 265, 270, 272, 277, 304, 321, 324-

326, 332, 333, II, 11, 12, 38, 74, 81-83, 86, 104, 112, 116-125, 133-134, 174, 187, 199, 202, 212, 226, 305, 316, III, 14, 92-99, 106, 107, 117-122, 125-129, 146, 157, 199-208, 212, 218-220, 235, 251-252, 271, 274, 318, 320, 329; see also *Banns, Wedding, Matrimony, Mate, Mock, Wedlock, Remarriage*

Married persons: I, 68, 71, 80, 85, 132, 136, 140, 141, 145-146, 149, 154, 160-163, 168, 192, 218, 204-205, 242, 252-254, 258, 267, 274-275, 287, 331, III, 62, 91, 199, 201, 209-210, 212, 230, 234, 238-239, 251, 259, 274; see also *Husband, Wife, Spouses,* etc.

Marryat, —: cited, II, 38, 45, 152, 160, 214, 246, 290 *note*, 300 *note*

Martineau, Miss —: cited, II, 24, 45, 55, 112, 126, 152, 176, 182, 188, 208, 238 *note*, 251, 278, 281, 285, 286, 290 *note*, 297, 301, 323-324, 326, 328

Martyn, —: on Ebenezer, I, 310; on Georgia settlement, I, 224; on land-holding, I, 240

Martyn, Mrs. S. T: cited, II, 118

Maryland: I, 196, 221, 229, 230, 232, 235, 240, 241, 244-261, 268-269, 271, 276-282, 286-298, 302-304, 308-309, 313-316, 322, 326, 327, II, 59, 176, 249, 265, 330-334, 339, 340, 344-345, 348, III, 38, 39; *Society for History of Germans in,* cited, I, 261

Massachusetts: I, 51, 57, 63-69, 72, 77, 80-83, 86, 88, 89, 93, 95, 100, 102, 105-106, 119-121, 124-126, 129-136, 141, 146, 149, 159, 170, 241, 251, 274, 291, II, 18, 45, 61, 125-126, 129, 144, 180, 181, 196, 211, III, 66-68, 72, 88-89, 113, 137-139, 151, 165, 202, 209-211, 226, 227, 233, 234, 240, 249, 276, 290, 317; *Bureau of Statistics,* cited, III, 68 *note*, 71, 78, 137-139, 202; *Historical Society Proceedings,* cited, I, 129 *note*, 134 *note*, II, 174 *note*; see also *Bay Colony*

things, I, 136, 164, 188, 205, 207, 315, III, 255, 307; see also *Church, Theology, Worship*, names of sects, *Clergy*, etc.

Remarriage: I, 40, 45, 52, 54, 59, 69-70, 78, 79, 88, 90, 96, 97, 142, 163, 169, 170, 176-177, 208-209, 238, 239, 245, 247-249, 253, 255, 310, II, 14, 17, 258, 327, 330, III, 40-41; divorce, etc., and, I, 26, 146-148, 181, 182, 195-196, 303, II, 46-48, III, 15, 106, 199, 258, 264, 268, 271, 272, 277, 279-280, 283, 294-301, 306, 307, 309, 311

Removal: I, 287, 307, 308, 311, 312, 317; see also *Moving*

Renaissance: I, 18, 37-38, 43-44

Rent: I, 171, III, 55, 56, 71, 75, 78-79, 181

Reproduction: III, 232, 248, 251, 254; see also *Generation*

Residence: I, 50, 156, 265, 290, 299, 300, 323, III, 78, 188, 266, 279, 289; see also *Moving*

Restaurant: III, 183, 184, 186

Revolution: I, 51, 93, 107, 110-111, 119, 130, 145-146, 161, 166, 174, 183, 201, 205, 234, 244, 246, 248, 252-253, 255, 265, 272, 275, 278, 281, 282, 293, 301, 303, 323, II, 332, 334, III, chap. xiv

Rhode Island: I, 51, 62, 71, 94-96, 110, 116, 123, 132, 133, 136, 139, 143, 146-148, 306, II, 18, 44-45, 174-176, III, 66, 231, 276

Rhodes, D. W: cited, III, 72 *note*

Rhodes, J. F: cited, II, 159 *note*, 362 *note*,

Richmond (Va.): I, 306, II, 329, 332, 341, 368, III, 57

Richmond *Enquirer*: cited, II, 269, 306

Rights: I, 44, 172, 176, 191, 239, 249, 255, 261, 276, 314, 326; see also under *Children; Woman*, movement, status, etc.

Rivalry: I, 52, 257, 326, II, 250-252, 292

Roads: I, 229, III, 18, 19, 24, 81

Robin, Abbé: I, 129, 145, 246; negro rapist, I, 328

Rock River conference: III, 284, 290

Rocky Mts: III, 105; states, III, 203

Roman: Catholic Church, I, 166, 264, III, 263, 270, 288-295, 300; see also *Catholic*; law, III, 224

Roosevelt, Theodore: II, 33 *note*, III, 308

Rose, Ernestine: II, 117

Rose, Geo: cited, III, 145-146, 179, 217, 230, 255

Runaway: I, 125, 211, 226, 249, 250, 261, 286, 306, 327-328, 331, II, 31, 313

Rural: I, 39, 166, 241, II, 11, 29, 58, 152, 159, 163, 196, 209, 229, 305, 331, 338 343, 366, III, 13, 21-23, 32, 37, 51-54, 65, 66, 80-83, 89-90, 187, 205, 241, 248, 259, 260, 263, 266, 267; see also *Country, Urban*

Rush, B: cited, I, 203, II, 58, 86

Russia: III, 320

Ryan, Father: cited, III, 285 *note*, 293-294, 313 *note*

SABBATH: I, 60, 64-65, 73, 75, 92, 99, 107, 110, 117, 126, 145, 148, 162, 175, 195, 207, III, 303, 320

Sacrament: I, 60, 148, 185, III, 278, 284-286, 295, 296, 299, 309

Saint: I, 100, 111

St. Anne's parish: I, 246

St. John's: *American Letters*, cited, II, 28; parish, I, 304; river, I, 230

St. Louis: III, 72, 141; Exposition, III, 315; *Republican*, cited, II, 248

St. Marie's: I, 249

St. Martin: I, 249

St. Mary's: I, 248

St. Méry: cited, II, 71

St. Thomas: I, 246

St. Victor: cited, II, 37-38, 131, 132 *note*, 208, 220

Salary: I, 123-124, 162, 246, 248-249, 301, III, 321; see also *Wages*

Sale: I, 96, 143, 237, 255, 275, 299, 327; of persons, I, 65, 80-82, 87, 149, 204, 205, 211-214, 220, 240,

86-88, 91, 105, 135, 137-139, 171, 188, 206-209, 249, 250, 268, 269, 302; see also *Salary*

Walker, F. A: cited, II, 25, 364 *note*, 366 *note*, III, 181, 244

War: I, 15, 61, 116, 117, 130, 161, 246, 323, II, 321-322, chap. XIV, III, 7, 31, 85, 106; see also *Army, Soldiers, Civil War*

Wardens: see under *Church*

Warfield, E. D: cited, I, 102-103, 153, II, 362 *note*

Warner, C. D: cited, II, 330 *note*

Washing: I, 78, 200, 230, 253, III, 82, 189; see also *Laundry*

Washington: army officer in, III, 223

Washington, Booker: cited, II, 251, 273

Washington, Bushrod: II, 268

Washington: city, II, 326, 362, III, 55-57

Washington family: I, 291

Washington, Geo: I, 229, 248, 254, II, 172

Washington: state and territory, III, 104, 105, 263, 273

Waste: I, 39, 49, 181, 236, 237, 266, III, 139

Wealth: I, 56-59, 64, 70, 78, 91, 132, 135, 140, 150, 154, 168, 169, 174, 187, 200-202, 217, 219, 221, 222, 231, 233, 235-237, 240, 242, 244, 249, 255, 273, 283, 291, 335, 336, II, 52, 66, 201, 209, 213, 217, 225, 233, 293, 338, III, 79-80, 117, 119, 124, 132-136, 143, 151, 165, 170, 181, 201, 204, 212, 213, 238-239, 242-244, 247, 248, 251, 270, 302; see also *Property*

Weatherford, W. D: cited, III, 33, 48, 50-51

Weaving: I, 125, 188, 229, 280, 281

Wedding: I, 64, 83, 162, 164, 178, 207, 209, 213, 242, 253, 264-266, II, 14, 15, 32, 34, 36, 39, 175, 201, 249, 257, 316, 373, III, 18, 40, 220; see also *Marriage, Ring*

Weeden: cited, I, 133

Weekly People: cited, III, 177 *note*, 223 *note*, 224 *note*

Wells, D. C: cited, III, 94 *note*

Wells, Kate G: cited, II, 262 *note*, III, 190-191, 194-195

Welsh Tract Baptist Meeting: I, 197

Wenches: I, 212, 230, 251, 320, 327; see also *Girl*

Wertenbaker, T. J: cited, I, 219 *note*, 220 *note*, 235 *note*, 243 *note*, 274 *note*, 275

Wesleyan: College, II, 343; University, III, 233

West: I, 60, 102, 130, 207, 227, 236, 241, 312, chap. XX, II, 13, 27, 29, 103-106, 109, chap. VIII, 243, 374, III, 17, 78, 79, 85, 105-107, 113, 142, 163, 165, 176, 180-181, 203, 228, 239, 240, 255-256, 262, 271, 273; western, Europe, III, 266; Reserve, III, 228

West India: I, 170, 173, 251

West Jersey: I, 186

West Point: II, 60-61

White: I, 65, 66, 81, 149, 176, 209-211, 225, 232, 251, 278, 282, 283, 286, 291, 305, 323-329, II, 245, 281, 294, 309-310, chap. XIII, III, chap. I, 29-31, 34, 38, 41, 62, 64, 233; see also *Race, Miscegenation, Slavery of whites*, etc.

White, F. M: cited, III, 141 *note*, 174 *note*

White, Susanna: I, 69

White, Thomas: I, 277

Whoredom: I, 133, 138, 149, 314, 316, 321; see also *Prostitution*

Widow: I, 45, 49, 52, 58, 69-70, 75, 77-79, 95-100, 140, 158, 160, 165, 169, 173, 176-177, 204, 206, 208-209, 235, 237-239, 247-249, 253, 255, 263, 276, 301, 304, 309, 310, 312, 321, II, 14, 17, 23, 28, 97, 109, 119, 125, 175, 185, 186, 190, 191, 199, 322, 329-330, 353-354, III, 11-13, 61, 86, 88, 183, 206, 216

Widowers: I, 54, 69-70, 78, 156, 163, 249, II, 14, 169, III, 61, 183

Wife: I, 85, 101, 250, 277; abroad, I, 141, 147, 149, 160, 292, 316, 321, 324; character of, I, 39, 44, 75, 81,